Juvenilia & Other Poems by George Crabbe

Also includes Midnight, The Library, The Village and other classic texts

George Crabbe was born on December 24th, 1754 in Aldeburgh, Suffolk. He was sent to school at a very young age and soon developed an avid and precocious interest in books.

Crabbe was sent first to a boarding-school at Bungay, and a few years later to a school at Stowmarket, where he learnt mathematics and Latin. His early reading included William Shakespeare, Alexander Pope, Abraham Cowley, Sir Walter Raleigh and Edmund Spenser.

Medicine had now been settled on as his future career and, after three years at Stowmarket, in 1768, he was apprenticed to a local doctor at Wickhambrook, near Bury St Edmunds.

In 1772, a lady's magazine offered a prize for the best poem on 'hope'. Crabbe entered and won. The magazine then printed other short pieces of his during the year.

His first major work, Inebriety, \ pleted his medical
training and returned to Aldebu lon to study at a
hospital was abandoned and ins

The following year, 1777, he did d home with financial
woes. Crabbe continued to prac received only the
poorest of patients, together wit

He moved to London again in Ap ...could make it as a poet, or, if that failed, as a doctor. By the end of May he had been forced to pawn his surgical instruments.

With the publication in May 1783 of his poem The Village, Crabbe achieved popularity with both the public and critics. Samuel Johnson said of it in a letter to Reynolds "I have sent you back Mr. Crabbe's poem, which I read with great delight. It is original, vigorous, and elegant."

In 1796 their third son, Edmund, died at the age of six. The death shredded Sarah's mental health and she never recovered. Crabbe, a devoted husband, tended her until her death many years later.

In September 1807, Crabbe published a new volume of poems which included The Library, The Newspaper, The Village and The Parish Register, to which were added Sir Eustace Grey and The Hall of Justice. It had been decades since his last publication but now he was seen as an important poet.

Crabbe's next volume of poetry, Tales, was published in 1812. It received a warm welcome from the poet's admirers, and critics. It is now considered Crabbe's masterpiece.

In the summer of 1813, Sarah felt well enough to visit London again. George, Sarah and their two sons spent nearly three months there. The family returned to Muston in September, and at October's end Sarah died at age 63.

In June 1819, Crabbe published his collection Tales of the Hall.

Around 1820 Crabbe began suffering from frequent severe attacks of neuralgia, and this, together with his age, made him less able to travel to London.

In November 1822 he went to see his son George. He was able to preach twice for his son, who congratulated him on the power of his voice. "I will venture a good sum, sir," he said, "that you will be assisting me ten years hence." "Ten weeks" was Crabbe's answer. The prediction proved eerily accurate.

George Crabbe died on February 3rd, 1832, aged 77 at Trowbridge, Wiltshire with his two sons by his side.

Index of Contents

PREFATORY NOTE

In the present edition of Crabbe's Poems the general arrangement adopted is that of the chronological order of publication. The poem entitled Midnight has been inserted at a conjectural date as belonging to the period of the Juvenile Poems (1772-1780); but all other poems contained in this edition which have hitherto remained unpublished will be printed after the published poems, in the sequence of their production so far as this is ascertainable.

JUVENILIA

(1772—1780)

SOLITUDE

September, 1772

Free from envy, strife and sorrow,
Jealous doubts, and heart-felt fears;
Free from thoughts of what to-morrow
May o'er-charge the soul with cares—

Live I in a peaceful valley,
By a neighbouring lonely wood;
Giving way to melancholy,
(Joy, when better understood).

Near me ancient ruins falling
From a worn-out castle's brow;
Once the greatest [chiefs] installing,
Where are all their honours now?

Here in midnight's gloomy terror
I enjoy the silent night;
Darkness shews the soul her error,
Darkness leads to inward light.

Here I walk in meditation,
Pond'ring all sublunar things,
From the silent soft persuasion,
Which from virtue's basis springs.

What, says truth, are pomp and riches?
Guilded baits to folly lent;
Honour, which the soul bewitches,
When obtain'd, we may repent.

By me plays the stream meand'ring
Slowly, as its waters glide;
And, in gentle murmurs wand'ring,
Lulls to downy rest my pride.

Silent as the gloomy graves are
Now the mansions once so loud;
Still and quiet as the brave, or
All the horrors of a croud.

This was once the seat of plunder,
Blood of heroes stain'd the floor;
Heroes, nature's pride and wonder,
Heroes heard of now no more.

Owls and ravens haunt the buildings,
Sending gloomy dread to all;
Yellow moss the summit yielding,
Pellitory decks the wall.

Time with rapid speed still wanders,
Journies on an even pace;

Fame of greatest actions squanders,
But perpetuates disgrace.

Sigh not then for pomp or glory;
What avails a heroe's name?
Future times may tell your story,
To your then disgrace and shame.

Chuse some humble cot as this is,
In sweet philosophic ease;
With dame Nature's frugal blisses
Live in joy, and die in peace.

G. EBBARE.

A SONG

September, 1772

I.
As Chloe fair, a new-made bride,
Sat knotting in an arbour,
To Colin now the damsel ty'd,
No strange affection harbour.

II.
"How poor," says she, "'s a single life,
A maid's affected carriage;
Spent in sighs and inward strife,
Things unknown in marriage.

III.
"Virgins vainly say they're free,
None so much confin'd are;
Lovers kind and good may be,
Husbands may be kinder.

IV.
"Then shun not wedlock's happy chain,
Nor wantonly still fly man;
A single life is care and pain,
Blessings wait on Hymen."

G. EBBARE.

CONCLUDING LINES OF PRIZE POEM ON HOPE

Before October, 1772

But, above all, the POET owns thy powers—
Hope leads him on, and every fear devours;
He writes, and, unsuccessful, writes again,
Nor thinks the last laborious work in vain;
New schemes he forms, and various plots he tries
To win the laurel, and possess the PRIZE.

TO EMMA

View, my fair, the fading flower,
Clad like thee in beauty's arms,
Idle pageant of an hour;
Soon shall time its tints devour,
And what are then its charms?

Early pluck'd, it might produce
A remedy to mortal pain,
Afford a balmy cordial juice,
That might celestial ease diffuse,
Nor blossom quite in vain.

So 'tis with thee, my Emma fair,
If nature's law's unpaid,
If thou refuse our vows to hear
And steel thy heart to ev'ry pray'r,
A cruel frozen maid.

But yield, my fair one, yield to love,
And joys unnumber'd find,
In Cupid's mystic circle move,
Eternal raptures thou shalt prove,
Which leave no pang behind.

G. EBBAAC.

Suffolk, Oct. 15, 1772.

'Multa cadunt inter calicem supremaque labra.'

DESPAIR

November, 1772

Heu mihi!
Quod nullis amor medicabilis herbis.   OVID.

Tyrsis and Damon

Damon
Begin, my Tyrsis; songs shall sooth our cares,
Allay our sorrows, and dispel our fears;
Shall glad thy heart, and bring its native peace,
And bid thy grief its weighty influence cease.
No more those tears of woe, dear shepherd, shed,
Nor ever mourn the lov'd Cordelia dead.

Tyrsis
In vain, my Damon, urge thy fond request
To still the troubles of an anxious breast:
Cordelia's gone! and now what pain is life
Without my fair, my friend, my lovely wife?
Hope! cheerful hope! to distant climes is fled,
And Nature mourns the fair Cordelia dead.

Damon
But can thy tears re-animate the earth,
Or give to sordid dust a second birth?
Mistaken mortal! learn to bear the ill,
Nor let that canker, grief, thy pleasures kill.
No more in Sorrow's sable garb array'd,
Still mourn thy lov'd, thy lost Cordelia dead.

Tyrsis
Can I forget the fairest of her kind,
Beauteous in person, fairer still in mind?
Can I forget she sooth'd my heart to rest,
And still'd the troubl'd motion in my breast?
Can I, by soothing song or friendship led,
Forget to mourn my lov'd Cordelia dead?

Damon
Another fair may court thee to her arms,
Display her graces, and reveal her charms;
May catch thy wand'ring eye, dispel thy woe,
And give to sorrow final overthrow.
No longer, then, thy heart-felt anguish shed,
Nor mourn, in solitude, Cordelia dead.

Tyrsis

Sooner shall lions fierce forget to roam,
And peaceful walk with gentle lambs at home;
Sooner shall Discord love her ancient hate,
And Peace and Love with Rage incorporate;
Sooner shall turtles with the sparrow wed,
Than I forget my lov'd Cordelia dead.

Damon

Must then Dorintha ever sigh in vain,
And Cælia breathe to echoing groves her pain?
Must Chloe hope in vain to steel that heart
In which each nymph would gladly share a part?
Must these, dejected shepherd, be betray'd.
And victims fall, because Cordelia's dead?

Tyrsis

By those who love, my friend, it stands confest,
No second flame can fill a lover's breast:
For me no more the idle scenes of life
Shall vex with envy, hatred, noise, or strife;
But here, in melancholy form array'd,
I'll ever mourn my lov'd Cordelia dead.

G. EBBARE.

CUPID

November, 1772

Whoe'er thou art, thy master know;
He has been, is, or shall be so.

What is he, who clad in arms,
Hither seems in haste to move,
Bringing with him soft alarms,
Fears the heart of man to prove;
Yet attended too by charms—
Is he Cupid, God of Love?

Yes, it is, behold him nigh,
Odd compound of ease and smart;
Near him stands a nymph, whose sigh
Grief and joy, and love impart;

Pleasure dances in her eye,
Yet she seems to grieve at heart.

Lo! a quiver by his side,
Arm'd with darts, a fatal store!
See him, with a haughty pride,
Ages, sexes, all devour;
Yet, as pleasure is describ'd,
Glad we meet the tyrant's power.

Doubts and cares before him go,
Canker'd jealousy behind;
Round about him spells he'll throw,
Scatt'ring with each gust of wind
On the motley crew below,
Who, like him, are render'd blind.

This is love! a tyrant kind,
Giving extacy and pain;
Fond deluder of the mind,
Ever feigning not to feign;
Whom no savage laws can bind,
None escape his pleasing chain.

G. EBBARE.

SONG

November, 1772

Cease to bid me not to sing.
Spite of Fate I'll tune my lyre:
Hither, god of music, bring
Food to feed the gentle fire;
And on Pægasean wing
Mount my soul enraptur'd higher.

Some there are who'd curb the mind,
And would blast the springing bays;
All essays are vain, they'll find,
Nought shall drown the muse's lays,
Nought shall curb a free-born mind,
Nought shall damp Apollo's praise.

G. EBBARE.

ON THE DEATH OF WILLIAM SPRINGALL LEVETT

[1774.]

What though no trophies peer above his dust,
Nor sculptured conquests deck his sober bust;
What though no earthly thunders sound his name,
Death gives him conquest, and our sorrows fame:
One sigh reflection heaves, but shuns excess—
More should we mourn him, did we love him less.

PARODY ON BYROM'S "MY TIME, OH YE MUSES"

Woodbridge, about 1774

My days, oh ye lovers, were happily sped
Ere you or your whimsies got into my head;
I could laugh, I could sing, I could trifle and jest,
And my heart play'd a regular tune in my breast.
But now, lack-a-day! what a change for the worse,
'Tis as heavy as lead, yet as wild as a horse.

My fingers, ere love had tormented my mind,
Could guide my pen gently to what I design'd.
I could make an enigma, a rebus, or riddle,
Or tell a short tale of a dog and a fiddle.
But, since this vile Cupid has got in my brain,
I beg of the gods to assist in my strain.
And whatever my subject, the fancy still roves,
And sings of hearts, raptures, flames, sorrows, and loves.

THE WISH

Woodbridge, about 1774

My Mira, shepherds, is as fair
As sylvan nymphs who haunt the vale,
As sylphs who dwell in purest air,
As fays who skim the dusky dale,
As Venus was when Venus fled
From watery Triton's oozy bed.

My Mira, shepherds, has a voice
As soft as Syrinx in her grove,
As sweet as echo makes her choice,
As mild as whispering virgin-love;
As gentle as the winding stream
Or fancy's song when poets dream.

INEBRIETY

The PREFACE

Presumption or Meanness are but too often the only articles to be discovered in a Preface. Whilst one author haughtily affects to despise the public attention, another timidly courts it. I would no more beg for than disdain applause, and therefore should advance nothing in Favor of the following little Poem, did it not appear a Cruelty and disregard to send a first Production naked into the WORLD.

The WORLD!—how pompous, and yet how trifling the sound. Every MAN, Gentle Reader, has a WORLD of his own, & whether it consists of half a score, or half a thousand Friends, 'tis his, and he loves to boast of it. Into my WORLD, therefore, I commit this, my Muse's earliest labor, nothing doubting the Clemency of the Climate, nor fearing the Partiality of the censorious.

Something by way of Apology for this trifle, is perhaps necessary; especially for those parts, wherein I have taken such great Liberties with Mr. POPE; that Gentleman, secure in immortal Fame, would forgive me; forgive me too, my friendly Critic; I promise thee, thou wilt find the Extracts from the Swan of Thames the best Parts of the Performance; Few, I dare venture to affirm, will pay me so great a Compliment, as to think I have injured Mr POPE; Fewer, I hope, will think I endeavoured to do it, and Fewest of all will think any thing about it.

The LADIES will doubtless favor my Attempt; for them indeed it was principally composed; I have endeavored to demonstrate that it is their own Faults, if they are not deemed as good MEN, as half the masculine World; that a personal Difference of Sex need not make a real Difference; and that a tender Languishment, a refin'd Delicacy, and a particular attention to shine in Dress, will render the Beau-Animal infinitely more feminine, than the generality of LADIES, whatever arcane Tokens of Manhood the said Animal may be indued with; and yet, ye FAIR! these creatures pass even in your catalogue for MEN; which I'm afraid is a Demonstration that the real MAN is very scarce.

Some grave Head or other may possibly tell me, that Vice is to be lash'd, not indulg'd; that true Poetry forbids, not encourages, Folly; and such other wise and weighty Sentences, picked from POPE and HORACE, as he shall think most appertaining to his own dignity. But this, my good Reader, is a trifle; People now a Days are not to be preach'd into Reflection, or they pay Parsons, not Poets for it, if they were; they listen indeed to a Discourse from the Pulpit, for MEN are too wise to give away their Money without any consideration; and though they don't mind what is said there, 'tis doubtless a great Satisfaction to think they might if they choose it; but a MAN reads a Poem for quite a different purpose: to be lul'd into ease from reflection, to be lul'd into an inclination for pleasure, and (where I confess it comes nearer the Sermon) to be lul'd—asleep.

But lest the Apology should have the latter effect in itself, and so take away the merit of the Performance by forestalling that agreeable Event: I without further ceremony bid thee Adieu!

PART the FIRST

The mighty Spirit and its power which stains
The bloodless cheek, and vivifies the brains,
I sing. Say ye, its fiery Vot'ries true,
The jovial Curate, and the shrill-tongu'd Shrew;
Ye, in the floods of limpid poison nurst,
Where Bowl the second charms like Bowl the first;
Say, how and why the sparkling ill is shed,
The Heart which hardens, and which rules the Head.
When Winter stern his gloomy front uprears,
A sable void the barren earth appears;
The meads no more their former verdure boast,
Fast bound their streams, and all their Beauty lost;
The herds, the flocks, their icy garments mourn,
And wildly murmur for the Spring's return;
The fallen branches from the sapless tree
With glittering fragments strow the glassy way;
From snow-top'd Hills the whirlwinds keenly blow,
Howl through the Woods, and pierce the vales below;
Through the sharp air a flaky torrent flies,
Mocks the slow sight, and hides the gloomy skies;
The fleecy clouds their chilly bosoms bare,
And shed their substance on the floating air;
The floating air their downy substance glides
Through springing Waters, and prevents their tides;
Seizes the rolling Waves, and, as a God,
Charms their swift race, and stops the refl'ent flood;
The opening valves, which fill the venal road,
Then scarcely urge along the sanguine flood;
The labouring Pulse a slower motion rules,
The Tendons stiffen, and the Spirit cools;
Each asks the aid of Nature's sister Art,
To Cher the senses, and to warm the Heart.
The gentle fair on nervous tea relies,
Whilst gay good-nature sparkles in her eyes;
An inoffensive Scandal fluttering round,
Too rough to tickle, and too light to wound;
Champain the Courtier drinks, the spleen to chase,
The Colonel burgundy, and port his Grace;
Turtle and 'rrack the city rulers charm,
Ale and content the labouring peasants warm;
O'er the dull embers happy Colin sits,

Colin, the prince of joke and rural wits;
Whilst the wind whistles through the hollow panes,
He drinks, nor of the rude assault complains;
And tells the Tale, from sire to son retold,
Of spirits vanishing near hidden gold;
Of moon-clad Imps, that tremble by the dew,
Who skim the air, or glide o'er waters blue.
The throng invisible, that doubtless float
By mould'ring Tombs, and o'er the stagnant moat;
Fays dimly glancing on the russet plain,
And all the dreadful nothing of the Green.
And why not these? Less fictious is the tale,
Inspir'd by Hel'con's streams, than muddy ale?
Peace be to such, the happiest and the best,
Who with the forms of fancy urge their jest;
Who wage no war with an Avenger's Rod,
Nor in the pride of reason curse their God.

When in the vaulted arch Lucina gleams,
And gaily dances o'er the azure streams;
When in the wide cerulean space on high
The vivid stars shoot lustre through the sky;
On silent Ether when a trembling sound
Reverberates, and wildly floats around,
Breaking through trackless space upon the ear—
Conclude the Bacchanalian Rustic near;
O'er Hills and vales the jovial Savage reels,
Fire in his head and Frenzy at his heels;
From paths direct the bending Hero swerves,
And shapes his way in ill-proportion'd curves;
Now safe arriv'd, his sleeping Rib he calls,
And madly thunders on the muddy walls;
The well-known sounds an equal fury move,
For rage meets rage, as love enkindles love;
The buxom Quean from bed of flocks descends
With vengeful ire, a civil war portends,
An oaken plant the Hero's breast defends.
In vain the 'waken'd infant's accents shrill
The humble regions of the cottage fill;
In vain the Cricket chirps the mansion through,
'Tis war, and Blood and Battle must ensue.
As when, on humble stage, him Satan hight
Defies the brazen Hero to the fight;
From twanging strokes what dire misfortunes rise,
What fate to maple arms, and glassen eyes;
Here lies a leg of elm, and there a stroke
From ashen neck has whirl'd a Head of oak.
So drops from either power, with vengeance big,

A remnant night-cap, and an old cut wig;
Titles unmusical, retorted round,
On either ear with leaden vengeance sound;
'Till equal Valour equal Wounds create,
And drowsy peace concludes the fell debate;
Sleep in her woolen mantle wraps the pair,
And sheds her poppies on the ambient air;
Intoxication flies, as fury fled,
On rocky pinions quits the aching head;
Returning Reason cools the fiery blood,
And drives from memory's seat the rosy God.
Yet still he holds o'er some his madd'ning rule,
Still sways his Sceptre, and still knows his Fool;
Witness the livid lip and fiery front,
With many a smarting trophy plac'd upon't;
The hollow Eye, which plays in misty springs,
And the hoarse Voice, which rough and broken rings.
These are his triumphs, and o'er these he reigns,
The blinking Deity of reeling brains.

See Inebriety! her wand she waves,
And lo! her pale, and lo! her purple slaves;
Sots in embroidery, and sots in crape,
Of every order, station, rank, and shape;
The King, who nods upon his rattle-throne;
The staggering Peer, to midnight revel prone;
The slow-tongu'd Bishop, and the Deacon sly,
The humble Pensioner, and Gownsman dry;
The proud, the mean, the selfish, and the great,
Swell the dull throng, and stagger into state.

Lo! proud Flaminius at the splendid board,
The easy chaplain of an atheist Lord,
Quaffs the bright juice, with all the gust of sense,
And clouds his brain in torpid elegance;
In china vases see the sparkling ill,
From gay Decanters view the rosy rill;
The neat-carv'd pipes in silver settle laid,
The screw by mathematic cunning made;
The whole a pompous and enticing scene,
And grandly glaring for the surplic'd Swain;
Oh! happy Priest whose God like Egypt's lies,
At once the Deity and sacrifice!
But is Flaminius, then, the man alone,
To whom the Joys of swimming brains are known?
Lo! the poor Toper whose untutor'd sense
Sees bliss in ale, and can with wine dispense;
Whose head proud fancy never taught to steer

Beyond the muddy extacies of Beer;
But simple nature can her longing quench
Behind the settle's curve, or humbler bench;
Some kitchen-fire diffusing warmth around,
The semi-globe by Hieroglyphics crown'd;
Where canvas purse displays the brass enroll'd,
Nor Waiters rave, nor Landlords thirst for gold;
Ale and content his fancy's bounds confine,
He asks no limpid Punch, no rosy Wine;
But sees, admitted to an equal share,
Each faithful swain the heady potion bear.
Go, wiser thou! and in thy scale of taste
Weigh gout and gravel against ale and rest.
Call vulgar palates, what thou judgest so;
Say, beer is heavy, windy, cold and slow;
Laugh at poor sots with insolent pretence,
Yet cry when tortur'd, where is Providence?
If thou alone art, head and heel, not clear,
Alone made steady here, untumour'd there;
Snatch from the Board the bottle and the bowl,
Curse the keen pain, and be a mad proud Fool.

PART the SECOND

In various forms the madd'ning Spirit moves,
This drinks and fights, another drinks and loves.
A bastard Zeal of different kinds it shows,
And now with rage, and now Religion glows;
The frantic Soul bright reason's path defies,
Now creeps on Earth, now triumphs in the Skies;
Swims in the seas of error and explores,
Through midnight mists, the fluctuating Shores;
From wave to wave in rocky Channel glides,
And sinks in woe, or on presumption slides;
In Pride exalted, or by Shame deprest,
An Angel-Devil, or a human-Beast.
Without a pilot who attempts to steer,
Has small discretion or has little care;
That pilot Reason, in the erring Soul,
Is lost, is blinded in the steaming Bowl,
Charm'd by its power, we cast our guide away,
And at the mercy of conjecture lay;
Discretion dies with reason, Revel wakes!
And o'er the head his fiery banners shakes.
With him come frenzy, folly and excess,
Blink-ey'd conceit and shallow emptiness;

At Folly's beck a train of Vices glide,
Murder in madness cloak'd, in choler, Pride;
Above, Impiety, with curses bound,
Lours at the skies, and whirls Damnation round.

Some rage, in all the strength of folly mad,
Some love stupidity, in silence clad,
Are never quarrelsome, are never gay,
But sleep and groan and drink the Night away;
Old Torpio nods, and, as the laugh goes round,
Grunts through the nasal Duct, and joins the sound;
Then sleeps again, and, as the liquors pass,
Wakes at the friendly Jog, and takes his Glass;
Alike to him who stands, or reels, or moves;
The elbow chair, good wine and Sleep he loves;
Nor cares of state disturb his easy head,
By grosser fumes and calmer follies fed;
Nor thoughts, of when, or where, or how to come,
The Canvass general, or the general Doom;
Extremes ne'er reach'd one passion of his Soul;
A villain tame, and an unmettled fool,
To half his Vices he has but pretence,
For they usurp the place of common sense;
To half his little Merits has no claim
But very Indolence has rais'd his name,
Happy in this, that under Satan's sway
His passions humble, but will not obey.

The Vicar at the table's front presides,
Whose presence a monastic life derides;
The reverend Wig, in sideway order plac'd,
The reverend Band, by rubric stains disgrac'd,
The leering Eye, in wayward circles roll'd,
Mark him the Pastor of a jovial Fold,
Whose various texts excite a loud applause,
Favouring the Bottle, and the good old Cause.
See! the dull smile which fearfully appears,
When gross Indecency her front uprears;
The joy conceal'd the fiercer burns within,
As masks afford the keenest gust to Sin;
Imagination helps the reverend Sire,
And spreads the sails of sub-divine desire.
But when the gay immoral joke goes round,
When Shame and all her blushing train are drown'd,
Rather than hear his God blasphem'd he takes
The last lov'd Glass, and then the board forsakes:
Not that Religion prompts the sober thought,
But slavish Custom has the practice taught.

Besides, this zealous son of warm devotion
Has a true levite Bias for promotion;
Vicars must with discretion go astray,
Whilst Bishops may be d—n'd the nearest way;
So puny robbers individuals kill,
When hector-Heroes murder as they will.

Good honest Curio elbows the divine,
And strives, a social sinner, how to shine;
The dull quaint tale is his, the lengthen'd tale,
That Wilton Farmers give you with their ale:
How midnight Ghosts o'er vaults terrific pass,
Dance o'er the Grave, and slide along the grass;
How Maids forsaken haunt the lonely wood,
And tye the Noose, or try the willow flood;
How rural Heroes overcame the giants,
And through the ramshorn trumpet blew defiance;
Or how pale Cicely, within the wood,
Call'd Satan forth and bargain'd with her blood.
These, honest Curio, are thine, and these
Are the dull Treasures of a brain at peace.
No wit intoxicates thy gentle skull,
Of heavy, native, unwrought folly full;
Bowl upon Bowl in vain exert their force;
The breathing Spirit takes a downward course,
Or, vainly soaring upwards to the head,
Meets an impenetrable tence of lead.

Hast thou, Oh Reader! search'd o'er gentle Gay,
Where various animals their powers display?
In one strange Group, a chattering race was hurl'd,
Led by the Monkey who had seen the world.
He, it is said, from woodland shepherds stole,
And went to Court, to greet each fellow fool.
Like him, Fabricio steals from guardian's side,
Swims not in pleasure's stream, but sips the tide
He hates the Bottle, yet but thinks it right
To boast next day the honours of the night;
None like your Coward can describe a fight.
See him, as down the sparkling potion goes,
Labor to grin away the horrid dose;
In joy-feign'd gaze his misty eye-balls float,
Th' uncivil Spirit gurgling at his throat;
So looks dim Titan through a wintry scene,
And faintly cheers the woe-foreboding swain;
But now, Alas! the hour, th'increasing flood,
Rolls round and round, and cannot be withstood;
Thrice he essays to stop the ruby flow,

To stem its Force, and keep it still below;
In vain his Art, it comes! at distance gaze,
Ye stancher Sots, and be not near the place.
As when a flood from Ossa's pendant brow
Rolls rapid to its fellow streams below,
It moves tempest'ous down the Mountain's sides,
O'er lesser hills and vales like light'ning glides,
And o'er their beauties fall'n triumphant rides,
Each verdant spot and sunny bank defaces,
And forms a minor Ocean at its basis;
So from his rueful lips Fabricio pours,
With melancholy Force, the tinctur'd showers;
O'er the embroider'd vest they take their way,
And in the grave its tinsel honours lay.
No Nymph was there, to hold the helpless face,
Or save from ruin's spoil the luckless lace;
No guardian Fair, to turn the head aside
And to securer paths the torrent glide;
From silk to silk it drove its wayward Course,
And on the diamond buckle spent its Force.
Ah! gentle Fop! what luckless fate was thine
To sin through fashion, and in woe to shine.
But all our Numbers why should rascals claim?
Rise, honest Muse, and sing a nobler name.
Pleas'd in his Eye good humour always smiles,
And Mirth unbought with strife the hour beguiles,
Who smoothed the frown on yonder surly brow?
From the dry Joke who bade gay Laughter flow?
Not of affected, empty rapture full,
Nor in proud Strain magnificently dull,
But gay and easy, giving without Art
Joy to each sense, and Solace to the heart.
Thrice happy Damon, able to pursue
What all so wish, but want the power to do.
No cares thy Head, no crimes thy Heart torment,
At home thou'rt happy, and abroad content;
Pleas'd with thyself, and therefore form'd to please,
With Moderation free, and gay with Ease,
Wise in a medium, just to an extreme,
"The soul of Humour, and the life of Whim,"
Plac'd from thy Sphere, amid the sons of shame,
Proud of thy Jest, but prouder of thy Name.

Pernicious streams from healthy fountains rise,
And Wit abus'd degenerates into vice;
Timon, long practic'd in the School of art,
Has lost each finer feeling of the Heart,
Triumphs o'er shame, and with delusive whiles,

Laughs at the Idiot he himself beguiles.
So matrons, past the awe of Censure's tongue,
Deride the blushes of the fair and young.
Few with more Fire on every subject spoke,
But chief he lov'd the gay immoral joke;
The Words most sacred, stole from holy writ,
He gave a newer form, and call'd them Wit;
Could twist a Sentence into various meaning,
And save himself in dubious explaining;
Could use a manner long taught art affords,
And hint Impiety in holy words.
Vice never had a more sincere ally,
So bold no Sinner, yet no Saint so sly;
Sophist and Cynic, mystically cool,
And still a very Sceptic at the soul;
Learn'd but not wise, and without Virtue brave,
A gay, deluding, philosophic Knave.
When Bacchus' joys his airy fancy fire,
They stir a new, but still a false desire;
The place of malice ridicule then holds,
And woe to teachers, ministers and scolds;
And, to the comfort of each untaught Fool,
Horace in English vindicates the Bowl.
"The man" (says Timon) "who is drunk is blest,
No fears disturb, no cares destroy his rest;
In thoughtless joy he reels away his life,
Nor dreads that worst of ills, a noisy wife.
Of late I sat within the jangling bar,
And heard my Rib's hoarse thunder from afar;
Careless I spoke, and, when she found me drunk,
She breath'd one Curse, and then away she slunk,
Oh! place me, Jove, where none but women come,
And thunders worse than thine afflict the room;
Where one eternal Nothing flutters round,
And senseless titt'rings sense of mirth confound;
Or lead me bound to Garret, babel-high,
Where frantic Poet rolls his crazy eye;
Tiring the Ear, with oft-repeated chimes,
And smiling at the never ending rhymes;
E'en here or there, I'll be as blest as Jove,
Give me tobacco, and the wine I love."
Applause from Hands the dying accents break
Of stagg'ring sots, who vainly try to speak;
From Milo, him who hangs upon each word,
And in loud praises splits the tortur'd board,
Collects each sentence, ere it's better known,
And makes the mutilated joke his own,
At weekly club to flourish, where he rules

The glorious president of grosser fools.

But cease, my Muse; of those or these enough,
The fools who listen, and the knaves who Scoff;
The jest profane, that mocks th' offended God,
Defies his power, and sets at nought his rod.
The empty Laugh, discretion's vainest foe,
From fool to fool re-echo'd to and fro;
The sly Indecency, that slowly springs
From barren wit, and halts on trembling wings:
Enough of these, and all the charms of Wine;
Be sober joys and social evenings mine,
Where peace and Reason unsoil'd mirth improve,
The powers of friendship and the joys of love;
Where thought meets thought ere Words its form array,
And all is sacred, elegant, and gay;
Such pleasure leaves no Sorrow on the mind,
Too great to pall, to sicken too refin'd,
Too soft for Noise, and too sublime for art,
The social solace of the feeling Heart,
For sloth too rapid, and for wit too high,
'Tis Virtue's Pleasure, and can never die.

PART the THIRD

Now soar, my Muse! and leave the meaner crew,
To aim at bliss, and vainly bliss pursue;
Let us (since Man no privilege can claim,
Than a contended, half superior name)
Expatiate o'er the raptures of the Fair,
Vot'ries to stolen joys, but yet sincere;
In secret Haunts, where never day-light gleams
By bottles, tempting with forbidden streams,
Together let us search; above, below,
Try what the Closets, what the Cellars show;
The latent vault with piercing view explore
Of her who hides the all reviving store.
Eye Beauty's walks, when round the welkin rolls,
And catch the stumbling Charmer as she falls;
Laugh where we must, but pity where we can,
And vindicate the sweet soft souls to Man.

Pardon, ye Fair, the Poet and his Muse,
And what ye can't approve, at least excuse;
Far be from him the iron lash of Wit,
The jokes of Humour, and the sneers that hit;

He speaks of Freedom, and he speaks to you,
His Verse is simple, but his Subject new;
And novelty, ye Fair, beyond a doubt,
Is philosophic truth, the World throughout.

Hard is the lot of Woman, so have sung
The pensive old, and the presuming young;
Born without privilege, in bondage bred,
Slave from the Cradle to the marriage Bed;
Slave from the hour hymeneal to the grave,
In age, in youth, in infancy a Slave.
Happy the Bard, who, bold in pride of song
Shall free the chain, by Custom bound so long,
And show the Fair, to mean tradition prone,
Though Virtue may have sex, yet Vice has none.
If Man is licenc'd to confuse his mind,
Say, why should female Frailty be confin'd?
Is't right that she who dearly bought the fruit,
Of all our wayward appetites the root,
Who first made Man a fool and then a brute;
Who fair in spells of tender kind can slay,
Like Israel's Judge, her thousands in a day;
Nay farther, has a far superior Pow'r,
And almost thousands in a day can cure;
She, the bright cause of fury in Man's breast;
And brighter cause who bids that fury rest;
Who raises peace or war at her command,
And bids a sword destroy a tipsy Land;
Say, is it right that she who kills and saves,
Makes wise Men mad, and takes the veil from Knaves,
Should want the pow'r, the magic, which alone,
Can Conquests boast more fatal than her own?
For Man alone did earth produce her fruit,
The sole, as well as the superior, brute;
Does he alone the glorious licence claim,
To put the human off, and loose his Name?
Woman in Knowledge was the earlier curst,
And tasted of forbidden Fruit the first;
Prior to Man, the law she disobey'd,
And shall she want the Freedom she convey'd?
By her first Theft each fiery ill we feel,
And yet compel the gen'rous Fair to steal;
First made by her for soaring actions fit,
Woman! the spring of super-human wit,
Shall we from her each dear bought bliss withhold,
As Spaniards use the Indians for their Gold?
Ungrateful Man! in pride so high to aim,
As to be sole inheritor of shame!

And you, ye Fair! why slumber on disdain,
Forbear to vindicate, yet can't refrain?
Why should Papilla seek the vaulted hoard,
And but in secret ape her honest Lord?
Why should'st thou, Celia, to thy stores repair,
And sip the generous Spirit in such fear?
Reform the Error, and revoke your plan,
And as ye dare to imitate, be—Man.

First know yourselves, and frame your passions all,
In proper order, how to rise and fall;
Woman's a Being, dubiously great,
Never contented with a passive state;
With too much Knowledge to give Man the sway,
With too much Pride his humours to obey,
She hangs in doubt, too humble or too brave;
In doubt to be a Mistress or a Slave;
In doubt herself or Husband to controul;
Born to be made a tyrant or a fool;
In one extreme, her Power is always such
Either to show too little, or too much;
Bred up in Passions, by their sway abus'd,
The weaker for the stronger still refus'd;
Created oft' to rise, and oft' to fall,
Changing in all things, yet alike in all;
Soft Judge of right or wrong, or blest or curst,
The happiest, saddest, holiest, or the worst.

And why? because your failings ye suppress,
And what ye dare to act, dare not confess.
Would you, ye Fair, as Man your vices boast,
And she be most admir'd, who sins the most;
Would ye in open revel gaily spring,
And o'er the wanton Banquet vaunting sing;
The doubtful Precedence we then should own,
And you be first in Error's mazes known.

But why to Vices of the boist'rous kind
Tye the soft Soul, and urge the gentle Mind?
Forbid it, Nature! to the Fair I speak,
By her made strong, by Custom rendered weak;
Whose passions, trembling for unbounded sway,
Will thank the Bard, who points the nearest way;
All Vice through Folly's regions first should pass,
And Folly holds her sceptre o'er the glass.
Drink then, ye Fair! and nature's laws fulfill;
Be ev'ry thing at once, and all ye will;

Put off the mask that hides the Sex's claim
And makes Distinction but an empty name.

Go, wond'rous Creature! where the potion glides
From Bowls unmeasured in illumin'd tides;
Instruct each other, in your due degrees;
Correct old Rules, and be e'en what you please;
Go, drink! for who shall jointed power contest?
Drink to the passable, the good, the best.
And, quitting Custom and her idle plan,
Call drowning reason imitating Man;
Like lovers' brains in giddy circles run,
And, all exhausting, imitate the Sun;
Go, and be Man in noise and glorious strife,
Then drop into his Arms and be a—Wife.

Ye Gods! what scenes upon my Fancy press,
The Consequence of unconfin'd excess;
When Vice in common has one general name,
And male and female Errors be the same;
For, as the strength of Spirit none contest,
That daring Ill shall introduce the rest;
Then, what a field of glory will arise,
What dazzling scenes, ye Fair, before your eyes:
As female duels, Jockies—what besides?
Gamblers in petticoats, and booted brides;
The tender Billet to the gentle swain,
That boldly dares avouch the am'rous pain;
Soft Beaux intreated, gentle Coxcombs prest,
And Fops asham'd half blush to be addrest.
Thus to sweet Strephon will his Chloris say,
One cup of Nectar having pav'd the way;
"Oh! why so dead to my emploring eyes,
Deaf to my prayer, and speechless to my sighs?
Sure never Nymph of old, my darling Boy,
When Men intreated, and when we were coy,
Was prest so warmly by a bleeding swain,
Or shot from killing eyes such cold disdain."
And thus will run wild Flavia's Billetdoux,
The writing bold, and e'en the spelling true:
"No more, my Belmour, shun these longing arms,
Thou quintessence of all thy Sex's charms;
At ten—behind the elm, where echoes sigh,
Shall, taught by me, teach thee my swain to die;
The conscious Moon shall fill her lucid horn,
And join thy Blush to mock the crimson morn;
The limpid Stream shall softly move along,
And hear its own sweet warble from thy tongue;

There come, dear boy, or vainly flow the streams,
There come, or vainly sheds the moon her beams;
Vainly on her my Moments I shall waste,
She who like thee is cold, and who like thee is chaste."
But then what tender Stripling shall escape?
What blushing Boy avoid a Lady-Rape?
Where shall each lisping creature hide his head,
To amazonian desires betray'd?
Where from the wily Heroine remove,
Clad in the fortitude of Wine and Love?
Oh! hapless Lad, what refuge canst thou find
Too soft, too mild, too tender to be kind?
Yet this is no objection understood,
"For partial Evil's universal Good."

Nor think of Nature's state I make a jest:
The state of Nature is a state undrest;
The love of Pleasure at our birth began,
Pleasure the aim of all things, and of Man.
Law then was not, the swelling flame to kill,
Man walk'd with beast, and—so he always will;
And Woman too, the same their board and bed,
And would be now, but Folks are better bred;
In some convenient grot, or tufted wood,
All human beings Nature's circuit trod;
The shrine was her's, with no gay vesture laid;
Unbrib'd, unmarried stood the willing maid;
Her attribute was universal Love,
And man's prerogative to range and rove.
But how unlike the Pairs of times to come,
Wedded, yet separate, abroad at home,
Who foes to Nature, and to evil prone,
Despising all, but hating most their own.
A wayward craving this Neglect succeeds,
As every Monster monst'rous children breeds;
Strange motly passions from this vice began,
And Man unnatural turn'd to worship Man.

For this the Muse now calls the Fair to rise,
To shew our failings, and to make us wise;
Be now to Bacchus, now to Venus prone,
And share each folly Man has thought his own;
Shame him from Vice, by shewing him your shame,
And part with yours, to reinstate his Fame;
Be generously vile, and this your view:
That Man may hate his errors seen in you.

Say, when the Coxcomb flatters and adores,

When (taking snuff) your pity he implores;
With many a gentle Dem'me swears to die,
And humbly begs Destruction from your eye;
When your own arts he takes, and speaks in smiles,
With Softness woos, and with a Voice beguiles;
Does it not move your pity and disdain,
Such flow'ry passion, and such mincing pain;
Your various Follies you with anger scan,
So shewn by one whom Nature meant for Man.
E'en so do we our faults in you despise,
And Vice has double malice in those Eyes.
When Chloe toasts her Beau, or raves too loud;
When Flavia leaves her home, and joins a croud;
When Silvia fearless rolls the roguish eye,
And Damon's want of confidence supply;
When betts, and duns, and every rougher name,
Sound in the ear of either Sex the same;
How should we tell, when thus you love and hate,
Who acts the Man, and who's effeminate?

Drink, then! disclaim your Sex, be Man in all,
Shew us at once, distinction ought to fall;
And from the humble things ye were of old,
Be reeling Cæsars in a cyprian mould.

Better for us, 'tis granted, it might be,
Were you all Softness, and all Honour we;
That never rougher Passion mov'd your mind;
That we were all or excellent or blind;
But, as we now subsist by passions strife,
Which are (POPE writes) the elements of life,
The general order, since the whole began,
Should be dissolv'd, and Manners make the Man.

Nor fear, if once ye break through general Laws,
To draw in thousands, and gain our applause;
Nor fear but Fame your merits shall make known,
And female Bravos trample Hectors down;
From Man himself you'll learn the art he boasts,
Rule in his room, and govern in his posts.

Thus does the Muse in vein didactic speak—
"Go, from proud Man thy full instructions take;
Learn from the Law, what gain its mazes yield;
Learn of the Brave the police of the field;
Thy arts of shuffling from the Courtier get;
Learn of his Grace to stare away a debt;
Learn from the Sot his poison to caress,

Shake the mad room, and revel in excess;
From Man all forms of grand deception find,
And so be tempted to delude Mankind.
Here frantic schemes of wild Ambition see;
There all the plots, my Fair! he lays for thee.
Learn each small People's genius, humours, aims,
The Jocky's dealing, and Newmarket games;
How there in common wealth in currents go,
And poverty and riches ebb and flow;
And these for ever, though a Saint deny'd,
To splendour or contempt their Masters guide;
Mark the nice rules of modern honour well,
Rules which the laws of Nature far excel.
In vain thy fancy finer whims shall draw;
Good-breeding is as difficult as Law,
And, form'd so complex, makes itself a science,
To bid the Scholar and the Clown defiance.
Go then, and thus thy present Lords survey,
And let the Creatures feel they must obey;
Learn all their Arts, be these thy choicest hoard,
Be fear'd for these, and be for these ador'd."

And where are these? within the Bowl they lie;
Thence spring ambitious thoughts, there doubtings die;
From thence we trace the horrors of a War,
Chaotic counsel, ministerial jar;
This makes a gambling Lord, a Patriot vain,
The Soldier's fury, and the Lover's pain;
Fills Bedlam's wards with souls of ærial mould;
This makes the Madman, this supplies the Scold;
Here rules the one grand Passion in extreme,
A love of lucre, or a love of fame;
The Scholar's boast, the Politician's plan;
Here shines the Bubble, and here falls the Man.

Oh! happy fall of insolence and pride,
Which makes the humblest with the great allied;
Which levels like the Grave all earthly things,
For drunken Coblers are as proud as Kings;
Which plucks the sons of grandeur from their sphere,
For who is lower than a stagg'ring Peer?
Yet here, ye Fair, tho' ev'ry Soul's the same,
And Prince and Pedlar differ but in name,
Folly with Fashion is discreetly grac'd,
And, if all sin, not all can sin in taste;
For who, ye Gods! would ever go astray,
If 'twas not something in a modish way?

Oh! Fashion, caprice, pride—whate'er we call—
Thou something, nothing, dear attractive all;
Thou serious trifle of the gentle Soul,
Worship'd, yet changing, varying to controul;
Sweet Child of wanton fancy, artful whim,
Bred in an instant, born in an Extreme;
Folly's best friend, and luxury's ally,
Who, dying always, prov'st thou canst not die;
Attend us here; let us grow mad in Form,
Rage with an Air, and elegantly storm;
Invoke destruction with a Grace divine,
And call for Satan as a child of thine;
Genteely stagger from the common road;
And ape the brute, but ape him in the mode;
With a Court-grace make every action known,
For who'd be d—n'd for sins they blush to own?

Far as the power of human vice extends,
Her scale of sensual vanity ascends;
Mark how it rises to the gilded Throne,
From the poor wretch who dully topes alone.
What modes of folly, each in one extreme,
The sots dim sense, th' Epicurean's dream;
Of scent, what difference 'twixt the pungent rum
And noxious vapours of fermenting stum;
Of hearing, to Champain's decanted swell
From the dull gurgle of expiring ale?
The touch, how distant in the mean and great,
Who feel all roughness, or who feed from plate;
In the nice Lord, behold what arts produce;
From vases carv'd is quaff'd the balmy juice;
How palates vary in the poor Divine,
Compar'd, half-reasoning Nobleman! with thine.

Thus every sense is fill'd in due degree,
And proper barriers bound his Grace and me;
Here every Passion is at length display'd,
Nations are ruin'd, Ministers betray'd;
And what, ye Fair, concerns your pleasures most,
Intrigues are plan'd, and Reputations lost:
By you persuaded, Man was overcome,
And conquer'd once, received a general doom;
Requite the deed, partake a general Curse;
We fell with you, and you should fall with us.

JUVENILIA

THE LEARNING OF LOVE

About 1776

Ah! blest be the days when with Mira I took
The learning of Love....
When we pluck'd the wild blossoms that blush'd in the grass,
And I taught my dear maid of their species and class;
For Conway, the friend of mankind, had decreed
That Hudson should show us the wealth of the mead.

YE GENTLE GALES

Woodbridge, 1776.

Ye gentle Gales, that softly move,
Go whisper to the Fair I love;
Tell her I languish and adore,
And pity in return implore.

But if she's cold to my request,
Ye louder Winds, proclaim the rest—
My sighs, my tears, my griefs proclaim,
And speak in strongest notes my flame.

Still, if she rests in mute disdain,
And thinks I feel a common pain—
Wing'd with my woes, ye Tempests, fly,
And tell the haughty Fair I die.

MIRA

Aldborough, 1777

A wanton chaos in my breast raged high,
A wanton transport darted in mine eye;
False pleasure urged, and ev'ry eager care,
That swell the soul to guilt and to despair.
My Mira came! be ever blest the hour,
That drew my thoughts half way from folly's power;
She first my soul with loftier notions fired;
I saw their truth, and as I saw admired;

With greater force returning reason moved,
And as returning reason urged, I loved;
Till pain, reflection, hope, and love allied
My bliss precarious to a surer guide—
To Him who gives pain, reason, hope, and love,
Each for that end that angels must approve.
One beam of light He gave my mind to see,
And gave that light, my heavenly fair, by thee;
That beam shall raise my thoughts, and mend my strain,
Nor shall my vows, nor prayers, nor verse be vain.

HYMN

Beccles, 1778

Oh, Thou! who taught my infant eye
To pierce the air, and view the sky,
To see my God in earth and seas,
To hear him in the vernal breeze,
To know him midnight thoughts among,
O guide my soul, and aid my song!
Spirit of Light! do thou impart
Majestic truths, and teach my heart;
Teach me to know how weak I am,
How vain my powers, how poor my frame;
Teach me celestial paths untrod—
The ways of glory and of God.

No more let me, in vain surprise,
To heathen art give up my eyes—
To piles laborious science rear'd
For heroes brave, or tyrants fear'd;
But quit Philosophy, and see
The Fountain of her works in Thee.

Fond man! yon glassy mirror eye—
Go, pierce the flood, and there descry
The miracles that float between
The rainy leaves of wat'ry green;
Old Ocean's hoary treasures scan;
See nations swimming round a span.

Then wilt thou say—and rear no more
Thy monuments in mystic lore—
My God! I quit my vain design,
And drop my work to gaze on Thine:

Henceforth I'll frame myself to be,
Oh, Lord! a monument of Thee.

THE WISH

Aldborough, 1778

Give me, ye Powers that rule in gentle hearts,
The full design, complete in all its parts,
Th' enthusiastic glow, that swells the soul—
When swell'd too much the judgment to control—
The happy ear that feels the flowing force
Of the smooth line's uninterrupted course;
Give me, oh give, if not in vain the prayer,
That sacred wealth, poetic worth, to share—
Be it my boast to please and to improve,
To warm the soul to virtue and to love;
To paint the passions, and to teach mankind
Our greatest pleasures are the most refined;
The cheerful tale with fancy to rehearse,
And gild the moral with the charm of verse.

THE COMPARISON

Parham, 1778

Friendship is like the gold refined,
And all may weigh its worth;
Love like the ore, brought undesign'd
In virgin beauty forth.

Friendship may pass from age to age,
And yet remain the same;
Love must in many a toil engage,
And melt in lambent flame.

GOLDSMITH TO THE AUTHOR

Aldborough, 1778

Felix quem faciunt aliena pericula cautum.

You're in love with the Muses? Well, grant it be true,
When, good Sir, were the Muses enamour'd of you?
Read first—if my lectures your fancy delight—
Your taste is diseased, can your cure be to write?

You suppose you're a genius, that ought to engage
The attention of wits and the smiles of the age:
Would the wits of the age their opinion make known,
Why—every man thinks just the same of his own.

You imagine that Pope—but yourself you beguile—
Would have wrote the same things, had he chose the same style.
Delude not yourself with so fruitless a hope—
Had he chose the same style, he had never been Pope.

You think of my muse with a friendly regard,
And rejoice in her author's esteem and reward:
But let not his glory your spirits elate,
When pleased with his honours, remember his fate.

FRAGMENT

Aldborough, 1778

Lord, what is man, that thou art mindful of him?

Proud, little Man, opinion's slave.
Error's fond child, too duteous to be free,
Say, from the cradle to the grave,
Is not the earth thou tread'st too grand for thee?
This globe that turns thee, on her agile wheel
Moves by deep springs, which thou canst never feel;
Her day and night, her centre and her sun,
Untraced by thee, their annual courses run.
A busy fly, thou sharest the march divine,
And flattering fancy calls the motion thine;
Untaught how soon some hanging grave may burst,
And join thy flimsy substance to the dust.

THE RESURRECTION

Aldborough, 1778.

The wintry winds have ceased to blow,

And trembling leaves appear;
And fairest flowers succeed the snow,
And hail the infant year.

So, when the world and all its woes
Are vanish'd far away,
Fair scenes and wonderful repose
Shall bless the new-born day—

When, from the confines of the grave,
The body too shall rise,
No more precarious passion's slave,
Nor error's sacrifice.

'Tis but a sleep—and Sion's king
Will call the many dead;
'Tis but a sleep—and then we sing
O'er dreams of sorrow fled.

Yes!—wintry winds have ceased to blow,
And trembling leaves appear,
And Nature has her types to show
Throughout the varying year.

MY BIRTH-DAY

Aldborough, December 24, 1778

Through a dull tract of woe, of dread,
The toiling year has pass'd and fled:
And, lo! in sad and pensive strain,
I sing my birth-day date again.

Trembling and poor, I saw the light,
New waking from unconscious night;
Trembling and poor I still remain,
To meet unconscious night again.

Time in my pathway strews few flowers,
To cheer or cheat the weary hours;
And those few strangers, dear indeed,
Are choked, are check'd, by many a weed.

TO ELIZA

Beccles, 1779

The Hebrew king, with spleen possest,
By David's harp was soothed to rest;
Yet, when the magic song was o'er,
The soft delusion charm'd no more;
The former fury fired the brain,
And every care return'd again.

But had he known Eliza's skill
To bless the sense and bind the will,
To bid the gloom of care retire,
And fan the flame of fond desire,
Remembrance then had kept the strain,
And not a care return'd again.

LIFE

Aldborough, 1779

Think ye, the joys that fill our early day,
Are the poor prelude to some full repast?
Think you, they promise?—ah! believe they pay;
The purest ever, they are oft the last.
The jovial swain that yokes the morning team,
And all the verdure of the field enjoys,
See him, how languid, when the noon-tide beam
Plays on his brow, and all his force destroys.
So 'tis with us, when, love and pleasure fled,
We at the summit of our hill arrive:
Lo! the gay lights of Youth are past—are dead,
But what still deepening clouds of Care survive!

THE SACRAMENT

Aldborough, 1779

O sacred gift of God to man,
A faith that looks above,
And sees the deep amazing plan
Of sanctifying love.

Thou dear and yet tremendous God,

Whose glory pride reviles;
How did'st thou change thy awful rod
To pard'ning grace and smiles!

Shut up with sin, with shame below,
I trust, this bondage past,
A great, a glorious change to know,
And to be bless'd at last.

I do believe, that, God of light!
Thou didst to earth descend,
With Satan and with Sin to fight—
Our great, our only friend.

I know thou did'st ordain for me,
Thy creature, bread and wine;
The depth of grace I cannot see,
But worship the design.

NIGHT

Aldborough, 1779

The sober stillness of the night
That fills the silent air,
And all that breathes along the shore,
Invite to solemn prayer.

Vouchsafe to me that spirit, Lord!
Which points the sacred way,
And let thy creatures here below
Instruct me how to pray.

FRAGMENT, WRITTEN AT MIDNIGHT

Aldborough, 1779

Oh, great Apollo! by whose equal aid
The verse is written and the med'cine made,
Shall thus a boaster, with his fourfold powers,
In triumph scorn this sacred art of ours?
Insulting quack! on thy sad business go,
And land the stranger on this world of woe.
Still I pass on, and now before me find

The restless ocean, emblem of my mind;
There wave on wave, here thought on thought succeeds,
Their produce idle works and idle weeds.
Dark is the prospect o'er the rolling sea,
But not more dark than my sad views to me;
Yet from the rising moon the light beams dance
In troubled splendour o'er the wide expanse;
So on my soul, whom cares and troubles fright,
The Muse pours comfort in a flood of light.—
Shine out, fair flood! until the day-star flings
His brighter rays on all sublunar things.
"Why in such haste? by all the powers of wit,
I have against thee neither bond nor writ.
If thou'rt a poet, now indulge the flight
Of thy fine fancy in this dubious light;
Cold, gloom, and silence shall assist thy rhyme,
And all things meet to form the true sublime."—
"Shall I, preserver deem'd around the place,
With abject rhymes a doctor's name disgrace?
Nor doctor solely, in the healing art
I'm all in all, and all in every part;
Wise Scotland's boast let that diploma be
Which gave me right to claim the golden fee.
Praise, then, I claim, to skilful surgeon due,
For mine th' advice and operation too;
And, fearing all the vile compounding tribe,
I make myself the med'cines I prescribe.
Mine, too, the chemic art; and not a drop
Goes to my patients from a vulgar shop.
But chief my fame and fortune I command
From the rare skill of this obstetric hand:
This our chaste dames and prudent wives allow,
With her who calls me from thy wonder now."

MIDNIGHT

A POEM

About 1779

Life is a Dream;—it steals upon the Man,
He knows not how, but thinks himself awake;
'Tis like a Bubble dancing on the Deep,
That turns its glossy surface to the Sun,
Catches a Rainbow-Vest, and sparkles, proud

Of momentary Being—then it breaks—
To some tremendous Billow drops a prey,
And joins th' eternal Source, from whence it sprang.

But ah! how dismal are the Dreams of Care,
How much of Care do e'en the happiest dream,
And some—hard Fortune theirs—of Care alone.

Forgive me then, ye Wise, who seem awake,
A Midnight Song, and let your Censure sleep;
While Sorrow's Theme, and Contemplation sad,
And Soul-dilating Fancy's pensive Flight
Through Star-crown'd Gloom, I sing; inspir'd by her,
Whom Virtue loves, whom Wisdom; from whose Touch
Grief borrows Charm, and Expectation sits
On the cold Bosom of the Tomb serene.
Pale Melancholy she; nor softer shines
The sabled Fair, her Votress, o'er the Grave
Of the departed Lover; nor more mild
Sits yonder Moon's chaste ray upon the Rock,
That, rising from the Bosom of the Wave,
Flings Awe on Night. Thou Grave-enamour'd Fair,
Attune my Song, and, languid as thou art,
The Song shall please; and I will paint the Dream
That Midnight gave thee, when with wintry Wing
She swept thy Grot, and shook her grisled Dew
Upon the frozen Garment of the pool;
And I will drown mine Eye in Tears like thine,
And give my hollow Cheek a dewy pale,
And dress me in the Livery of the Dead;
And o'er their dreary Mansions walk with thee;
Bidding a brief Farewell to little Cares,
And Visionary Honour's frantic Sons,
Who feed on Adulation—let them feed,
Till the full Soul disdains the nauseous Trash,
And sickens with Repletion.—

I will ask,
No Voice of Fame to spread abroad my Song,
Nor Court Applause—Meonides had Fame,
And with her poverty and pain and Care,
Attendants on the Bard-deluding Nymph,
Who mock the Babbling of her loudest Note;
From Heaven he stole Description, Nature's Key,
And loosen'd into Light her Mysteries;
Ambition started when he sang of War,
In Language all her own; and o'er his Lyre
Hung Devastation, glowing at the Sound,

And frantic for the Field; and there Distress,
As if enamour'd of the Mighty Man,
With cruel Constancy repaid his Muse;
And chiding Fame, by whispering to the Soul
Domestic Ills, she triumph'd over praise,
And, through th' untasted Plaudit of a World,
Led the blind Bard in Sadness to the Tomb.—

I ask no Mantuan Muse with silver Wing
To bear me in some rapid even flight
Thro' distant Ages, tho' so sweet her Bard
That yet the Traveller o'er each Hill he sang,
Transported, wanders, feeling power divine
New-rising on his Soul to chain its Cares.
Imagination turns the Tide of Time,
Unwinds each year, and, thro' reviving Light,
And thro' the vandal Gloom of Centuries drear,
And falling Rome works back, till Nature smiles
And Tityrus sings anew; then laughs each Scene,
And cloudless skies appear, and Beachen Boughs
That Shade the Nereids listning from their Streams.—

Nor Milton's muse I boast, to whom the Morn
And all her rosy Train, and blazing Noon,
Dipping his fiery Tresses in the Stream
Of Pison, bank'd with Gold, and tepid Eve,
Who in her soft recesses cradles Thought,
And Worlds unsung pay Homage, and the Suns,
From which the Light yet wings its rapid Way,
Nor on the gloomy Bosom of the Earth,
Sleeps from the Labour of its long Career.

Nor feels my Bosom that ambiguous Flame,
That now from Skies, and now from central Gloom,
Shot devious o'er the fervent Page of Young—
Young, Thought's Oeconomist, who wove reproof
Her gloomiest Vest, and yet a Vest that shone;
Whose Invitation was assault: he found
The World asleep and rent its drowsy Ear.

Nor shares my Soul the soft enchanting Stream,
The lambent Blaze, that Thomson knew to blend
With his Creation; when he led the Eye
Through the year's Verdant Gate, the budding Spring;
And from the Willow o'er the tuneless Stream,
And from the Aspen Rind, ere yet her Leaf
Unfolding flicker'd, and from limpid rills
Unmantled, cull'd Simplicity and Grace.

Ah! who with mingled Modesty and Love
So paints the bathing Maid; who so describes
The new-mown Meadow, and the new shorn Lamb?
Hard is the Task to strip the Muse's Wing
Of Learning's plume, yet leave enough to charm;
But this was thine! Grace beautify'd thy page,
And led thy weary plowman from the field,
And spread thy simple Foliage on the Sod,
And hung thy ponderous Treasures on the Bough,
And rov'd with thy Lavinia where the Winds,
Rustling along the golden Valley, bear
The Grain just dropping from its withering Glume.
And Winter too was thine! permit me there
To bear a part, for mine are wintry Thoughts.—

Nor dare I hope his Dignity and Fire,
Who led the soul thro' Nature, and display'd
Imagination's pleasures to its Eye;
His the blest Task, a gloomier task is mine;
His were the Smiles of Fortune, mine her Frowns;
And when her Frowns and Smiles shall charm alike,
At that dread Hour when the officious Friend,
Stammering his Idiot-Comfort, soothes amiss,
May Joys he painted dart upon the Soul,
And, more than Fancy pointing to the Skies,
Whisper a noble Challenge to the Tomb.—
Tho' far behind my Song, my Hope the same,
And not behind my Song; with Vulgar souls,
Both sentenc'd to Contempt—unletter'd pride—
Grins the pale Bard Disgrace alike to him
Who soars above or labours in the Clouds,
Who travels the sublime, or dives profound
In the Wild Chaos of a School-boy's Dream:
He, tyed to some poor Spot, where e'en the rill
That owns him Lord untasted steals away,
Hallows a Clod, and spurns Immensity.

Ye gentle, nameless Bards, who float a-down
The soft smoothe Stream of silver poesy
And dream your pretty Dreams, permit my Song
Cold inspiration from a Winter's Night.
This is no Stanza'd Birth-Day of his Grace,
Your patron; no sad Satire of the Lord,
Your Foe; no Dunciad arm'd with power,
To dive into the Depths of your profound,
And with a vile assemblage gather'd there
Whip the pale Moonshine from your with'ring Bays.—

Is there, who sick of Pleasure's daily Draught,
In repetition mawkish, or who tir'd
Thinks Life an Idiot's Tale? or whom the Hand
Of Disappointment snatches from the Vice
That waits on power? or who has lost a friend,
And mingles with the dew that wets his Tomb
A frequent Tear? or who by Nature's mild
And melancholy Bias from the Womb
Was fashioned for the View of serious Things,
And with the sober chiding of his eye,
Freezes the Current within Laughter's Cheek,
And awes the Voice of loud Garrulity?
Let him approach, and I will tell my Soul,
EUGENIO rises from the Grave, and give
The Living Youth the Manners of my Friend.
From the Enshrouded Tenant of the Sod
I'll call the speaking Eye, the open Heart,
The Tongue belov'd of Knowledge, and the Form
That, could Deceit put on, Grey-headed Guile,
That judges from his own embosom'd Guilt,
Would yet be won, and lend a ductile Ear.

Together, while the Echo's feeble Sound,
Halting in frozen regions of the Air,
Mocks our slow Step, we from the Mountain's Brow,
Will look around and court the Stars of Heav'n
For as much Light as guides the Miser's hand,
To grasp Delusion in her Guise of Gold.—

The Morn is banish'd now, nor down the Hill
Slopes the faint Shadow; now in other Realms
She drinks the Dew that on the Vi'lets Lip
Slept thro' the Night; and, with her golden Dart
Bays the pale Moon, retiring from the View.
In other Climates, from the rays of Noon
Embower'd, Content lies sleeping; and the palm
Drinking the fiery Stream, plays o'er the Brow
Of shadied Weariness; and distant now
Draws meek-ey'd Eve, with even hand and slow,
The fringed Curtain of the setting Sun,
Ting'd with the golden Splendour he bequeaths,
The brief, but beauteous Legacy of Light.
'Tis Midnight round us, canopied by Dim
And twinkling Orbs that, gleaming ghastly, gild
The restless Bosom of the briny Deep.
The fiery Meteor in the foggy Air
Rides emulous of Fame and apes the Star,
Till, in the Compass of a Maiden's Wish,

It mocks the Eye, and sheds an igneous Stream,
Within the bosom of Oblivion.

The Sea-Bird sleeps upon yon hoary Cliff,
Unconscious of the Surge that grates below
The frozen Shore; and Icy Friendship binds,
As Danger Wretches Destitute of Soul,
The wave-worn pebbles, which the ebbing Tide,
Left with the Salt-Flood shining; dark is now
The awfull Deep, and o'er the Seaman's Grave
Rolls pouring, and forbids the lucid Stream,
That silvers oft the way, a shining Vest,
Sprung from the scaly people's putrid Dead,
Hanging unhers'd upon the Coral Bough;
Or, as the Sage explains, from Stores of Light
Imprizon'd in the Bowels of the Deep,
And now escaping, when the parent Sun
Flings out his fiery Noon with Beam direct,
Upon the Glossy Surface of the wave.

Cold Vapour, falling on the putrid Fen,
Condenses grey, and wraps with glassy net
The wintry Fern, and throws along the Heath
A Hoary Garment, nor less fair than Spring
Drops on the Sod, of Texture near as frail.
The icy Atoms thro' the burden'd Air
Shed Languor, and enwrap with double Fleece
The Slumbering Fold; they cloathe the knotted oak,
Stretching its naked arms, as if to chide,
With age's stern and touching Eloquence
The ruthless Skies for Summer's slow return.
The winds that in converging Furrows plough
The freezing pool, and shake the rattling Wood,
Are arm'd with pain, and vitrified their Wings.
In Winter's Livery sleeps this earthly Scene—
And, save where Ocean rolls his restless Flood,
The horizontal Eye grasps all things grey.—

Eugenio, see—for thou shalt bear His Name
Who sleeps beneath yon Sod, and was my Friend—
The Grave o'er which I weep; and give not thou
A Glance contemptuous to the grassy Tomb;
For oft the vaulted Chambers of the Dead,
Where Vanity amid the Mouldring Scrolls
Of Genealogy and mingled Bones
Moves in a formal join'd Solemnity,
House wretched Remnants of degenerate Man;
And oft the Green Turf's temporary swell,

Sepulchring all that Virtue leaves the Earth,
Stirs busy Memory to con o'er Deeds
Of high Renown in Heaven, the Deeds of Love;
Which in th' eternal Records of the Just,
Are written with an Angels pen, and sung
With Symphony of Harp, and there is Joy
And Gratulation with the Sons of God.—

Alas! how chang'd the Verdure of this Scene,
How lost the Flowers, how winter-struck the Blade!
No more the wild Thyme wings the passing Gale
With Fragrance, nor invites the roving Bee
To taste its Sweets—and why this direful waste
Of Verdure? why this Vegetable Death?
Did all with Man commit mysterious Sin?
All in rebellion rise?—and tepid Meads,
And Lawns irriguous, and the blooming field,
And Hills, and Vallies, and intangling Woods,
Spurn GOD'S Command and drink forbidden Dew?—

There was a Time, and Poets paint it fair,
(A wild, uncertain, musing, madning Race)
A Golden Age, when wealth was only Love:
Not even Fancy dreamt a Dream of Care,
The Sward was not—and Desolation slept
Till by a Crime awaken'd; not e'en Song
Wore Semblatude of War;—Eternal Spring
From the unfurrow'd Field the heavy Ear
Drew smiling, and the undistinguish'd year
Brought willing plenty forth, nor scorn'd she then
A Common Call, enamour'd of her plough.
The Clinging Vine prest down the branching Elm
E'en to the Earth, and in her verdant Lap
The tributary Grape, yet growing, laid.
The simple Shepherd pip'd a silvan Lay;
Or, while the Fair who charm'd him prest beside,
The listning Vale sung hymeneal Strains,
And woo'd with melting Themes a ten years' Bride.

Eugenio, thus they taught; and after this
A silver age arose, and hers the Scenes
Not Gold could purchase now: when Vice, afraid,
Hid his pale Visage in the womb of Night,
And blush'd, if but a Moon-beam met his Eye.
The Seasons alter'd, but the Change was slow,
And Man forgot they chang'd; then Care began
To plow his Furrows on the Brow of Age,
And Falshood from the female Eye to steal

The silent Tear; then prudence took her Seat
Within the Soul, and reign'd in Virtue's room.
Then Vanity, a Child, first learn'd to bend
The ready Ear to tales of her own praise;
Nor knew she yet the Gross of Flattery,
But was, as Modesty is now, afraid
The Verse she lov'd should tickle her too much.
Then young Ambition wore his Russet Gown
Only in better Form, and Infant pomp
But saw his Garden smile in richer Bloom,
And propt his Cottage with a taller pier.—

Since these, dread Sorrow, consequent of Sin
And foul Deformity, the Breast of Man
And the Sad Surface of the Earth enrobes.—

From the Dark Bosom of the Giant Guilt
Leak'd all Things terrible, and Murder first,
Who proul'd about the Earth and groan'd for Blood;
And treachery, breaking up the League of Friends
And rending Nature's Bond, a solemn writ,
With Heaven's own Seal imprest: and Avarice pale,
A Woolfish-Visag'd Fiend and fang'd with Care.
Hence War, in all her guilty Majesty
In slow pomp riding o'er a threat'ned Land,
With all the murderous Whispers of the Camp
And shout of Ambush, castigates the Night.—

And hence the Spirits from th' Abyss of Hell,
That prey upon Mankind.—Eugenio, give
Thy Soul's pure Eye, that sees immortal things,
To the grim Spectres hovering in the Air,
And we will mark the dreary Train that vex
The mortal Man, and ride with ghostly pomp,
Frowning upon the Midnight's murky Wing.—

And who is he, from yonder antient roof,
With Horror in his Eye, who steals around
Each hollow Isle; and with a fierce Embrace
Clasps the encrumbling ruin? 'Tis the Foe
Of Men and Virtue, Eldest-born of Night,
And Superstition call'd, a Giant fond
Of Dead-Men's Bones, and vagrant Rottenness,
Denied a Tomb; around him turns the wheel,
And faggots blaze; and prizons, with a Groan
Resounding loud, affright the Coward Soul
From Reason's Law, and Nature's. Hark! he Mourns
The fretted Abby where he reign'd Secure,

With Indolence and Folly, social pair,
Nurses to shrine-enamour'd Zeal, who built
The Cavern deep and dark, in which he chain'd
The drowsy Nine; who yet at Morn or Eve
Hail'd the arising or descending Sun
With gothic Note, harmoniously sad.
But now no more the Votive Maiden clasps
The clay cold Saint, and mingles with her Vow
The Heaven-reproaching Sigh; in these blest realms
No more the power-compelling Bigot plucks
The robe from Kings, and consecrates the Tomb
That hides a Brother-Saint with Zeal-enforc'd
And ceremonious Solemnity.—

O'er the Opaque of Nature and of Night
Fair Truth rose smiling, with the Heaven-born Art
That shews the Man his Fellow's Thought imprest
Within the Volumes' varied Character,
Where to the wondering Eye the Soul reveals
Her Store immortal. Hence a Bacon shone
And Newton thro' the World, and Light on Light
Pour'd on the human Breast, as when of old,
From the Eternal Fountains of the God,
Etherial Streams assail'd the groaning Mass;
Then Chaos and the Sun's large Eye survey'd
The first distinguish'd Forms of mortal Things,
Till then in Congregate Confusion hurl'd
Without a Station, and without a Name.
Then Wit began, the younger-born of Light,
To sport in hallow'd Cloysters, where the arm
Of Superstition, red with slaughter'd Foes,
Held high the Torch of Discord. Stroke on Stroke
The smiling Boy repeated with his Sword,
Sharp as the Whirlwind's Eye: yet fear'd the fight,
And oft drew back, his silver wing born down
By the foul Breath of Malice; till at length
The Monster, rousing in Collected Might,
Shook with his Roar the Earth, and at the Sound
Red Tyranny, and Torture, with his Limbs
Disjoint, and Ignorance that blows the blast
For every Fire, prepar'd each bloody Form
Of Death, and woo'd Destruction for her Wheel.—

Then on the Father dead the dying Son
Implor'd Heavn's Vengence. Execration shrill
Shot from the lurid Flame, and to the Skies
Sail'd with the Speed of Light. The Virgin's Eye
Met the grey Ruffian's, speaking Nature's Fear

Of Death and Pain: the Bigot's stern Reply,
Forbidding Hope, on the affrightned Soul
Flung Terror; till, in pity to the World,
Came Wisdom, whispering to the Ear of power,
And peace arose; and then the Brother wept
A Brother's Death, for distant seem'd his own.

And now the Spirit of uneasy Man,
That weds Extreme, and, ever on the Wing
For Wonder, baffles peace, high o'er the Cells
Of monkish Zeal, built with the base remains
The tow'ring Palace of Impiety.
There Jest profane, and Quibbling Mockery
Of all divine grew fast, as from the Earth
Enrich'd Ill-Weeds first spring; and here the Fools,
Of Laughter vain, despis'd the Voice of Truth,
And labour'd in the ludicrous obscene.

To these succeed, and ah! with sad Success,
A Sceptic herd more cool, and fair of form,
And smoothe of Tongue and apt to gloss a Lye
With Semblance strong of Nature and the Truth;
They shine as Serpents, and as Serpents bite,
With poison'd Tooth. Alas! the State of Man,
Or doom'd the Victim of ungovern'd Zeal,
Or led the Captive of unquiet Doubt!—

And now, Eugenio, turn thine Eye, and view
Yon Sire bare-headed to the ruthless Wind,
And heedless of its Force. Upon the Brow
Of yon huge shapeless Ruin, see, he kneels,
And urges the departed Saints who sleep,
To lend a Prayer; Repentance sent him forth,
Her Son, but late th' adopted of her dark
And gloomy Train. Ah! heavy weighs the Crime
Of Murder on his Soul, and haunts his Bed!
And, shrieking by, unseals the Eye of Sleep,
Or scatters on the dark and restless Mind
A thousand sooty Images of Death,
All horrible, and making Guilt's repose
Like to the fearfull rest the Vessel feels
In the dread Chasm of the tempestuous Sea,
Arch'd by the Wave that pauses o'er the Gulph,
While Sea-men urge their momentary prayer,
And with Heart-shrinking Horror view their Grave.

But hark, he speaks—attend the Wretches Tale—
Spreading his Soul upon the Wings of Night,

And seeking peace by giving Themes of pain
To the rude Air:

"Come, all ye little Ills,
Contempt, and poverty, and pale Disease
With Dewy Front, and Envy-struck applause
That sickens on the World, and all of Care
That shed your daily Drops of bitter Dew
Upon the Brow of mortal Man, here strike,
That I may feel your force, and call it Joy,
So made when weigh'd against the Load that Guilt,
With leaden Hand, deposits on my Heart,
And when a momentary Comfort strives,
Lifted by hope, to spread her downy Wing,
Dispair, with Icy palm, arrests the Thought,
And nips the still-born Joy.—

"To me no more
The Good I coveted brings Joy, brings peace,
Or stifles Truth's reproof that will be heard;
And did I think a base and sordid Heap
Had in it the Ability to pluck
The Sting from Guilt, and smother how it came
In the vile Knowledge that it came to me?
It was a Madman's Dream—O ye good Gods!
If Envy knew her Mark, she would beset
The poor Man's Table and the Shepherd's Hut,
Unroof'd to the cold Winter's wildest Blast,
Or the Embay'd Explorers of the Deep,
At their still howling North; and leave the Throne,
The Sceptre and the chested Gold to plant
The Thorn of Care upon the Brow of State,
On which Distraction drives his plow-share deep,
And helps the Scythe of Time to wrinkle there.—

"When shall I rest—O! let me, Night, besiege
Thy drowsy Ear with wailing, but be thou
Tenacious of my Guilt; and with her Band
Let everlasting Silence Tye thy Tongue;
The pent-up Woe now struggles to o'er-leap
Murder's Discretion, and with fearfull Speech
To free the Heart by telling Deeds of Death:
Death, Thought's repose, whom the abhor'd of Man,
The base assassin, gives, and after longs
With Lover's Ardour to embrace, be mine,
And I will yield all Hope of After-Life,
All Saints have promis'd, and all poets sung—
Elysium water'd with immortal Streams,

And gifted with Eternity of peace,
Balm-breathing Fields, and Bowers of soft repose,
Walks amaranthine, and the pillowy Moss,
On Banks where Harpers, to celestial Strings
Attuning Nature, warble Notes of Love,
The Anodyne to all-rebellious Thought.—

"These, for Oblivion, I forego, with these
Foregoing pain eternal. Why then strive
From off Life's galling Load to elbow Care,
When Life and Care may be remov'd together?—
If I were not a very Coward Wretch,
A very Shadow of the Man, a thing
Made to feel Burdens of my Fear, and drag
A hated Being on—'twere but to leap
From this rough Eminence, and all is done—
All that is done on this Side of the Bier.
But there, surrounded with impervious Fog,
Sits Doubt and Questions of the Scenes to come;
Oh! Death, what moves beyond thee? Fears and Hopes,
Dread and Confusion, Envy and Disease,
Sleeping and waking Lusts, War-moving Pride,
Windy Ambition, and slow Avarice,
Slay in thy path; within thy Sepulchre
Mould Dead Men's Bones, feed worms, rust Epitaphs,
Sleep brainless Skulls in blest Vacuity!
But what comes then? O for a Seraph's Eye
That, piercing thro' the Mask of Mortal Things,
Might scale the cloudless Battlements of Light,
And in its Immaterial Robe detect
The Spirit, stript of the encumbring Clay."—

Alas, Eugenio! Life, Deception's Child,
Gives us her fairer Side, and gives no more;
The rest we seek in our reflecting View
Of Self, and Guilt's o'erheard Soliloquy.
How smiles the World in pain, and smiles believ'd!
Yon Wretch who, muffled in the Garb of Night,
Gave her the Tortures of a weary Soul,
Meets—may he not?—the jovial Eye of Day,
With a depictur'd Laughter in his Cheek,
Or the smoothe Visage of habitual Ease?

How have I mourn'd my Lot, as if the Fates
Cull'd me, the vilest from their pitchy Stores
That ere in Mortal Bosom planted Woe,
And pain'd the Care-fraught Soul! I'll grieve no more,
But, take it patient with a sober hope,

That soon Distress may vary his assault,
Or soon the Welcome Tomb exclude Distress.—

But see another Son of Night and Care,
A Shepherd watching o'er his frozen Fold,
Himself benumb'd and murmuring at his Fate.
Sigh not, fond Man; thy bosom only feels
The gentler Blows of Nature, and receives
The Common Visit of Calamity.

JUVENILIA

A FAREWELL

1779?

The hour arrived! I sigh'd and said,
How soon the happiest hours are fled!
On wings of down they lately flew,
But then their moments pass'd with you;
And still with you could I but be,
On downy wings they'd always flee.

Say, did you not, the way you went,
Feel the soft balm of gay content?
Say, did you not all pleasures find,
Of which you left so few behind?
I think you did: for well I know
My parting prayer would make it so.

"May she," I said, "life's choicest goods partake;
Those, late in life, for nobler still forsake—
The bliss of one, th' esteem'd of many live,
With all that Friendship would, and all that Love can give!"

TIME

London, February, 1780

"The clock struck one! we take no thought of Time,"
Wrapt up in Night, and meditating rhyme.
All big with vision, we despise the powers
That vulgar beings link to days and hours—
Those vile, mechanic things that rule our hearts,

And cut our lives in momentary parts.
That speech of Time was Wisdom's gift, said Young.
Ah, Doctor! better, Time would hold his tongue:
What serves the clock? "To warn the careless crew,
How much in little space they have to do;
To bid the busy world resign their breath,
And beat each moment a soft call for death—
To give it, then, a tongue, was wise in man."
Support the assertion, Doctor, if you can.
It tells the ruffian when his comrades wait;
It calls the duns to crowd my hapless gate;
It tells my heart the paralysing tale
Of hours to come, when Misery must prevail.

THE CHOICE

London, February, 1780

What vulgar title thus salutes the eye,
The schoolboy's first attempt at poesy?
The long-worn theme of every humbler Muse,
For wits to scorn and nurses to peruse;
The dull description of a scribbler's brain,
And sigh'd-for wealth, for which he sighs in vain;
A glowing chart of fairy-land estate,
Romantic scenes, and visions out of date,
Clear skies, clear streams, soft banks, and sober bowers,
Deer, whimpering brooks, and wind-perfuming flowers?

Not thus! too long have I in fancy wove
My slender webs of wealth, and peace, and love;
Have dream'd of plenty, in the midst of want,
And sought, by Hope, what Hope can never grant;
Been fool'd by wishes, and still wish'd again,
And loved the flattery, while I knew it vain!
"Gain by the Muse!"—alas! thou might'st as soon
Pluck gain (as Percy honour) from the moon;
As soon grow rich by ministerial nods,
As soon divine by dreaming of the gods,
As soon succeed by telling ladies truth,
Or preaching moral documents to youth;
To as much purpose, mortal! thy desires,
As Tully's flourishes to country squires;
As simple truth within St. James's state,
Or the soft lute in shrill-tongued Billingsgate.
"Gain by the Muse!" alas, preposterous hope!

Who ever gain'd by poetry—but Pope?
And what art thou? No St. John takes thy part;
No potent Dean commends thy head or heart!
What gain'st thou but the praises of the poor?
They bribe no milkman to thy lofty door,
They wipe no scrawl from thy increasing score.
What did the Muse, or Fame, for Dryden, say?
What for poor Butler? what for honest Gay?
For Thomson, what? or what to Savage give?
Or how did Johnson—how did Otway live?
Like thee, dependent on to-morrow's good,
Their thin revénue never understood;
Like thee, elate at what thou canst not know;
Like thee, repining at each puny blow;
Like thee they lived, each dream of Hope to mock,
Upon their wits—but with a larger stock.
No, if for food thy unambitious pray'r,
With supple acts to supple minds repair;
Learn of the base in soft grimace to deal,
And deck thee with the livery genteel;
Or trim the wherry, or the flail invite,
Draw teeth, or any viler thing but write.
Writers, whom once th' astonish'd vulgar saw
Give nations language, and great cities law;
Whom gods, they said—and surely gods—inspired,
Whom emp'rors honour'd, and the world admired,
Now common grown, they awe mankind no more,
But vassals are, who judges were before.
Blockheads on wits their little talents waste,
As files gnaw metal that they cannot taste;
Though still some good the trial may produce,
To shape the useful to a nobler use.
Some few of these a statue and a stone
Has Fame decreed—but deals out bread to none.
Unhappy art! decreed thine owner's curse,
Vile diagnostic of consumptive purse;
Members by bribes, and ministers by lies,
Gamesters by luck, by courage soldiers rise:
Beaux by the outside of their heads may win,
And wily sergeants by the craft within:
Who but the race, by Fancy's demon led,
Starve by the means they use to gain their bread?
Oft have I read, and, reading, mourn'd the fate
Of garret-bard, and his unpitied mate;
Of children stinted in their daily meal,—
The joke of wealthier wits who could not feel.
Portentous spoke that pity in my breast,
And pleaded self—who ever pleads the best.

No! thank my stars, my misery's all my own—
To friends, to family, to foes unknown;
Who hates my verse, and damns the mean design,
Shall wound no peace—shall grieve no heart but mine.
One trial past, let sober Reason speak:
Here shall we rest, or shall we further seek?
Rest here, if our relenting stars ordain
A placid harbour from the stormy main;
Or, that denied, the fond remembrance weep,
And sink, forgotten, in the mighty deep.

A HUMBLE INVOCATION

1780

When summer's tribe, her rosy tribe, are fled,
And drooping beauty mourns her blossoms shed,
Some humbler sweet may cheer the pensive swain,
And simpler beauties deck the withering plain.
And thus, when Verse her wintry prospect weeps,
When Pope is gone, and mighty Milton sleeps,
When Gray in lofty lines has ceased to soar,
And gentle Goldsmith charms the town no more,
An humbler Bard the widow'd Muse invites,
Who led by hope and inclination writes;
With half their art, he tries the soul to move,
And swell the softer strain with themes of love.

FROM AN EPISTLE TO MIRA

April, 1780

Of substance I've thought, and the varied disputes
On the nature of man and the notions of brutes;
Of systems confuted, and systems explain'd;
Of science disputed, and tenets maintain'd.
These, and such speculations on these kind of things,
Have robb'd my poor Muse of her plume and her wings;
Consumed the phlogiston you used to admire,
The spirit extracted, extinguish'd the fire;
Let out all the ether, so pure and refined,
And left but a mere caput mortuum behind.

CONCLUDING LINES OF AN EPISTLE TO PRINCE WILLIAM HENRY, AFTERWARDS KING WILLIAM IV

April, 1780

Who thus aspiring sings, would'st thou explore?
A Bard replies, who ne'er assumed before—
One taught in hard affliction's school to bear
Life's ills, where every lesson costs a tear;
Who sees from thence the proper point of view,
What the wise heed not, and the weak pursue.

"And now farewell," the drooping Muse exclaims;
She lothly leaves thee to the shock of war,
And, fondly dwelling on her princely tar,
Wishes the noblest good her Harry's share,
Without her misery and without her care.
For, ah! unknown to thee, a rueful train,
Her hapless children sigh, and sigh in vain;
A numerous band, denied the boon to die,
Half-starved, half-fed by fits of charity.
Unknown to thee! and yet, perhaps, thy ear
Has chanced each sad, amusing tale to hear,
How some, like Budgell, madly sank for ease;
How some, like Savage, sicken'd by degrees;
How a pale crew, like helpless Otway, shed
The proud, big tear on song-extorted bread;
Or knew, like Goldsmith, some would stoop to choose
Contempt, and for the mortar quit the Muse.

One of this train—and of these wretches one—
Slave to the Muses, and to Misery son—
Now prays the Father of all Fates to shed
On Henry, laurels, on his poet, bread!
Unhappy art! decreed thine owner's curse;
Vile diagnostic of consumptive purse;
Still shall thy fatal force my soul perplex,
And every friend, and every brother vex—
Each fond companion?—No, I thank my God.
There rests my torment—there is hung the rod.
To friend, to fame, to family unknown,
Sour disappointments frown on me alone.
Who hates my song, and damns the poor design,
Shall wound no peace—shall grieve no heart but mine!

Pardon, sweet Prince! the thoughts that will intrude,
For want is absent, and dejection rude.
Methinks I hear, amid the shouts of Fame,

Each jolly victor hail my Henry's name;
And Heaven forbid that, in that jovial day,
One British bard should grieve when all are gay.
No! let him find his country has redress,
And bid adieu to every fond distress;
Or, touch'd too near, from joyful scenes retire,
Scorn to complain, and with one sigh expire!

DRIFTING

May, 1780

Like some poor bark on the rough ocean tost,
My rudder broken, and my compass lost,
My sails the coarsest, and too thin to last,
Pelted by rains, and bare to many a blast,
My anchor, Hope, scarce fix'd enough to stay
Where the strong current Grief sweeps all away,
I sail along, unknowing how to steer,
Where quicksands lie and frowning rocks appear.
Life's ocean teems with foes to my frail bark,
The rapid sword-fish, and the rav'ning shark,
Where torpid things crawl forth in splendid shell,
And knaves and fools and sycophants live well.
What have I left in such tempestuous sea?
No Tritons shield, no Naiads shelter me!
A gloomy Muse, in Mira's absence, hears
My plaintive prayer, and sheds consoling tears—
Some fairer prospect, though at distance, brings,
Soothes me with song, and flatters as she sings.

TO THE RIGHT HONOURABLE THE EARL OF SHELBURNE

June, 1780

Ah! SHELBURNE, blest with all that's good or great
T'adorn a rich, or save a sinking, state—
If public Ills engross not all thy care,
Let private Woe assail a patriot's ear;
Pity confined, but not less warm, impart,
And unresisted win thy noble heart;
Nor deem I rob thy soul of Britain's share,
Because I hope to have some interest there.
Still wilt thou shine on all a fostering sun,

Though with more fav'ring beams enlight'ning one;
As Heaven will oft make some more amply blest,
Yet still in general bounty feeds the rest.
Oh, hear the Virtue thou reverest plead;
She'll swell thy breast, and there applaud the deed.
She bids thy thoughts one hour from greatness stray,
And leads thee on to fame a shorter way;
Where, if no withering laurel's thy reward,
There's shouting Conscience, and a grateful Bard;
A bard untrained in all but misery's school,
Who never bribed a knave or praised a fool.
'Tis Glory prompts, and, as thou read'st, attend;
She dictates pity, and becomes my friend;
She bids each cold and dull reflection flee,
And yields her Shelburne to distress and me!

AN EPISTLE TO A FRIEND

June, 1780

Why, true, thou say'st the fools, at Court denied,
Growl vengeance—and then take the other side;
The unfed flatterer borrows satire's power,
As sweets unshelter'd run to vapid sour.
But thou, the counsel to my closest thought,
Beheld'st it ne'er in fulsome stanzas wrought.
The Muse I court ne'er fawn'd on venal souls,
Whom suppliants angle, and poor praise controls;
She, yet unskill'd in all but fancy's dream,
Sang to the woods, and Mira was her theme.
But, when she sees a titled nothing stand
The ready cipher of a trembling land—
Not of that simple kind that, placed alone,
Are useless, harmless things, and threaten none;
But those which, join'd to figures, well express
A strengthen'd tribe that amplify distress,
Grow in proportion to their number great,
And help each other in the ranks of state—
When this and more the pensive Muses see,
They leave the vales and willing nymphs to thee;
To Court on wings of agile anger speed,
And paint to freedom's sons each guileful deed.
Hence rascals teach the virtues they detest,
And fright base action from sin's wavering breast;
For, though the Knave may scorn the Muse's arts,
Her sting may haply pierce more timid hearts.

Some, though they wish it, are not steel'd enough,
Nor is each would-be villain conscience-proof.

And what, my friend, is left my song besides?
No school-day wealth that roll'd in silver tides,
No dreams of hope that won my early will,
Nor love, that pain'd in temporary thrill;
No gold to deck my pleasure-scorn'd abode,
No friend to whisper peace, to give me food.
Poor to the World, I'd yet not live in vain,
But show its lords their hearts, and my disdain.

Yet shall not Satire all my song engage
In indiscriminate and idle rage;
True praise, where Virtue prompts, shall gild each line,
And long—if Vanity deceives not—shine.
For, though in harsher strains, the strains of woe,
And unadorn'd my heart-felt murmurs flow,
Yet time shall be when this thine humbled friend
Shall to more lofty heights his notes extend.
A Man—for other title were too poor—
Such as 'twere almost virtue to adore,
He shall the ill that loads my heart exhale,
As the sun vapours from the dew-press'd vale;
Himself uninjuring, shall new warmth infuse,
And call to blossom every want-nipp'd Muse.
Then shall my grateful strains his ear rejoice,
His name harmonious thrill'd on Mira's voice;
Round the reviving bays new sweets shall spring,
And SHELBURNE'S fame through laughing valleys ring.

THE CANDIDATE; A POETICAL EPISTLE TO THE AUTHORS OF THE MONTHLY REVIEW

Multa quidem nobis facimus mala sæpe poetæ,
(Ut vineta egomet cædam mea) cum tibi librum
Sollicito damus, aut fesso, &c.

HOR. Lib. ii. Ep. I.

London, 1780

AN INTRODUCTORY ADDRESS OF THE AUTHOR TO HIS POEMS

Ye idler things, that soothed my hours of care,

Where would ye wander, triflers, tell me where?
As maids neglected, do ye fondly dote
On the fair type, or the embroider'd coat;
Detest my modest shelf, and long to fly,
Where princely POPES and mighty MILTONS lie?
Taught but to sing, and that in simple style,
Of Lycia's lip, and Musidora's smile,
Go, then! and taste a yet unfelt distress,
The fear that guards the captivating press;
Whose maddening region should ye once explore,
No refuge yields my tongueless mansion more.
But thus ye'll grieve, Ambition's plumage stript,
"Ah, would to Heaven, we'd died in manuscript!"
Your unsoil'd page each yawning wit shall flee
—For few will read, and none admire like me.—
Its place, where spiders silent bards enrobe.
Squeezed betwixt Cibber's Odes and Blackmore's Job;
Where froth and mud, that varnish and deform,
Feed the lean critic and the fattening worm;
Then sent disgraced—the unpaid printer's bane—
To mad Moorfields, or sober Chancery Lane,
On dirty stalls I see your hopes expire,
Vex'd by the grin of your unheeded sire,
Who half reluctant has his care resign'd,
Like a teased parent, and is rashly kind.

Yet rush not all, but let some scout go forth.
View the strange land, and tell us of its worth;
And, should he there barbarian usage meet,
The patriot scrap shall warn us to retreat.

And thou, the first of thy eccentric race,
A forward imp, go, search the dangerous place,
Where Fame's eternal blossoms tempt each bard,
Though dragon-wits there keep eternal guard.
Hope not unhurt the golden spoil to seize,
The Muses yield, as the Hesperides;
Who bribes the guardian, all his labour's done,
For every maid is willing to be won.

Before the lords of verse a suppliant stand,
And beg our passage through the fairy land:
Beg more—to search for sweets each blooming field,
And crop the blossoms woods and valleys yield;
To snatch the tints that beam on Fancy's bow,
And feel the fires on Genius' wings that glow;
Praise without meanness, without flattery stoop,
Soothe without fear, and without trembling hope.

TO THE READER

The following Poem being itself of an introductory nature, its author supposes it can require but little preface.

It is published with a view of obtaining the opinion of the candid and judicious reader on the merits of the writer as a poet; very few, he apprehends, being in such cases sufficiently impartial to decide for themselves.

It is addressed to the Authors of the Monthly Review, as to critics of acknowledged merit; an acquaintance with whose labours has afforded the writer of this Epistle a reason for directing it to them in particular, and, he presumes, will yield to others a just and sufficient plea for the preference.

Familiar with disappointment, he shall not be much surprised to find he has mistaken his talent. However, if not egregiously the dupe of his vanity, he promises to his readers some entertainment, and is assured that, however little in the ensuing Poem is worthy of applause, there is yet less that merits contempt.

TO THE AUTHORS OF THE MONTHLY REVIEW

The pious pilot, whom the Gods provide,
Through the rough seas the shatter'd bark to guide,
Trusts not alone his knowledge of the deep,
Its rocks that threaten, and its sands that sleep;
But, whilst with nicest skill he steers his way,
The guardian Tritons hear their favourite pray.
Hence borne his vows to Neptune's coral dome,
The God relents, and shuts each gulfy tomb.

Thus as on fatal floods to fame I steer,
I dread the storm, that ever rattles here;
Nor think enough, that long my yielding soul
Has felt the Muse's soft, but strong, control;
Nor think enough that manly strength and ease,
Such as have pleased a friend, will strangers please;
But, suppliant, to the critic's throne I bow,
Here burn my incense, and here pay my vow;
That censure hush'd, may every blast give o'er,
And the lash'd coxcomb hiss contempt no more.
And ye, whom authors dread or dare in vain,
Affecting modest hopes or poor disdain,
Receive a bard, who, neither mad nor mean,
Despises each extreme, and sails between;

Who fears; but has, amid his fears confess'd,
The conscious virtue of a Muse oppressed;
A Muse in changing times and stations nursed,
By nature honour'd and by fortune cursed.

No servile strain of abject hope she brings,
Nor soars presumptuous, with unwearied wings;
But, pruned for flight—the future all her care—
Would know her strength, and, if not strong, forbear.

The supple slave to regal pomp bows down,
Prostrate to power, and cringing to a crown;
The bolder villain spurns a decent awe,
Tramples on rule, and breaks through every law;
But he whose soul on honest truth relies,
Nor meanly flatters power, nor madly flies.
Thus timid authors bear an abject mind,
And plead for mercy they but seldom find.
Some, as the desperate to the halter run,
Boldly deride the fate they cannot shun;
But such there are, whose minds, not taught to stoop,
Yet hope for fame, and dare avow their hope;
Who neither brave the judges of their cause,
Nor beg in soothing strains a brief applause.
And such I'd be;—and, ere my fate is past,
Ere clear'd with honour, or with culprits cast,
Humbly at Learning's bar I'll state my case,
And welcome then distinction or disgrace!

When in the man the flights of fancy reign,
Rule in the heart, or revel in the brain,
As busy Thought her wild creation apes,
And hangs delighted o'er her varying shapes,
It asks a judgment, weighty and discreet,
To know where wisdom prompts, and where conceit;
Alike their draughts to every scribbler's mind
(Blind to their faults as to their danger blind)—
We write enraptured, and we write in haste,
Dream idle dreams, and call them things of taste;
Improvement trace in every paltry line,
And see, transported, every dull design;
Are seldom cautious, all advice detest,
And ever think our own opinions best;
Nor shows my Muse a muse-like spirit here,
Who bids me pause, before I persevere.

But she—who shrinks, while meditating flight
In the wide way, whose bounds delude her sight,

Yet tired in her own mazes still to roam,
And cull poor banquets for the soul at home—
Would, ere she ventures, ponder on the way,
Lest dangers yet unthought-of flight betray;
Lest her Icarian wing, by wits unplumed,
Be robb'd of all the honours she assumed,
And Dulness swell—a black and dismal sea,
Gaping her grave, while censures madden me.

Such was his fate, who flew too near the sun,
Shot far beyond his strength, and was undone;
Such is his fate, who creeping at the shore
The billow sweeps him, and he's found no more.
Oh! for some God, to bear my fortunes fair
Midway betwixt presumption and despair!

"Has then some friendly critic's former blow
Taught thee a prudence authors seldom know?"

Not so! their anger and their love untried,
A wo-taught prudence deigns to tend my side:
Life's hopes ill-sped, the Muse's hopes grow poor,
And though they flatter, yet they charm no more;
Experience points where lurking dangers lay,
And as I run, throws caution in my way.

There was a night, when wintry winds did rage,
Hard by a ruin'd pile I met a sage;
Resembling him the time-struck place appear'd,
Hollow its voice, and moss its spreading beard;
Whose fate-lopp'd brow, the bat's and beetle's dome,
Shook, as the hunted owl flew hooting home.
His breast was bronzed by many an eastern blast,
And fourscore winters seem'd he to have past;
His thread-bare coat the supple osier bound,
And with slow feet he press'd the sodden ground;
Where, as he heard the wild-wing'd Eurus blow,
He shook, from locks as white, December's snow;
Inured to storm, his soul ne'er bid it cease,
But lock'd within him meditated peace.

"Father," I said—for silver hairs inspire,
And oft I call the bending peasant Sire—
"Tell me, as here beneath this ivy bower,
That works fantastic round its trembling tower,
We hear Heaven's guilt-alarming thunders roar,
Tell me the pains and pleasures of the poor;
For Hope, just spent, requires a sad adieu,

And Fear acquaints me I shall live with you.

"There was a time when, by Delusion led,
A scene of sacred bliss around me spread;
On Hope's, as Pisgah's lofty top, I stood,
And saw my Canaan there, my promised good.
A thousand scenes of joy the clime bestow'd,
And wine and oil through vision's valleys flow'd;
As Moses his, I call'd my prospect bless'd,
And gazed upon the good I ne'er possess'd:
On this side Jordan doom'd by fate to stand,
Whilst happier Joshuas win the promised land."
"Son," said the Sage—"be this thy care suppressed;
The state the Gods shall choose thee is the best:
Rich if thou art, they ask thy praises more,
And would thy patience, when they make thee poor.
But other thoughts within thy bosom reign,
And other subjects vex thy busy brain;
Poetic wreaths thy vainer dreams excite,
And thy sad stars have destined thee to write.
Then, since that task the ruthless fates decree,
Take a few precepts from the Gods and me!

"Be not too eager in the arduous Chase:
Who pants for triumph seldom wins the race;
Venture not all, but wisely hoard thy worth,
And let thy labours one by one go forth;
Some happier scrap capricious wits may find
On a fair day, and be profusely kind;
Which, buried in the rubbish of a throng,
Had pleased as little as a new-year's song,
Or lover's verse, that cloy'd with nauseous sweet,
Or birth-day ode, that ran on ill-pair'd feet.
Merit not always—Fortune feeds the bard,
And, as the whim inclines, bestows reward;
None without wit, nor with it numbers gain;
To please is hard, but none shall please in vain.
As a coy mistress is the humour'd town,
Loth every lover with success to crown;
He who would win must every effort try,
Sail in the mode, and to the fashion fly;
Must gay or grave to every humour dress,
And watch the lucky Moment of Success;
That caught, no more his eager hopes are crost;
But vain are Wit and Love, when that is lost."

Thus said the God; for now a God he grew,
His white locks changing to a golden hue,

And from his shoulders hung a mantle azure-blue.
His softening eyes the winning charm disclosed
Of dove-like Delia, when her doubts reposed;
Mira's alone a softer lustre bear,
When wo beguiles them of an angel's tear;
Beauteous and young the smiling phantom stood,
Then sought on airy wing his blest abode.

Ah! truth distasteful in poetic theme,
Why is the Muse compell'd to own her dream?
Whilst forward wits had sworn to every line,
I only wish to make its moral mine.

Say then, O ye who tell how authors speed,
May Hope indulge her flight, and I succeed?
Say, shall my name, to future song prefix'd,
Be with the meanest of the tuneful mix'd?
Shall my soft strains the modest maid engage,
My graver numbers move the silver'd sage,
My tender themes delight the lover's heart,
And comfort to the poor my solemn songs impart?

For O! thou, Hope's—thou, Thought's eternal King,
Who gav'st them power to charm, and me to sing,
Chief to thy praise my willing numbers soar,
And in my happier transports I adore;
Mercy thy softest attribute proclaim,
Thyself in abstract, thy more lovely name;
That flings o'er all my grief a cheering ray,
As the foil moon-beam gilds the watery way.
And then too, Love, my soul's resistless lord,
Shall many a gentle, generous strain afford,
To all the soil of sooty passions blind,
Pure as embracing angels, and as kind;
Our Mira's name in future times shall shine,
And—though the harshest—Shepherds envy mine.

Then let me (pleasing task!) however hard,
Join, as of old, the prophet and the bard;
If not, ah! shield me from the dire disgrace
That haunts the wild and visionary race;
Let me not draw my lengthen'd lines along,
And tire in untamed infamy of song;
Lest, in some dismal Dunciad's future page,
I stand the CIBBER of this tuneless age;
Lest, if another POPE th' indulgent skies
Should give, inspired by all their deities,
My luckless name, in his immortal strain,

Should, blasted, brand me as a second Cain;
Doom'd in that song to live against my will,
Whom all must scorn, and yet whom none could kill.

The youth, resisted by the maiden's art,
Persists, and time subdues her kindling heart;
To strong entreaty yields the widow's vow,
As mighty walls to bold besiegers bow;
Repeated prayers draw bounty from the sky,
And heaven is won by importunity.
Ours, a projecting tribe, pursue in vain,
In tedious trials, an uncertain gain;
Madly plunge on through every hope's defeat,
And with our ruin only, find the cheat.

"And why then seek that luckless doom to share?"
Who, I?—To shun it is my only care.

I grant it true, that others better tell
Of mighty WOLFE, who conquer'd as he fell;
Of heroes born their threaten'd realms to save,
Whom Fame anoints, and Envy tends whose grave;
Of crimson'd fields, where Fate, in dire array,
Gives to the breathless the short-breathing clay;
Ours, a young train, by humbler fountains dream,
Nor taste presumptuous the Pierian stream;
When Rodney's triumph comes on eagle-wing,
We hail the victor, whom we fear to sing;
Nor tell we how each hostile chief goes on,
The luckless Lee, or wary Washington;
How Spanish bombast blusters—they were beat,
And French politeness dulcifies—defeat.
My modest Muse forbears to speak of kings,
Lest fainting stanzas blast the name she sings;
For who, the tenant of the beechen shade,
Dares the big thought in regal breasts pervade?
Or search his soul, whom each too-favouring God
Gives to delight in plunder, pomp, and blood?
No; let me, free from Cupid's frolic round,
Rejoice, or more rejoice by Cupid bound;
Of laughing girls in smiling couplets tell,
And paint the dark-brow'd grove, where wood-nymphs dwell,
Who bid invading youths their vengeance feel,
And pierce the votive hearts they mean to heal.
Such were the themes I knew in school-day ease,
When first the moral magic learn'd to please;
Ere Judgment told how transports warm'd the breast,
Transported Fancy there her stores imprest;

The soul in varied raptures learn'd to fly,
Felt all their force, and never question'd why.
No idle doubts could then her peace molest;
She found delight, and left to heaven the rest.
Soft joys in Evening's placid shades were born,
And where sweet fragrance wing'd the balmy morn.
When the wild thought roved vision's circuit o'er,
And caught the raptures, caught, alas! no more:
No care did then a dull attention ask,
For study pleased, and that was every task;
No guilty dreams stalk'd that heaven-favour'd round,
Heaven-guarded too; no Envy entrance found;
Nor numerous wants, that vex advancing age,
Nor Flattery's silver'd tale, nor Sorrow's sage;
Frugal Affliction kept each growing dart,
T' o'erwhelm in future days the bleeding heart.
No sceptic art veil'd Pride in Truth's disguise,
But prayer, unsoil'd of doubt, besieged the skies;
Ambition, avarice, care, to man retired,
Nor came desires more quick, than joys desired.

A summer morn there was, and passing fair;
Still was the breeze, and health perfumed the air;
The glowing east in crimson'd splendour shone,
What time the eye just marks the pallid moon;
Vi'let-wing'd Zephyr fann'd each opening flower,
And brush'd from fragrant cups the limpid shower;
A distant huntsman fill'd his cheerful horn,
The vivid dew hung trembling on the thorn,
And mists, like creeping rocks, arose to meet the morn.
Huge giant shadows spread along the plain,
Or shot from towering rocks o'er half the main.
There to the slumbering bark the gentle tide
Stole soft, and faintly beat against its side;
Such is that sound, which fond designs convey,
When, true to love, the damsel speeds away;
The sails, unshaken, hung aloft unfurl'd,
And, simpering nigh, the languid current curl'd;
A crumbling ruin, once a city's pride,
The well-pleased eye through withering oaks descried,
Where Sadness, gazing on time's ravage, hung,
And Silence to Destruction's trophy clung—
Save that, as morning songsters swell'd their lays,
Awaken'd Echo humm'd repeated praise.
The lark on quavering pinion woo'd the day,
Less towering linnets fill'd the vocal spray,
And song-invited pilgrims rose to pray.
Here at a pine-prest hill's embroider'd base

I stood, and hail'd the Genius of the place.
Then was it doom'd by fate, my idle heart,
Soften'd by Nature, gave access to Art;
The Muse approach'd, her syren-song I heard,
Her magic felt, and all her charms revered:
E'er since she rules in absolute control,
And Mira only dearer to my soul.
Ah! tell me not these empty joys to fly;
If they deceive, I would deluded die;
To the fond themes my heart so early wed,
So soon in life to blooming visions led,
So prone to run the vague uncertain course—
'Tis more than death to think of a divorce.

What wills the poet of the favouring gods,
Led to their shrine, and blest in their abodes?
What, when he fills the glass, and to each youth
Names his loved maid, and glories in his truth?
Not India's spoils, the splendid nabob's pride,
Not the full trade of Hermes' own Cheapside,
Nor gold itself, nor all the Ganges laves,
Or shrouds, well shrouded in his sacred waves;
Nor gorgeous vessels deck'd in trim array,
Which the more noble Thames bears far away.
Let those whose nod makes sooty subjects flee,
Hack with blunt steel the savory callipee;
Let those whose ill-used wealth their country fly,
Virtue-scorn'd wines from hostile France to buy:
Favour'd by fate, let such in joy appear,
Their smuggled cargoes landed thrice a year;
Disdaining these, for simpler food I'll look,
And crop my beverage at the mantled brook.

O Virtue! brighter than the noon-tide ray,
My humble prayers with sacred joys repay!
Health to my limbs may the kind Gods impart,
And thy fair form delight my yielding heart!
Grant me to shun each vile inglorious road,
To see thy way, and trace each moral good;
If more—let Wisdom's sons my page peruse,
And decent credit deck my modest Muse.

Nor deem it pride that prophesies, my song
Shall please the sons of taste, and please them long.
Say, ye, to whom my Muse submissive brings
Her first-fruit offering, and on trembling wings,
May she not hope in future days to soar,
Where fancy's sons have led the way before?

Where genius strives in each ambrosial bower
To snatch with agile hand the opening flower?
To cull what sweets adorn the mountain's brow,
What humbler blossoms crown the vales below?
To blend with these the stores by art refined,
And give the moral Flora to the mind?

Far other scenes my timid hour admits,
Relentless critics, and avenging wits;
E'en coxcombs take a licence from their pen,
And to each "let-him-perish" cry Amen!
And thus, with wits or fools my heart shall cry,
For if they please not, let the trifles die—
Die, and be lost in dark oblivion's shore,
And never rise to vex their author more.

I would not dream o'er some soft liquid line,
Amid a thousand blunders form'd to shine;
Yet rather this, than that dull scribbler be,
From every fault, and every beauty free,
Curst with tame thoughts and mediocrity.
Some have I found so thick beset with spots,
'Twas hard to trace their beauties through their blots;
And these, as tapers round a sick-man's room,
Or passing chimes, but warn'd me of the tomb!

O! if you blast, at once consume my bays,
And damn me not with mutilated praise.
With candour judge; and, a young bard in view.
Allow for that, and judge with kindness too.
Faults he must own, though hard for him to find,
Not to some happier merits quite so blind;
These if mistaken Fancy only sees,
Or Hope, that takes Deformity for these;
If Dunce, the crowd-befitting title, falls
His lot, and Dulness her new subject calls:
To the poor bard alone your censures give—
Let his fame die, but let his honour live;
Laugh if you must—be candid as you can,
And when you lash the Poet, spare the Man.

POEMS

Ipse per Ausonias Æneïa carmina gentes
Qui sonat, ingenti qui nomine pulsat Olympum,
Mæoniumque senem Romano provocat ore:

Forsitan illius nemoris latuisset in umbrâ
Quod canit, et sterili tantum cantâsset avenâ
Ignotus populi, si Mæcenate careret.

Paneg. ad Pisones.

TO THE RIGHT HONOURABLE HENRY RICHARD FOX, LORD HOLLAND, OF HOLLAND, IN LINCOLNSHIRE; LORD HOLLAND OF FOXLEY; AND FELLOW OF THE SOCIETY OF ANTIQUARIES.

MY LORD,

That the longest poem in this collection was honoured by the notice of your Lordship's right honourable and ever-valued relation, Mr. FOX; that it should be the last which engaged his attention; and that some parts of it were marked with his approbation: are circumstances productive of better hopes of ultimate success than I had dared to entertain before I was gratified with a knowledge of them; and the hope thus raised leads me to ask permission that I may dedicate this book to your Lordship, to whom that truly great and greatly lamented personage was so nearly allied in family, so closely bound in affection, and in whose mind presides the same critical taste which he exerted to the delight of all who heard him. He doubtless united with his unequalled abilities a fund of good-nature; and this possibly led him to speak favourably of, and give satisfaction to writers, with whose productions he might not be entirely satisfied; nor must I allow myself to suppose his desire of obliging was withholden, when he honoured any effort of mine with his approbation. But, my Lord, as there was discrimination in the opinion he gave; as he did not veil indifference for insipid mediocrity of composition under any general expression of cool approval: I allow myself to draw a favourable conclusion from the verdict of one who had the superiority of intellect few would dispute, which he made manifest by a force of eloquence peculiar to himself; whose excellent judgment no one of his friends found cause to distrust, and whose acknowledged candour no enemy had the temerity to deny.

With such encouragement, I present my book to your Lordship: the Account of the Life and Writings of Lopez de Vega has taught me what I am to expect; I there perceive how your Lordship can write, and am there taught how you can judge of writers: my faults, however numerous, I know will none of them escape through inattention, nor will any merit be lost for want of discernment; my verses are before him who has written elegantly, who has judged with accuracy, and who has given unequivocal proof of abilities in a work of difficulty—a translation of poetry, which few persons in this kingdom are able to read, and in the estimation of talents not hitherto justly appreciated. In this view, I cannot but feel some apprehension; but I know also, that your Lordship is apprised of the great difficulty of writing well; that you will make much allowance for failures, if not too frequently repeated; and, as you can accurately discern, so you will readily approve, all the better and more happy efforts of one who places the highest value upon your Lordship's approbation, and who has the honour to be,

My LORD,

Your Lordship's most faithful
and obliged humble servant,
GEORGE CRABBE.

PREFACE

About twenty-five years since was published a poem called "The Library," which, in no long time, was followed by two others, "The Village," and "The Newspaper." These, with a few alterations and additions, are here reprinted; and are accompanied by a poem of greater length, and several shorter attempts, now, for the first time, before the public; whose reception of them creates in their author something more than common solicitude, because he conceives that, with the judgment to be formed of these latter productions, upon whatever may be found intrinsically meritorious or defective, there will be united an inquiry into the relative degree of praise or blame which they may be thought to deserve, when compared with the more early attempts of the same writer.

And certainly, were it the principal employment of a man's life to compose verses, it might seem reasonable to expect that he would continue to improve as long as he continued to live; though, even then, there is some doubt whether such improvement would follow, and perhaps proof might be adduced to show it would not. But when, to this "idle trade" is added some "calling," with superior claims upon his time and attention, his progress in the art of versification will probably be in proportion neither to the years he has lived, nor even to the attempts he has made.

While composing the first-published of these poems, the author was honoured with the notice and assisted by the advice of the Right Honourable Edmund Burke; part of it was written in his presence, and the whole submitted to his judgment; receiving, in its progress, the benefit of his correction. I hope, therefore, to obtain pardon of the reader, if I eagerly seize the occasion, and, after so long a silence, endeavour to express a grateful sense of the benefits I have received from this gentleman, who was solicitous for my more essential interests, as well as benevolently anxious for my credit as a writer.

I will not enter upon the subject of his extraordinary abilities; it would be vanity, it would be weakness, in me to believe that I could make them better known or more admired than they now are. But of his private worth, of his wishes to do good, of his affability and condescension; his readiness to lend assistance when he knew it was wanted, and his delight to give praise where he thought it was deserved: of these I may write with some propriety. All know that his powers were vast, his acquirements various; and I take leave to add, that he applied them with unremitted attention to those objects which he believed tended to the honour and welfare of his country. But it may not be so generally understood that he was ever assiduous in the more private duties of a benevolent nature; that he delighted to give encouragement to any promise of ability, and assistance to any appearance of desert. To what purposes he employed his pen, and with what eloquence he spake in the senate, will be told by many, who yet may be ignorant of the solid instruction, as well as the fascinating pleasantry, found in his common conversation, amongst his friends, and his affectionate manners, amiable disposition, and zeal for their happiness, which he manifested in the hours of retirement with his family.

To this gentleman I was indebted for my knowledge of Sir Joshua Reynolds, who was as well known to his friends for his perpetual fund of good-humour and his unceasing wishes to oblige, as he was to the public for the extraordinary productions of his pencil and his pen. By him I was favoured with an introduction to Doctor Johnson, who honoured me with his notice, and assisted me, as Mr. Boswell has told, with remarks and emendations for a poem I was about to publish. The doctor had been often wearied by applications, and did not readily comply with requests for his opinion: not from any unwillingness to oblige, but from a painful contention in his mind between a desire of giving pleasure and a determination to speak truth. No man can, I think, publish a work without some expectation of satisfying those who are to judge of its merit; but I can, with the utmost regard to veracity, speak my fears, as predominating over every pre-indulged thought of a more favourable nature, when I was told that a judge so discerning had consented to read and give his opinion of "The Village," the poem I had prepared for publication. The time of suspense was not long protracted; I was soon favoured with a few words from Sir Joshua, who observed, "If I knew how cautious Doctor Johnson was in giving commendation, I should be well satisfied with the portion dealt to me in his letter." Of that letter the following is a copy:

"SIR,

"I have sent you back Mr. Crabbe's poem, which I read with great delight. It is original, vigorous, and elegant. The alterations which I have made, I do not require him to adopt; for my lines are, perhaps, not often better than his own: but he may take mine and his own together, and perhaps, between them, produce something better than either.—He is not to think his copy wantonly defaced; a wet sponge will wash all the red lines away, and leave the pages clean.—His Dedication will be least liked: it were better to contract it into a short sprightly address.—I do not doubt of Mr. Crabbe's success.

"I am, Sir, your most humble servant,

"SAM. JOHNSON."
"March 4, 1783."

That I was fully satisfied, my readers will do me the justice to believe; and I hope they will pardon me, if there should appear to them any impropriety in publishing the favourable opinion expressed in a private letter: they will judge, and truly, that by so doing, I wish to bespeak their good opinion, but have no design of extorting their applause. I would not hazard an appearance so ostentatious to gratify my vanity, but I venture to do it in compliance with my fears.

After these was published "The Newspaper": it had not the advantage of such previous criticism from any friends, nor perhaps so much of my own attention as I ought to have given to it; but the impression was disposed of, and I will not pay so little respect to the judgment of my readers as now to suppress they then approved.

Since the publication of this poem more than twenty years have elapsed, and I am not without apprehension, lest so long a silence should be construed into a blamable neglect of my own interest, which those excellent friends were desirous of promoting; or, what is yet worse, into a want of gratitude for their assistance, since it becomes me to suppose, they considered these first attempts as promises of better things, and their favours as stimulants to future exertion. And here, be the construction put upon my apparent negligence what it may, let me not suppress my testimony to the liberality of those who are looked up to as patrons and encouragers of literary merit, or indeed of merit of any kind: their patronage has never been refused, I conceive, when it has been reasonably expected or modestly required; and it would be difficult, probably, to instance, in these times and in this country, any one who merited or was supposed to merit assistance, but who nevertheless languished in obscurity or necessity for want of it; unless in those cases where it was prevented by the resolution of impatient pride, or wearied by the solicitations of determined profligacy. And, while the subject is before me, I am unwilling to pass silently over the debt of gratitude which I owe to the memory of two deceased noblemen, His Grace the late Duke of Rutland, and the Right Honourable the Lord Thurlow: sensible of the honour done me by their notice, and the benefits received from them, I trust this acknowledgment will be imputed to its only motive, a grateful sense of their favours.

Upon this subject I could dwell with much pleasure; but, to give a reason for that appearance of neglect, as it is more difficult, so, happily, it is less required. In truth, I have, for many years, intended a republication of these poems, as soon as I should be able to join with them such other of later date as might not deprive me of the little credit the former had obtained. Long indeed has this purpose been procrastinated; and, if the duties of a profession, not before pressing upon me—if the claims of a situation, at that time untried—if diffidence of my own judgment, and the loss of my earliest friends, will not sufficiently account for my delay, I must rely upon the good-nature of my reader, that he will let them avail as far as he can, and find an additional apology in my fears of his censure.

These fears being so prevalent with me, I determined not to publish any thing more, unless I could first obtain the sanction of such an opinion as I might with some confidence rely upon. I looked for a friend who, having the discerning taste of Mr. Burke, and the critical sagacity of Doctor Johnson, would bestow upon my MS. the attention requisite to form his opinion, and would then favour me with the result of his observations; and it was my singular good fortune to gain such assistance; the opinion of a critic so qualified, and a friend so disposed to favour me. I had been honoured by an introduction to the Right Honourable Charles James Fox some years before, at the seat of Mr. Burke; and, being again with him, I received a promise that he would peruse any work I might send to him previous to its publication, and would give me his opinion. At that time, I did not think myself sufficiently prepared; and when, afterwards, I had collected some poems for his inspection, I found my right honourable friend engaged by the affairs of a great empire, and struggling with the inveteracy of a fatal disease; at such time, upon such mind, ever disposed to oblige as that mind was, I could not obtrude the petty business of criticising verses; but he remembered the promise he had kindly given, and repeated an offer, which, though I had not presumed to expect, I was happy to receive. A copy of the poems, now first published, was immediately sent to him, and (as I have the information from Lord Holland, and his Lordship's permission to inform my readers) the poem which I have named "The Parish Register" was heard by Mr. Fox, and it excited interest enough, by some of its parts, to gain for me the benefit of his judgment upon the whole. Whatever he approved, the reader will readily believe, I have carefully retained; the parts he disliked are totally expunged, and others are substituted, which I hope resemble those, more conformable to the taste of so admirable a judge. Nor can I deny myself the melancholy satisfaction of adding, that this poem (and more especially the story of Phoebe Dawson, with some parts of the second book), were the last compositions of their kind that engaged and amused the capacious, the candid, the benevolent mind of this great man.

The above information I owe to the favour of the Right Honourable Lord Holland; nor this only, but to his Lordship I am indebted for some excellent remarks upon the other parts of my MS. It was not indeed my good fortune then to know that my verses were in the hands of a nobleman who had given proof of his accurate judgment as a critic, and his elegance as a writer, by favouring the public with an easy and spirited translation of some interesting scenes of a dramatic poet, not often read in this kingdom. The Life of Lopez de Vega was then unknown to me; I had, in common with many English readers, heard of him, but could not judge whether his far-extended reputation was caused by the sublime efforts of a mighty genius, or the unequalled facility of a rapid composer, aided by peculiar and fortunate circumstances. That any part of my MS. was honoured by the remarks of Lord Holland yields me a high degree of satisfaction, and his Lordship will perceive the use I have made of them; but I must feel some regret when I know to what small portion they were limited; and discerning, as I do, the taste and judgment bestowed upon the verses of Lopez de Vega, I must perceive how much my own needed the assistance afforded to one who cannot be sensible of the benefit he has received.

But how much soever I may lament the advantages lost, let me remember with gratitude the helps I have obtained. With a single exception, every poem in the ensuing collection has been submitted to the critical sagacity of a gentleman, upon whose skill and candour their author could rely. To publish by advice of friends has been severely ridiculed, and that too by a poet, who probably, without such advice, never made public any verses of his own: in fact, it may not be easily determined who acts with less discretion, the writer who is encouraged to publish his works, merely by the advice of friends whom he consulted, or he who, against advice, publishes from the sole encouragement of his own opinion. These are deceptions to be carefully avoided; and I was happy to escape the latter, by the friendly attentions of the Reverend Richard Turner, minister of Great Yarmouth. To this gentleman I am indebted more than I am able to describe, or than he is willing to allow, for the time he has bestowed upon the attempts I have made. He is, indeed, the kind of critic for whom every poet should devoutly wish, and the friend whom every man would be happy to acquire; he has taste to discern all that is meritorious, and sagacity to detect whatsoever should be discarded; he gives just the opinion an author's wisdom should covet, however his vanity might prompt him to reject it; what altogether to expunge and what to improve he has repeatedly taught me, and, could I have obeyed him in the latter direction, as I invariably have in the former, the public would have found this collection more worthy its attention, and I should have sought the opinion of the critic more void of apprehension.

But whatever I may hope or fear, whatever assistance I have had or have needed, it becomes me to leave my verses to the judgment of the reader, without my endeavour to point out their merit, or an apology for their defects. Yet as, among the poetical attempts of one who has been for many years a priest, it may seem a want of respect for the legitimate objects of his study, that nothing occurs, unless it be incidentally, of the great subjects of religion: so it may appear a kind of ingratitude of a beneficed clergyman, that he has not employed his talent (be it estimated as it may) to some patriotic purpose—as in celebrating the unsubdued spirit of his countrymen in their glorious resistance of those enemies, who would have no peace throughout the world, except that which is dictated to the drooping spirit of suffering humanity by the triumphant insolence of military success.

Credit will be given to me, I hope, when I affirm that subjects so interesting have the due weight with me, which the sacred nature of the one, and the national importance of the other, must impress upon every mind not seduced into carelessness for religion by the lethargic influence of a perverted philosophy, nor into indifference for the cause of our country by hyperbolical or hypocritical professions of universal philanthropy; but, after many efforts to satisfy myself by various trials on these subjects, I declined all further attempt, from a conviction that I should not be able to give satisfaction to my readers. Poetry of religious nature must indeed ever be clogged with almost insuperable difficulty; but there are doubtless to be found poets who are well qualified to celebrate the unanimous and heroic spirit of our countrymen, and to describe in appropriate colours some of those extraordinary scenes, which have been and are shifting in the face of Europe, with such dreadful celerity; and to such I relinquish the duty.

It remains for me to give the reader a brief view of those articles in the following collection, which for the first time solicit his attention.

In the "Parish Register," he will find an endeavour once more to describe village-manners, not by adopting the notion of pastoral simplicity or assuming ideas of rustic barbarity, but by more natural views of the peasantry, considered as a mixed body of persons, sober or profligate, and hence, in a great measure, contented or miserable. To this more general description are added the various characters which occur in the three parts of a Register: Baptism, Marriages, and Burials.

If the "Birth of Flattery" offer no moral, as an appendage to the fable, it is hoped that nothing of an immoral, nothing of improper, tendency will be imputed to a piece of poetical playfulness. In fact, genuine praise, like all other species of truth, is known by its bearing full investigation: it is what the giver is happy that he can justly bestow, and the receiver conscious that he may boldly accept; but adulation must ever be afraid of inquiry, and must, in proportion to their degrees of moral sensibility,

Be shame "to him that gives and him that takes."

The verses in later pages want a title; nor does the motto, although it gave occasion to them, altogether express the sense of the writer, who meant to observe that some of our best acquisitions, and some of our nobler conquests, are rendered ineffectual, by the passing away of opportunity, and the changes made by time: an argument that such acquirements and moral habits are reserved for a state of being in which they have the uses here denied them.

In the story of "Sir Eustace Grey," an attempt is made to describe the wanderings of a mind first irritated by the consequences of error and misfortune, and afterwards soothed by a species of enthusiastic conversion, still keeping him insane: a task very difficult, and, if the presumption of the attempt may find pardon, it will not be refused to the failure of the poet. It is said of our Shakspeare, respecting madness,

"In that circle none dare walk but he."

Yet be it granted to one who dares not to pass the boundary fixed for common minds, at least to step near to the tremendous verge, and form some idea of the terrors that are stalking in the interdicted space.

When first I had written "Aaron, or The Gipsy," I had no unfavourable opinion of it; and, had I been collecting my verses at that time for publication, I should certainly have included this tale. Nine years have since elapsed, and I continue to judge the same of it, thus literally obeying one of the directions given by the prudence of criticism to the eagerness of the poet; but how far I may have conformed to rules of more importance must be left to the less partial judgment of the readers.

The concluding poem, entitled "Woman!" was written at the time when the quotation from Mr. Ledyard was first made public; the expression has since become hackneyed; but the sentiment is congenial with our feelings, and though somewhat amplified in these verses, it is hoped they are not so far extended as to become tedious.

After this brief account of his subjects, the author leaves them to their fate, not presuming to make any remarks upon the kinds of versification he has chosen, or the merit of the execution. He has indeed brought forward the favourable opinion of his friends, and for that he earnestly hopes his motives will be rightly understood; it was a step of which he felt the advantage while he foresaw the danger; he was aware of the benefit, if his readers would consider him as one who puts on a defensive armour against hasty and determined severity; but he feels also the hazard, lest they should suppose he looks upon himself to be guarded by his friends, and so secure in the defence, that he may defy the fair judgment of legal criticism. It will probably be said, "he has brought with him his testimonials to the bar of the public," and he must admit the truth of the remark; but he begs leave to observe in reply, that of those who bear testimonials of any kind the greater numbers feel apprehension, and not security: they are indeed so far from the enjoyment of victory, of the exultation of triumph, that, with all they can do for themselves, with all their friends have done for them, they are, like him, in dread of examination, and in fear of disappointment.

Muston, Leicestershire,
September, 1807.

THE LIBRARY

Books afford Consolation to the troubled Mind, by substituting a lighter Kind of Distress for its own—They are productive of other Advantages—An Author's Hope of being known in distant Times—Arrangement of the Library—Size and Form of the Volumes—The ancient Folio, clasped and chained—Fashion prevalent even in this Place—The Mode of publishing in Numbers, Pamphlets, &c.—Subjects of the different Classes—Divinity—Controversy—The Friends of Religion often more dangerous than her Foes—Sceptical Authors—Reason too much rejected by the former Converts; exclusively relied upon by the latter—Philosophy ascending through the Scale of Being to moral Subjects—Books of Medicine: their Variety, Variance, and Proneness to System: the Evil of this, and the Difficulty it causes—Farewell to this Study—Law: the increasing Number of its Volumes—Supposed happy State of Man without Laws—Progress of Society—Historians: their Subjects—Dramatic Authors, Tragic and Comic—Ancient Romances—The Captive Heroine—Happiness in the Perusal of such Books: why—Criticism—Apprehensions of the Author, removed by the Appearance of the Genius of the Place; whose Reasoning and Admonition conclude the Subject.

When the sad soul, by care and grief oppress'd,
Looks round the world, but looks in vain for rest;
When every object that appears in view,
Partakes her gloom and seems dejected too:
Where shall affliction from itself retire?
Where fade away and placidly expire?
Alas! we fly to silent scenes in vain;
Care blasts the honours of the flow'ry plain:
Care veils in clouds the sun's meridian beam,
Sighs through the grove and murmurs in the stream.
For, when the soul is labouring in despair,
In vain the body breathes a purer air:
No storm-toss'd sailor sighs for slumbering seas—
He dreads the tempest, but invokes the breeze;
On the smooth mirror of the deep resides
Reflected wo, and o'er unruffled tides
The ghost of every former danger glides.
Thus, in the calms of life, we only see
A steadier image of our misery;
But lively gales and gently-clouded skies

Disperse the sad reflections as they rise;
And busy thoughts and little cares avail
To ease the mind, when rest and reason fail.
When the dull thought, by no designs employ'd,
Dwells on the past, or suffer'd or enjoy'd,
We bleed anew in every former grief,
And joys departed furnish no relief.
Not Hope herself, with all her flattering art,
Can cure this stubborn sickness of the heart:
The soul disdains each comfort she prepares,
And anxious searches for congenial cares—
Those lenient cares, which, with our own combined,
By mix'd sensations ease th' afflicted mind.
And steal our grief away and leave their own behind:
A lighter grief! which feeling hearts endure
Without regret, nor e'en demand a cure.
But what strange art, what magic can dispose
The troubled mind to change its native woes?
Or lead us willing from ourselves, to see
Others more wretched, more undone than we?
This, books can do—nor this alone: they give
New views to life, and teach us how to live;
They soothe the grieved, the stubborn they chastise;
Fools they admonish, and confirm the wise.
Their aid they yield to all: they never shun
The man of sorrow, nor the wretch undone;
Unlike the hard, the selfish, and the proud,
They fly not sullen from the suppliant crowd;
Nor tell to various people various things,
But show to subjects, what they show to kings.
Come, Child of Care! to make thy soul serene,
Approach the treasures of this tranquil scene;
Survey the dome, and, as the doors unfold,
The soul's best cure in all her cares behold!
Where mental wealth the poor in thought may find,
And mental physic the diseased in mind.
See here the balms that passion's wounds assuage;
See coolers here, that damp the fire of rage;
Here alt'ratives by slow degrees control
The chronic habits of the sickly soul;
And round the heart, and o'er the aching head,
Mild opiates here their sober influence shed.
Now bid thy soul man's busy scenes exclude,
And view composed this silent multitude:—
Silent they are, but, though deprived of sound,
Here all the living languages abound,
Here all that live no more; preserved they lie,
In tombs that open to the curious eye.

Bless'd be the gracious Power, who taught mankind
To stamp a lasting image of the mind!—
Beasts may convey, and tuneful birds may sing,
Their mutual feelings in the opening spring;
But man alone has skill and power to send
The heart's warm dictates to the distant friend;
'Tis his alone to please, instruct, advise
Ages remote, and nations yet to rise.
In sweet repose, when labour's children sleep,
When joy forgets to smile and care to weep,
When passion slumbers in the lover's breast,
And fear and guilt partake the balm of rest—
Why then denies the studious man to share
Man's common good, who feels his common care?
Because the hope is his, that bids him fly
Night's soft repose, and sleep's mild power defy;
That after-ages may repeat his praise,
And fame's fair meed be his for length of days.
Delightful prospect! when we leave behind
A worthy offspring of the fruitful mind,
Which, born and nursed through many an anxious day,
Shall all our labour, all our care repay.
Yet all are not these births of noble kind,
Not all the children of a vigorous mind;
But, where the wisest should alone preside,
The weak would rule us, and the blind would guide;
Nay, man's best efforts taste of man, and show
The poor and troubled source from which they flow:
Where most he triumphs, we his wants perceive,
And for his weakness in his wisdom grieve.
But, though imperfect all, yet wisdom loves
This seat serene, and virtue's self approves;   1
Here come the grieved, a change of thought to find,
The curious here, to feed a craving mind;
Here the devout their peaceful temple choose;
And here the poet meets his favouring muse.
With awe around these silent walks I tread:
These are the lasting mansions of the dead.—
"The dead," methinks, a thousand tongues reply;
"These are the tombs of such as cannot die!
Crown'd with eternal fame, they sit sublime,
And laugh at all the little strife of time."
Hail, then, immortals! ye who shine above,
Each in his sphere the literary Jove;
And ye, the common people of these skies,
A humbler crowd of nameless deities:
Whether 'tis yours to lead the willing mind
Through history's mazes, and the turnings find;

Or whether, led by science, ye retire,
Lost and bewilder'd in the vast desire;
Whether the Muse invites you to her bowers,
And crowns your placid brows with living flowers;
Or godlike wisdom teaches you to show
The noblest road to happiness below;
Or men and manners prompt the easy page
To mark the flying follies of the age:
Whatever good ye boast, that good impart;
Inform the head and rectify the heart!

Lo! all in silence, all in order stand;
And mighty folios first, a lordly band,
Then quartos, their well-order'd ranks maintain,
And light octavos fill a spacious plain;
See yonder, ranged in more frequented rows,
A humbler band of duodecimos;
While undistinguished trifles swell the scene,
The last new play and fritter'd magazine.
Thus 'tis in life, where first the proud, the great,
In leagued assembly keep their cumbrous state;
Heavy and huge, they fill the world with dread,
Are much admired, and are but little read:
The commons next, a middle rank, are found;
Professions fruitful pour their offspring round;
Reasoners and wits are next their place allow'd,
And last, of vulgar tribes a countless crowd.
First, let us view the form, the size, the dress;
For these the manners, nay the mind express;
That weight of wood, with leathern coat o'erlaid;
Those ample clasps, of solid metal made;
The close-press'd leaves, unclosed for many an age;
The dull red edging of the well-fill'd page;
On the broad back the stubborn ridges roll'd,
Where yet the title stands in tarnish'd gold;
These all a sage and labour'd work proclaim,
A painful candidate for lasting fame:
No idle wit, no trifling verse can lurk
In the deep bosom of that weighty work;
No playful thoughts degrade the solemn style,
Nor one light sentence claims a transient smile.
Hence, in these times, untouch'd the pages lie,
And slumber out their immortality:
They had their day, when, after all his toil,
His morning study, and his midnight oil,
At length an author's ONE great work appear'd,
By patient hope, and length of days, endear'd:
Expecting nations hail'd it from the press;

Poetic friends prefix'd each kind address;
Princes and kings received the pond'rous gift,
And ladies read the work they could not lift.
Fashion, though Folly's child, and guide of fools,
Rules e'en the wisest, and in learning rules;
From crowds and courts to Wisdom's seat she goes,
And reigns triumphant o'er her mother's foes.
For lo! these fav'rites of the ancient mode
Lie all neglected like the Birth-day Ode;
Ah! needless now this weight of massy chain;
Safe in themselves, the once-loved works remain;
No readers now invade their still retreat,
None try to steal them from their parent-seat;
Like ancient beauties, they may now discard
Chains, bolts, and locks, and lie without a guard.
Our patient fathers trifling themes laid by,
And roll'd o'er labour'd works th' attentive eye;
Page after page, the much-enduring men
Explored the deeps and shallows of the pen;
Till, every former note and comment known,
They mark'd the spacious margin with their own:
Minute corrections proved their studious care;
The little index, pointing, told us where;
And many an emendation show'd the age
Look'd far beyond the rubric title-page.
Our nicer palates lighter labours seek,
Cloy'd with a folio-Number once a week;
Bibles, with cuts and comments, thus go down:
E'en light Voltaire is number'd through the town:
Thus physic flies abroad, and thus the law,
From men of study, and from men of straw;
Abstracts, abridgments, please the fickle times,
Pamphlets and plays, and politics and rhymes:
But though to write be now a task of ease,
The task is hard by manly arts to please,
When all our weakness is exposed to view,
And half our judges are our rivals too.

Amid these works, on which the eager eye
Delights to fix, or glides reluctant by,
When all combined, their decent pomp display,
Where shall we first our early offering pay?

To thee, DIVINITY! to thee, the light
And guide of mortals through their mental night;
By whom we learn our hopes and fears to guide;
To bear with pain, and to contend with pride;
When grieved, to pray; when injured, to forgive;

And with the world in charity to live.
Not truths like these inspired that numerous race,
Whose pious labours fill this ample space;
But questions nice, where doubt on doubt arose,
Awaked to war the long-contending foes.
For dubious meanings, learn'd polemics strove.
And wars on faith prevented works of love;
The brands of discord far around were hurl'd,
And holy wrath inflamed a sinful world—
Dull though impatient, peevish though devout,
With wit disgusting and despised without;
Saints in design, in execution men,
Peace in their looks, and vengeance in their pen.

Methinks, I see, and sicken at the sight,
Spirits of spleen from yonder pile alight:
Spirits who prompted every damning page,
With pontiff pride and still-increasing rage.
Lo! how they stretch their gloomy wings around,
And lash with furious strokes the trembling ground!
They pray, they fight, they murder, and they weep—
Wolves, in their vengeance, in their manners sheep;
Too well they act the prophet's fatal part,
Denouncing evil with a zealous heart;
And each, like Jonas, is displeased, if God
Repent his anger, or withhold his rod.
But here the dormant fury rests unsought,
And Zeal sleeps soundly by the foes she fought;
Here all the rage of controversy ends,
And rival zealots rest like bosom-friends:
An Athanasian here, in deep repose,
Sleeps with the fiercest of his Arian foes;
Socinians here with Calvinists abide,
And thin partitions angry chiefs divide;
Here wily Jesuits simple Quakers meet,
And Bellarmine has rest at Luther's feet.
Great authors, for the church's glory fired,
Are, for the church's peace, to rest retired;
And close beside, a mystic, maudlin race,
Lie, "Crums of Comfort for the Babes of Grace."
Against her foes Religion well defends
Her sacred truths, but often fears her friends;
If learn'd, their pride, if weak, their zeal she dreads,
And their hearts' weakness, who have soundest heads.
But most she fears the controversial pen,
The holy strife of disputatious men;
Who the bless'd Gospel's peaceful page explore,
Only to fight against its precepts more.

Near to these seats, behold yon slender frames,
All closely fill'd and mark'd with modern names;
Where no fair science ever shows her face,
Few sparks of genius, and no spark of grace.
There sceptics rest, a still-increasing throng,
And stretch their widening wings ten thousand strong:
Some in close fight their dubious claims maintain;
Some skirmish lightly, fly and fight again;
Coldly profane, and impiously gay;
Their end the same, though various in their way.
When first Religion came to bless the land,
Her friends were then a firm believing band;
To doubt was, then, to plunge in guilt extreme,
And all was gospel that a monk could dream;
Insulted Reason fled the grov'ling soul,
For Fear to guide, and visions to control.
But now, when Reason has assumed her throne,
She, in her turn, demands to reign alone;
Rejecting all that lies beyond her view,
And, being judge, will be a witness too.
Insulted Faith then leaves the doubtful mind,
To seek for truth, without a power to find;
Ah! when will both in friendly beams unite,
And pour on erring man resistless light?

Next to the seats, well stored with works divine,
An ample space, PHILOSOPHY! is thine;
Our reason's guide, by whose assisting light
We trace the moral bounds of wrong and right;
Our guide through nature, from the sterile clay,
To the bright orbs of yon celestial way!
'Tis thine, the great, the golden chain to trace,
Which runs through all, connecting race with race;
Save where those puzzling, stubborn links remain,
Which thy inferior light pursues in vain:—
How vice and virtue in the soul contend;
How widely differ, yet how nearly blend!
What various passions war on either part,
And now confirm, now melt the yielding heart;
How Fancy loves around the world to stray,
While Judgment slowly picks his sober way!
The stores of memory, and the flights sublime
Of genius, bound by neither space nor time—
All these divine Philosophy explores,
Till, lost in awe, she wonders and adores.
From these, descending to the earth, she turns,
And matter, in its various form, discerns;
She parts the beamy light with skill profound,

Metes the thin air, and weighs the flying sound;
'Tis hers the lightning from the clouds to call,
And teach the fiery mischief where to fall.
Yet more her volumes teach—on these we look
As abstracts drawn from Nature's larger book:
Here, first described, the torpid earth appears,
And next, the vegetable robe it wears:
Where flow'ry tribes, in valleys, fields and groves,
Nurse the still flame, and feed the silent loves—
Loves, where no grief, nor joy, nor bliss, nor pain,
Warm the glad heart or vex the labouring brain;
But as the green blood moves along the blade,
The bed of Flora on the branch is made;
Where, without passion, love instinctive lives,
And gives new life, unconscious that it gives.
Advancing still in Nature's maze, we trace,
In dens and burning plains, her savage race;
With those tame tribes who on their lord attend,
And find in man, a master and a friend;
Man crowns the scene, a world of wonders new,
A moral world, that well demands our view.
This world is here; for, of more lofty kind,
These neighbouring volumes reason on the mind;
They paint the state of man, ere yet endued
With knowledge—man, poor, ignorant, and rude;
Then, as his state improves, their pages swell,
And all its cares, and all its comforts, tell:
Here we behold how inexperience buys,
At little price, the wisdom of the wise;
Without the troubles of an active state,
Without the cares and dangers of the great,
Without the miseries of the poor, we know
What wisdom, wealth, and poverty bestow;
We see how reason calms the raging mind,
And how contending passions urge mankind.
Some, won by virtue, glow with sacred fire;
Some, lured by vice, indulge the low desire;
Whilst others, won by either, now pursue
The guilty chase, now keep the good in view;
For ever wretched, with themselves at strife,
They lead a puzzled, vex'd, uncertain life;
For transient vice bequeaths a lingering pain,
Which transient virtue seeks to cure in vain.

Whilst thus engaged, high views enlarge the soul,
New interests draw, new principles control:
Nor thus the soul alone resigns her grief,
But here the tortured body finds relief;

For see where yonder sage Arachnè shapes
Her subtile gin, that not a fly escapes!
There PHYSIC fills the space, and far around,
Pile above pile, her learned works abound:
Glorious their aim—to ease the labouring heart;
To war with death, and stop his flying dart;
To trace the source whence the fierce contest grew,
And life's short lease on easier terms renew;
To calm the frenzy of the burning brain;
To heal the tortures of imploring pain;
Or, when more powerful ills all efforts brave,
To ease the victim no device can save,
And smooth the stormy passage to the grave.
But man, who knows no good unmix'd and pure,

Oft finds a poison where he sought a cure;
For grave deceivers lodge their labours here,
And cloud the science they pretend to clear.
Scourges for sin, the solemn tribe are sent;
Like fire and storms, they call us to repent;
But storms subside, and fires forget to rage,
These are eternal scourges of the age.
'Tis not enough that each terrific hand
Spreads desolation round a guilty land;
But, train'd to ill, and harden'd by its crimes,
Their pen relentless kills through future times.
Say ye, who search these records of the dead,
Who read huge works, to boast what ye have read:
Can all the real knowledge ye possess,
Or those (if such there are) who more than guess,
Atone for each impostor's wild mistakes,
And mend the blunders pride or folly makes?
What thought so wild, what airy dream so light,
That will not prompt a theorist to write?
What art so prevalent, what proof so strong,
That will convince him his attempt is wrong?
One in the solids finds each lurking ill,
Nor grants the passive fluids power to kill;
A learned friend some subtler reason brings
Absolves the channels, but condemns their springs;
The subtile nerves, that shun the doctor's eye,
Escape no more his subtler theory;
The vital heat, that warms the labouring heart,
Lends a fair system to these sons of art;
The vital air, a pure and subtile stream,
Serves a foundation for an airy scheme,
Assists the doctor, and supports his dream.
Some have their favourite ills, and each disease

Is but a younger branch that kills from these.
One to the gout contracts all human pain;
He views it raging in the frantic brain;
Finds it in fevers all his efforts mar,
And sees it lurking in the cold catarrh.
Bilious by some, by others nervous seen,
Rage the fantastic demons of the spleen;
And every symptom of the strange disease
With every system of the sage agrees.
Ye frigid tribe, on whom I wasted long
The tedious hours, and ne'er indulged in song;
Ye first seducers of my easy heart,
Who promised knowledge ye could not impart;
Ye dull deluders, truth's destructive foes;
Ye sons of fiction, clad in stupid prose;
Ye treacherous leaders, who, yourselves in doubt,
Light up false fires, and send us far about—
Still may yon spider round your pages spin,
Subtile and slow, her emblematic gin!
Buried in dust and lost in silence, dwell;
Most potent, grave, and reverend friends—farewell!

Near these, and where the setting sun displays
Through the dim window his departing rays,
And gilds yon columns, there, on either side,
The huge abridgments of the LAW abide.
Fruitful as vice the dread correctors stand,
And spread their guardian terrors round the land;
Yet, as the best that human care can do,
Is mix'd with error, oft with evil too,
Skill'd in deceit, and practised to evade,
Knaves stand secure, for whom these laws were made;
And justice vainly each expedient tries,
While art eludes it, or while power defies.
"Ah! happy age," the youthful poet sings,
"When the free nations knew not laws nor kings;
When all were bless'd to share a common store,
And none were proud of wealth, for none were poor;
No wars nor tumults vex'd each still domain,
No thirst of empire, no desire of gain;
No proud great man, nor one who would be great,
Drove modest merit from its proper state;
Nor into distant climes would avarice roam,
To fetch delights for luxury at home:
Bound by no ties which kept the soul in awe,
They dwelt at liberty, and love was law!"
"Mistaken youth! each nation first was rude,
Each man a cheerless son of solitude,

To whom no joys of social life were known;
None felt a care that was not all his own;
Or in some languid clime his abject soul
Bow'd to a little tyrant's stern control;
A slave, with slaves his monarch's throne he raised,
And in rude song his ruder idol praised;
The meaner cares of life were all he knew;
Bounded his pleasures, and his wishes few.
But when by slow degrees the Arts arose,
And Science waken'd from her long repose;
When Commerce, rising from the bed of ease,
Ran round the land, and pointed to the seas;
When Emulation, born with jealous eye,
And Avarice, lent their spurs to industry;
Then one by one the numerous laws were made,
Those to control, and these to succour trade;
To curb the insolence of rude command,
To snatch the victim from the usurer's hand;
To awe the bold, to yield the wrong'd redress,
And feed the poor with Luxury's excess."
Like some vast flood, unbounded, fierce, and strong,
His nature leads ungovern'd man along;
Like mighty bulwarks made to stem that tide,
The laws are form'd and placed on ev'ry side:
Whene'er it breaks the bounds by these decreed,
New statutes rise, and stronger laws succeed;
More and more gentle grows the dying stream,
More and more strong the rising bulwarks seem;
Till, like a miner working sure and slow,
Luxury creeps on, and ruins all below;
The basis sinks, the ample piles decay;
The stately fabric shakes and falls away;
Primeval want and ignorance come on,
But freedom, that exalts the savage state, is gone.

Next, HISTORY ranks;—there full in front she lies,
And every nation her dread tale supplies.
Yet History has her doubts, and every age
With sceptic queries marks the passing page;
Records of old nor later date are clear—
Too distant those, and these are placed too near;
There time conceals the objects from our view,
Here our own passions and a writer's too.
Yet, in these volumes, see how states arose,
Guarded by virtue from surrounding foes;
Their virtue lost, and of their triumphs vain,
Lo! how they sunk to slavery again!
Satiate with power, of fame and wealth possess'd,

A nation grows too glorious to be bless'd;
Conspicuous made, she stands the mark of all,
And foes join foes to triumph in her fall.
Thus speaks the page that paints ambition's race,
The monarch's pride, his glory, his disgrace;
The headlong course, that madd'ning heroes run,
How soon triumphant, and how soon undone;
How slaves, turn'd tyrants, offer crowns to sale,
And each fall'n nation's melancholy tale.
Lo! where of late the Book of Martyrs stood,
Old pious tracts, and Bibles bound in wood:
There, such the taste of our degenerate age,
Stand the profane delusions of the STAGE.
Yet virtue owns the TRAGIC MUSE a friend—
Fable her means, morality her end;
For this she rules all passions in their turns,
And now the bosom bleeds, and now it burns;
Pity with weeping eye surveys her bowl;
Her anger swells, her terror chills the soul;
She makes the vile to virtue yield applause,
And own her sceptre while they break her laws;
For vice in others is abhorr'd of all,
And villains triumph when the worthless fall.
Not thus her sister COMEDY prevails,
Who shoots at folly, for her arrow fails:
Folly, by dulness arm'd, eludes the wound,
And harmless sees the feather'd shafts rebound;
Unhurt she stands, applauds the archer's skill,
Laughs at her malice, and is folly still.
Yet well the Muse portrays in fancied scenes
What pride will stoop to, what profession means;
How formal fools the farce of state applaud;
How caution watches at the lips of fraud;
The wordy variance of domestic life;
The tyrant husband, the retorting wife,
The snares for innocence, the lie of trade,
And the smooth tongue's habitual masquerade.
With her the virtues too obtain a place,
Each gentle passion, each becoming grace;
The social joy in life's securer road,
Its easy pleasure, its substantial good;
The happy thought that conscious virtue gives.
And all that ought to live, and all that lives.

But who are these? Methinks, a noble mien
And awful grandeur in their form are seen—
Now in disgrace. What, though by time is spread
Polluting dust o'er every reverend head;

What, though beneath yon gilded tribe they lie,
And dull observers pass insulting by:
Forbid it shame, forbid it decent awe,
What seems so grave, should no attention draw!
Come, let us then with reverent step advance,
And greet—the ancient worthies of ROMANCE.
Hence, ye profane! I feel a former dread;
A thousand visions float around my head.
Hark! hollow blasts through empty courts resound,
And shadowy forms with staring eyes stalk round;
See! moats and bridges, walls and castles rise,
Ghosts, fairies, demons, dance before our eyes;
Lo! magic verse inscribed on golden gate,
And bloody hand that beckons on to fate:—
"And who art thou, thou little page, unfold!
Say, doth thy lord my Claribel withhold?
Go tell him straight, Sir Knight, thou must resign
The captive queen—for Claribel is mine."
Away he flies; and now for bloody deeds,
Black suits of armour, masks, and foaming steeds;
The giant falls, his recreant throat I seize,
And from his corslet take the massy keys;
Dukes, lords, and knights in long procession move,
Released from bondage with my virgin love;
She comes! she comes! in all the charms of youth,
Unequall'd love and unsuspected truth!
Ah! happy he who thus, in magic themes,
O'er worlds bewitch'd in early rapture dreams,
Where wild Enchantment waves her potent wand,
And Fancy's beauties fill her fairy land;
Where doubtful objects strange desires excite,
And Fear and Ignorance afford delight.
But lost, for ever lost, to me these joys,
Which Reason scatters, and which Time destroys—
Too dearly bought: maturer judgment calls
My busied mind from tales and madrigals;
My doughty giants all are slain or fled,
And all my knights, blue, green, and yellow, dead!
No more the midnight fairy tribe I view,
All in the merry moonshine tippling dew;
E'en the last lingering fiction of the brain,
The church-yard ghost, is now at rest again;
And all these wayward wanderings of my youth
Fly Reason's power and shun the light of truth.
With fiction, then, does real joy reside,
And is our reason the delusive guide?
Is it, then, right to dream the syrens sing,
Or mount enraptured on the dragon's wing?

No, 'tis the infant mind, to care unknown,
That makes th' imagined paradise its own;
Soon as reflections in the bosom rise,
Light slumbers vanish from the clouded eyes;
The tear and smile, that once together rose,
Are then divorced; the head and heart are foes:
Enchantment bows to Wisdom's serious plan,
And Pain and Prudence make and mar the man.

While thus, of power and fancied empire vain,
With various thoughts my mind I entertain;
While books, my slaves, with tyrant hand I seize,
Pleased with the pride that will not let them please;
Sudden I find terrific thoughts arise,
And sympathetic sorrow fills my eyes;
For, lo! while yet my heart admits the wound,
I see the CRITIC army ranged around.
Foes to our race! if ever ye have known
A father's fears for offspring of your own.—
If ever, smiling o'er a lucky line,
Ye thought the sudden sentiment divine,
Then paused and doubted, and then, tired of doubt,
With rage as sudden dash'd the stanza out—
If, after fearing much and pausing long,
Ye ventured on the world your labour'd song,
And from the crusty critics of those days
Implored the feeble tribute of their praise:
Remember now the fears that moved you then,
And, spite of truth, let mercy guide your pen!
What vent'rous race are ours! what mighty foes
Lie waiting all around them to oppose!
What treacherous friends betray them to the fight!
What dangers threaten them—yet still they write:
A hapless tribe! to every evil born,
Whom villains hate, and fools affect to scorn;
Strangers they come amid a world of wo,
And taste the largest portion ere they go.

Pensive I spoke, and cast mine eyes around;
The roof, methought, return'd a solemn sound;
Each column seem'd to shake, and clouds, like smoke,
From dusty piles and ancient volumes broke;
Gathering above, like mists condensed they seem,
Exhaled in summer from the rushy stream;
Like flowing robes they now appear, and twine
Round the large members of a form divine;
His silver beard, that swept his aged breast,
His piercing eye, that inward light express'd,

Were seen—but clouds and darkness veil'd the rest.
Fear chill'd my heart: to one of mortal race,
How awful seem'd the Genius of the place!
So, in Cimmerian shores, Ulysses saw
His parent-shade, and shrunk in pious awe;
Like him I stood, and wrapt in thought profound,
When from the pitying power broke forth a solemn sound:—
"Care lives with all; no rules, no precepts save
The wise from wo, no fortitude the brave;
Grief is to man as certain as the grave:
Tempests and storms in life's whole progress rise,
And hope shines dimly through o'erclouded skies;
Some drops of comfort on the favour'd fall,
But showers of sorrow are the lot of all:
Partial to talents, then, shall Heav'n withdraw
Th' afflicting rod, or break the general law?
Shall he who soars, inspired by loftier views,
Life's little cares and little pains refuse?
Shall he not rather feel a double share
Of mortal wo, when doubly arm'd to bear?
"Hard is his fate who builds his peace of mind
On the precarious mercy of mankind;
Who hopes for wild and visionary things,
And mounts o'er unknown seas with vent'rous wings:
But as, of various evils that befall
The human race, some portion goes to all:
To him perhaps the milder lot's assign'd,
Who feels his consolation in his mind;
And, lock'd within his bosom, bears about
A mental charm for every care without.
E'en in the pangs of each domestic grief,
Or health or vigorous hope affords relief;
And every wound the tortured bosom feels,
Or virtue bears, or some preserver heals;
Some generous friend, of ample power possess'd;
Some feeling heart that bleeds for the distress'd;
Some breast that glows with virtues all divine;
Some noble RUTLAND, Misery's friend and thine.
"Nor say, the Muse's song, the Poet's pen,
Merit the scorn they meet from little men.
With cautious freedom if the numbers flow,
Not wildly high, nor pitifully low;
If vice alone their honest aims oppose,
Why so ashamed their friends, so loud their foes?
Happy for men in every age and clime,
If all the sons of vision dealt in rhyme!
Go on then, Son of Vision! still pursue
Thy airy dreams; the world is dreaming too.

Ambition's lofty views, the pomp of state,
The pride of wealth, the splendour of the great,
Stripp'd of their mask, their cares and troubles known,
Are visions far less happy than thy own:
Go on! and, while the sons of care complain,
Be wisely gay and innocently vain;
While serious souls are by their fears undone,
Blow sportive bladders in the beamy sun,
And call them worlds! and bid the greatest show
More radiant colours in their worlds below;
Then, as they break, the slaves of care reprove,
And tell them, Such are all the toys they love."

THE VILLAGE

IN TWO BOOKS

BOOK I

The Subject proposed—Remarks upon Pastoral Poetry—A Tract of Country near the Coast described—
An impoverished Borough—Smugglers and their Assistants—Rude Manners of the Inhabitants—Ruinous
Effects of a high Tide—The Village Life more generally considered: Evils of it—The youthful Labourer—
The old Man: his Soliloquy—The Parish Workhouse: its Inhabitants—The sick Poor: their Apothecary—
The dying Pauper—The Village Priest.

The Village Life, and every care that reigns
O'er youthful peasants and declining swains;
What labour yields, and what, that labour past,
Age, in its hour of languor, finds at last;
What form the real picture of the poor,
Demand a song—the Muse can give no more.
Fled are those times when, in harmonious strains,
The rustic poet praised his native plains.
No shepherds now, in smooth alternate verse,
Their country's beauty or their nymphs' rehearse;
Yet still for these we frame the tender strain,
Still in our lays fond Corydons complain,
And shepherds' boys their amorous pains reveal,
The only pains, alas! they never feel.
On Mincio's banks, in Cæsar's bounteous reign,
If Tityrus found the Golden Age again,
Must sleepy bards the flattering dream prolong,
Mechanic echoes of the Mantuan song?
From Truth and Nature shall we widely stray,
Where Virgil, not where Fancy, leads the way?

Yes, thus the Muses sing of happy swains,
Because the Muses never knew their pains.
They boast their peasants' pipes; but peasants now
Resign their pipes and plod behind the plough;
And few, amid the rural-tribe, have time
To number syllables, and play with rhyme;
Save honest Duck, what son of verse could share
The poet's rapture, and the peasant's care?
Or the great labours of the field degrade,
With the new peril of a poorer trade?
From this chief cause these idle praises spring,
That themes so easy few forbear to sing;
For no deep thought the trifling subjects ask:
To sing of shepherds is an easy task.
The happy youth assumes the common strain,
A nymph his mistress, and himself a swain;
With no sad scenes he clouds his tuneful prayer,
But all; to look like her, is painted fair.
I grant indeed that fields and flocks have charms
For him that grazes or for him that farms;
But, when amid such pleasing scenes I trace
The poor laborious natives of the place,
And see the mid-day sun, with fervid ray,
On their bare heads and dewy temples play;
While some, with feebler heads and fainter hearts,
Deplore their fortune, yet sustain their parts:
Then shall I dare these real ills to hide
In tinsel trappings of poetic pride?
No; cast by Fortune on a frowning coast,
Which neither groves nor happy valleys boast;
Where other cares than those the Muse relates,
And other shepherds dwell with other mates;
By such examples taught, I paint the Cot,
As Truth will paint it, and as Bards will not:
Nor you, ye poor, of letter'd scorn complain,
To you the smoothest song is smooth in vain;
O'ercome by labour, and bow'd down by time,
Feel you the barren flattery of a rhyme?
Can poets soothe you, when you pine for bread,
By winding myrtles round your ruin'd shed?
Can their light tales your weighty griefs o'erpower,
Or glad with airy mirth the toilsome hour?
Lo! where the heath, with withering brake grown o'er,
Lends the light turf that warms the neighbouring poor;
From thence a length of burning sand appears,
Where the thin harvest waves its wither'd ears;
Rank weeds, that every art and care defy,
Reign o'er the land, and rob the blighted rye:

There thistles stretch their prickly arms afar,
And to the ragged infant threaten war;
There poppies, nodding, mock the hope of toil;
There the blue bugloss paints the sterile soil;
Hardy and high, above the slender sheaf,
The slimy mallow waves her silky leaf;
O'er the young shoot the charlock throws a shade,
And clasping tares cling round the sickly blade;
With mingled tints the rocky coasts abound,
And a sad splendour vainly shines around.
So looks the nymph whom wretched arts adorn,
Betray'd by man, then left for man to scorn;
Whose cheek in vain assumes the mimic rose,
While her sad eyes the troubled breast disclose;
Whose outward splendour is but folly's dress,
Exposing most, when most it gilds distress.
Here joyless roam a wild amphibious race,
With sullen wo display'd in every face;
Who far from civil arts and social fly,
And scowl at strangers with suspicious eye.
Here too the lawless merchant of the main
Draws from his plough th' intoxicated swain;
Want only claim'd the labour of the day,
But vice now steals his nightly rest away.
Where are the swains, who, daily labour done,
With rural games play'd down the setting sun;
Who struck with matchless force the bounding ball,
Or made the pond'rous quoit obliquely fall;
While some huge Ajax, terrible and strong,
Engaged some artful stripling of the throng,
And fell beneath him, foil'd, while far around
Hoarse triumph rose, and rocks return'd the sound?
Where now are these?—Beneath yon cliff they stand,
To show the freighted pinnace where to land;
To load the ready steed with guilty haste;
To fly in terror o'er the pathless waste;
Or, when detected in their straggling course,
To foil their foes by cunning or by force;
Or, yielding part (which equal knaves demand),
To gain a lawless passport through the land.
Here, wand'ring long amid these frowning fields,
I sought the simple life that Nature yields;
Rapine and Wrong and Fear usurp'd her place,
And a bold, artful, surly, savage race;
Who, only skill'd to take the finny tribe,
The yearly dinner, or septennial bribe,
Wait on the shore, and, as the waves run high,
On the tost vessel bend their eager eye,

Which to their coast directs its vent'rous way;
Their, or the ocean's, miserable prey.
As on their neighbouring beach yon swallows stand,
And wait for favouring winds to leave the land,
While still for flight the ready wing is spread:
So waited I the favouring hour, and fled—
Fled from these shores where guilt and famine reign,
And cried, Ah! hapless they who still remain;
Who still remain to hear the ocean roar,
Whose greedy waves devour the lessening shore;
Till some fierce tide, with more imperious sway,
Sweeps the low hut and all it holds away;
When the sad tenant weeps from door to door,
And begs a poor protection from the poor!
But these are scenes where Nature's niggard hand
Gave a spare portion to the famish'd land;
Hers is the fault, if here mankind complain
Of fruitless toil and labour spent in vain.
But yet in other scenes, more fair in view,
Where Plenty smiles—alas! she smiles for few—
And those who taste not, yet behold her store,
Are as the slaves that dig the golden ore,
The wealth around them makes them doubly poor
Or will you deem them amply paid in health,
Labour's fair child, that languishes with wealth?
Go, then! and see them rising with the sun,
Through a long course of daily toil to run;
See them beneath the dog-star's raging heat,
When the knees tremble and the temples beat;
Behold them, leaning on their scythes, look o'er
The labour past, and toils to come explore;
See them alternate suns and showers engage,
And hoard up aches and anguish for their age;
Through fens and marshy moors their steps pursue,
When their warm pores imbibe the evening dew;
Then own that labour may as fatal be
To these thy slaves, as thine excess to thee.
Amid this tribe too oft a manly pride
Strives in strong toil the fainting heart to hide;
There may you see the youth of slender frame
Contend with weakness, weariness, and shame;
Yet, urged along, and proudly loth to yield,
He strives to join his fellows of the field;
Till long-contending nature droops at last,
Declining health rejects his poor repast,
His cheerless spouse the coming danger sees,
And mutual murmurs urge the slow disease.
Yet grant them health, 'tis not for us to tell,

Though the head droops not, that the heart is well;
Or will you praise that homely, healthy fare,
Plenteous and plain, that happy peasants share?
Oh! trifle not with wants you cannot feel,
Nor mock the misery of a stinted meal—
Homely, not wholesome; plain, not plenteous; such
As you who praise would never deign to touch.
Ye gentle souls, who dream of rural ease,
Whom the smooth stream and smoother sonnet please;
Go! if the peaceful cot your praises share,
Go, look within, and ask if peace be there:
If peace be his—that drooping weary sire,
Or theirs, that offspring round their feeble fire;
Or hers, that matron pale, whose trembling hand
Turns on the wretched hearth th' expiring brand!
Nor yet can Time itself obtain for these
Life's latest comforts, due respect and ease:
For yonder see that hoary swain, whose age
Can with no cares except his own engage;
Who, propp'd on that rude staff, looks up to see
The bare arms broken from the withering tree,
On which, a boy, he climb'd the loftiest bough,
Then his first joy, but his sad emblem now.
He once was chief in all the rustic trade;
His steady hand the straightest furrow made;
Full many a prize he won, and still is proud
To find the triumphs of his youth allow'd.
A transient pleasure sparkles in his eyes;
He hears and smiles, then thinks again and sighs:
For now he journeys to his grave in pain;
The rich disdain him, nay, the poor disdain;
Alternate masters now their slave command,
Urge the weak efforts of his feeble hand;
And, when his age attempts its task in vain,
With ruthless taunts, of lazy poor complain.
Oft may you see him, when he tends the sheep,
His winter-charge, beneath the hillock weep;
Oft hear him murmur to the winds that blow
O'er his white locks and bury them in snow,
When, roused by rage and muttering in the morn,
He mends the broken hedge with icy thorn:—
"Why do I live, when I desire to be
At once from life and life's long labour free?
Like leaves in spring, the young are blown away,
Without the sorrows of a slow decay;
I, like yon wither'd leaf, remain behind,
Nipp'd by the frost, and shivering in the wind;
There it abides till younger buds come on,

As I, now all my fellow-swains are gone;
Then, from the rising generation thrust,
It falls, like me, unnoticed to the dust.
"These fruitful fields, these numerous flocks I see,
Are others' gain, but killing cares to me:
To me the children of my youth are lords,
Cool in their looks, but hasty in their words:
Wants of their own demand their care; and who
Feels his own want and succours others too?
A lonely, wretched man, in pain I go,
None need my help, and none relieve my wo;
Then let my bones beneath the turf be laid,
And men forget the wretch they would not aid!"
Thus groan the old, till, by disease oppress'd,
They taste a final wo, and then they rest.
Theirs is yon house that holds the parish poor,
Whose walls of mud scarce bear the broken door;
There, where the putrid vapours, flagging, play,
And the dull wheel hums doleful through the day—
There children dwell, who know no parents' care;
Parents, who know no children's love, dwell there!
Heart-broken matrons on their joyless bed,
Forsaken wives, and mothers never wed;
Dejected widows with unheeded tears,
And crippled age with more than childhood fears;
The lame, the blind, and, far the happiest they!
The moping idiot and the madman gay.
Here too the sick their final doom receive,
Here brought, amid the scenes of grief, to grieve,
Where the loud groans from some sad chamber flow,
Mix'd with the clamours of the crowd below;
Here, sorrowing, they each kindred sorrow scan,
And the cold charities of man to man:
Whose laws indeed for ruin'd age provide,
And strong compulsion plucks the scrap from pride;
But still that scrap is bought with many a sigh,
And pride embitters what it can't deny.
Say ye, oppress'd by some fantastic woes,
Some jarring nerve that baffles your repose;
Who press the downy couch, while slaves advance
With timid eye to read the distant glance;
Who with sad prayers the weary doctor tease,
To name the nameless ever-new disease;
Who with mock patience dire complaints endure,
Which real pain, and that alone, can cure—
How would ye bear in real pain to lie,
Despised, neglected, left alone to die?
How would ye bear to draw your latest breath,

Where all that's wretched paves the way for death?
Such is that room which one rude beam divides,
And naked rafters form the sloping sides;
Where the vile bands that bind the thatch are seen,
And lath and mud are all that lie between,
Save one dull pane, that, coarsely patch'd, gives way
To the rude tempest, yet excludes the day.
Here, on a matted flock, with dust o'erspread,
The drooping wretch reclines his languid head;
For him no hand the cordial cup applies,
Or wipes the tear that stagnates in his eyes;
No friends with soft discourse his pain beguile,
Or promise hope till sickness wears a smile.
But soon a loud and hasty summons calls,
Shakes the thin roof, and echoes round the walls.
Anon, a figure enters, quaintly neat,
All pride and business, bustle and conceit;
With looks unalter'd by these scenes of wo,
With speed that, entering, speaks his haste to go,
He bids the gazing throng around him fly,
And carries fate and physic in his eye:
A potent quack, long versed in human ills,
Who first insults the victim whom he kills;
Whose murd'rous hand a drowsy Bench protect.
And whose most tender mercy is neglect.
Paid by the parish for attendance here,
He wears contempt upon his sapient sneer;
In haste he seeks the bed where Misery lies,
Impatience mark'd in his averted eyes;
And, some habitual queries hurried o'er,
Without reply, he rushes on the door.
His drooping patient, long inured to pain,
And long unheeded, knows remonstrance vain;
He ceases now the feeble help to crave
Of man; and silent sinks into the grave.
But ere his death some pious doubts arise,
Some simple fears, which "bold bad" men despise:
Fain would he ask the parish-priest to prove
His title certain to the joys above;
For this he sends the murmuring nurse, who calls
The holy stranger to these dismal walls;
And doth not he, the pious man, appear,
He, "passing rich with forty pounds a year"?
Ah! no; a shepherd of a different stock,
And far unlike him, feeds this little flock:
A jovial youth, who thinks his Sunday's task
As much as God or man can fairly ask;
The rest he gives to loves and labours light,

To fields the morning, and to feasts the night;
None better skill'd the noisy pack to guide,
To urge their chase, to cheer them or to chide;
A sportsman keen, he shoots through half the day,
And, skill'd at whist, devotes the night to play.
Then, while such honours bloom around his head,
Shall he sit sadly by the sick man's bed,
To raise the hope he feels not, or with zeal
To combat fears that e'en the pious feel?
Now once again the gloomy scene explore,
Less gloomy now; the bitter hour is o'er,
The man of many sorrows sighs no more.—
Up yonder hill, behold how sadly slow
The bier moves winding from the vale below;
There lie the happy dead, from trouble free,
And the glad parish pays the frugal fee.
No more, O Death! thy victim starts to hear
Churchwarden stern, or kingly overseer;
No more the farmer claims his humble bow,
Thou art his lord, the best of tyrants thou!
Now to the church behold the mourners come,
Sedately torpid and devoutly dumb;
The village children now their games suspend,
To see the bier that bears their ancient friend:
For he was one in all their idle sport,
And like a monarch ruled their little court;
The pliant bow he form'd, the flying ball,
The bat, the wicket, were his labours all;
Him now they follow to his grave, and stand
Silent and sad, and gazing, hand in hand;
While bending low, their eager eyes explore
The mingled relics of the parish poor.
The bell tolls late, the moping owl flies round,
Fear marks the flight and magnifies the sound;
The busy priest, detain'd by weightier care,
Defers his duty till the day of prayer;
And, waiting long, the crowd retire distress'd,
To think a poor man's bones should lie unbless'd.

BOOK II

There are found, amid the Evils of a laborious Life, some Views of Tranquillity and Happiness—The
Repose and Pleasure of a Summer Sabbath: interrupted by Intoxication and Dispute—Village
Detraction—Complaints of the 'Squire—The Evening Riots—Justice—Reasons for this unpleasant View
of Rustic Life: the Effect it should have upon the Lower Classes; and the Higher—These last have their

peculiar Distresses: Exemplified in the Life and heroic Death of Lord Robert Manners—Concluding Address to His Grace the Duke of Rutland.

No longer truth, though shown in verse, disdain,
But own the Village Life a life of pain.
I too must yield, that oft amid these woes
Are gleams of transient mirth and hours of sweet repose,
Such as you find on yonder sportive Green,
The 'squire's tall gate and churchway-walk between;
Where loitering stray a little tribe of friends,
On a fair Sunday when the sermon ends.
Then rural beaux their best attire put on,
To win their nymphs, as other nymphs are won;
While those long wed go plain, and, by degrees,
Like other husbands, quit their care to please.
Some of the sermon talk, a sober crowd,
And loudly praise, if it were preach'd aloud;
Some on the labours of the week look round,
Feel their own worth, and think their toil renown'd;
While some, whose hopes to no renown extend,
Are only pleased to find their labours end.
Thus, as their hours glide on, with pleasure fraught,
Their careful masters brood the painful thought;
Much in their mind they murmur and lament,
That one fair day should be so idly spent;
And think that Heaven deals hard, to tithe their store
And tax their time for preachers and the poor.
Yet still, ye humbler friends, enjoy your hour,
This is your portion, yet unclaim'd of power;
This is Heaven's gift to weary men oppress'd,
And seems the type of their expected rest.
But yours, alas! are joys that soon decay;
Frail joys, begun and ended with the day;
Or yet, while day permits those joys to reign,
The village vices drive them from the plain.
See the stout churl, in drunken fury great,
Strike the bare bosom of his teeming mate!
His naked vices, rude and unrefined,
Exert their open empire o'er the mind;
But can we less the senseless rage despise,
Because the savage acts without disguise?
Yet here disguise, the city's vice, is seen,
And Slander steals along and taints the Green:
At her approach domestic peace is gone,
Domestic broils at her approach come on;
She to the wife the husband's crime conveys,
She tells the husband when his consort strays,

Her busy tongue through all the little state
Diffuses doubt, suspicion, and debate;
Peace, tim'rous goddess! quits her old domain,
In sentiment and song content to reign.
Nor are the nymphs that breathe the rural air
So fair as Cynthia's, nor so chaste as fair:
These to the town afford each fresher face,
And the clown's trull receives the peer's embrace;
From whom, should chance again convey her down,
The peer's disease in turn attacks the clown.
Here too the 'squire, or 'squire-like farmer, talk,
How round their regions nightly pilferers walk;
How from their ponds the fish are borne, and all
The rip'ning treasures from their lofty wall;
How meaner rivals in their sports delight,
Just rich enough to claim a doubtful right;
Who take a licence round their fields to stray,
A mongrel race! the poachers of the day.
And hark! the riots of the Green begin,
That sprang at first from yonder noisy inn;
What time the weekly pay was vanish'd all,
And the slow hostess scored the threatening wall;
What time they ask'd, their friendly feast to close,
A final cup, and that will make them foes;
When blows ensue that break the arm of toil,
And rustic battle ends the boobies' broil.
Save when to yonder Hall they bend their way,
Where the grave justice ends the grievous fray;
He who recites, to keep the poor in awe,
The law's vast volume—for he knows the law:—
To him with anger or with shame repair
The injured peasant and deluded fair.
Lo! at his throne the silent nymph appears,
Frail by her shape, but modest in her tears;
And while she stands abash'd, with conscious eye,
Some favourite female of her judge glides by,
Who views with scornful glance the strumpet's fate,
And thanks the stars that made her keeper great;
Near her the swain, about to bear for life
One certain evil, doubts 'twixt war and wife;
But, while the falt'ring damsel takes her oath,
Consents to wed, and so secures them both.
Yet, why, you ask, these humble crimes relate,
Why make the poor as guilty as the great?
To show the great, those mightier sons of pride,
How near in vice the lowest are allied;
Such are their natures and their passions such,
But these disguise too little, those too much:

So shall the man of power and pleasure see
In his own slave as vile a wretch as he;
In his luxurious lord the servant find
His own low pleasures and degenerate mind:
And each in all the kindred vices trace
Of a poor, blind, bewilder'd, erring race;
Who, a short time in varied fortune past,
Die, and are equal in the dust at last.
And you, ye poor, who still lament your fate,
Forbear to envy those you call the great;
And know, amid those blessings they possess,
They are, like you, the victims of distress;
While sloth with many a pang torments her slave,
Fear waits on guilt, and danger shakes the brave.
Oh! if in life one noble chief appears,
Great in his name, while blooming in his years;
Born to enjoy whate'er delights mankind,
And yet to all you feel or fear resign'd;
Who gave up joys and hopes, to you unknown,
For pains and dangers greater than your own:
If such there be, then let your murmurs cease,
Think, think of him, and take your lot in peace.
And such there was:—Oh! grief, that checks our pride!
Weeping we say, there was—for Manners died:
Beloved of Heaven, these humble lines forgive,
That sing of Thee, and thus aspire to live.
As the tall oak, whose vigorous branches form
An ample shade and brave the wildest storm,
High o'er the subject wood is seen to grow,
The guard and glory of the trees below;
Till on its head the fiery bolt descends,
And o'er the plain the shatter'd trunk extends;
Yet then it lies, all wond'rous as before,
And still the glory, though the guard no more:
So THOU, when every virtue, every grace,
Rose in thy soul, or shone within thy face;
When, though the son of Granby, thou wert known
Less by thy father's glory than thy own;
When Honour loved and gave thee every charm,
Fire to thy eye and vigour to thy arm;
Then from our lofty hopes and longing eyes,
Fate and thy virtues call'd thee to the skies;
Yet still we wonder at thy tow'ring fame,
And, losing thee, still dwell upon thy name.
Oh! ever honour'd, ever valued! say,
What verse can praise thee, or what work repay?
Yet verse (in all we can) thy worth repays,
Nor trusts the tardy zeal of future days;—

Honours for thee thy country shall prepare,
Thee in their hearts, the good, the brave shall bear;
To deeds like thine shall noblest chiefs aspire,
The Muse shall mourn thee, and the world admire.
In future times, when, smit with Glory's charms,
The untried youth first quits a father's arms;—
"Oh! be like him," the weeping sire shall say;
"Like Manners walk, who walk'd in Honour's way;
In danger foremost, yet in death sedate,
Oh! be like him in all things, but his fate!"
If for that fate such public tears be shed,
That Victory seems to die now THOU art dead;
How shall a friend his nearer hope resign,
That friend a brother, and whose soul was thine?
By what bold lines shall we his grief express,
Or by what soothing numbers make it less?
'Tis not, I know, the chiming of a song,
Nor all the powers that to the Muse belong,
Words aptly cull'd and meanings well express'd,
Can calm the sorrows of a wounded breast;
But Virtue, soother of the fiercest pains,
Shall heal that bosom, Rutland, where she reigns.
Yet hard the task to heal the bleeding heart,
To bid the still-recurring thoughts depart,
Tame the fierce grief and stem the rising sigh,
And curb rebellious passion with reply;
Calmly to dwell on all that pleased before,
And yet to know that all shall please no more—
Oh! glorious labour of the soul, to save
Her captive powers, and bravely mourn the brave.
To such these thoughts will lasting comfort give—
Life is not measured by the time we live:
'Tis not an even course of threescore years,
A life of narrow views and paltry fears,
Gray hairs and wrinkles and the cares they bring,
That take from death the terrors or the sting;
But 'tis the gen'rous spirit, mounting high
Above the world, that native of the sky;
The noble spirit, that, in dangers brave,
Calmly looks on, or looks beyond the grave:—
Such Manners was, so he resign'd his breath,
If in a glorious, then a timely death.
Cease then that grief, and let those tears subside;
If Passion rule us, be that passion pride;
If Reason, Reason bids us strive to raise
Our fallen hearts, and be like him we praise;
Or, if Affection still the soul subdue,
Bring all his virtues, all his worth in view,

And let Affection find its comfort too:
For how can Grief so deeply wound the heart,
When Admiration claims so large a part?
Grief is a foe; expel him, then, thy soul;
Let nobler thoughts the nearer views control!
Oh! make the age to come thy better care;
See other Rutlands, other Granbys there!
And, as thy thoughts through streaming ages glide,
See other heroes die as Manners died:
And, from their fate, thy race shall nobler grow,
As trees shoot upwards that are pruned below;
Or as old Thames, borne down with decent pride,
Sees his young streams run warbling at his side;
Though some, by art cut off, no longer run,
And some are lost beneath the summer's sun—
Yet the pure stream moves on, and, as it moves,
Its power increases and its use improves;
While plenty round its spacious waves bestow,
Still it flows on, and shall for ever flow.

THE NEWSPAPER

E quibus, hi vacuas implent sermonibus aures,
Hi narrata ferunt alio: Mensuraque ficti
Crescit, et auditis aliquid novus adjicit auctor:
Illic Credulitas, illic temerarius Error,
Vanaque Lætitia est, consternatique Timores,
Seditioque recens, dubioque auctore Susurri.

Ovid. Metamorph. lib. xii.

TO THE RIGHT HONOURABLE EDWARD LORD THURLOW, LORD HIGH CHANCELLOR OF GREAT BRITAIN; ONE OF HIS MAJESTY'S MOST HONOURABLE PRIVY COUNCIL, ETC. ETC.

MY LORD,

My obligations to your Lordship, great as they are, have not induced me to prefix your name to the following Poem; nor is it your Lordship's station, exalted as that is, which prevailed upon me to solicit the honour of your protection for it. But, when I considered your Lordship's great abilities and good taste, so well known and so universally acknowledged, I became anxious for the privilege with which you have indulged me; well knowing that the Public would not be easily persuaded to disregard a performance, marked, in any degree, with your Lordship's approbation.

It is, my Lord, the province of superior rank, in general, to bestow this kind of patronage; but superior talents only can render it valuable. Of the value of your Lordship's I am fully sensible; and, while I make my acknowledgments for that, and for many other favours, I cannot suppress the pride I have in thus publishing my gratitude, and declaring how much I have the honour to be,

MY LORD,
Your Lordship's most obedient,
most obliged,
and devoted servant,
GEORGE CRABBE.

Belvoir Castle,
February 20th, 1785.

TO THE READER

The Poem which I now offer to the Public, is, I believe, the only one written on the subject; at least, it is the only one which I have any knowledge of; and, fearing there may not be found in it many things to engage the Reader's attention, I am willing to take the strongest hold I can upon him, by offering something which has the claim of novelty.

When the subject first occurred to me, I meant, in a few lines only, to give some description of that variety of dissociating articles which are huddled together in our Daily Papers. As the thought dwelt upon me, I conceived this might be done methodically, and with some connection of parts, by taking a larger scope; which notwithstanding I have done, I must still apologize for a want of union and coherence in my Poem. Subjects like this will not easily admit of them: we cannot slide from theme to theme in an easy and graceful succession; but, on quitting one thought, there will be an unavoidable hiatus, and in general an awkward transition into that which follows.

That, in writing upon the subject of our Newspapers, I have avoided every thing which might appear like the opinion of a party, is to be accounted for from the knowledge I have gained from them; since, the more of these Instructors a man reads, the less he will infallibly understand; nor would it have been very consistent in me, at the same time to censure their temerity and ignorance, and to adopt their rage.

I should have been glad to have made some discrimination in my remarks on these productions. There is, indeed, some difference; and I have observed, that one editor will sometimes convey his abuse with more decency, and colour his falsehood with more appearance of probability, than another: but till I see that paper, wherein no great character is wantonly abused, nor groundless insinuation wilfully disseminated, I shall not make any distinction in my remarks upon them.

It must, however, be confessed, that these things have their use, and are, besides, vehicles of much amusement; but this does not outweigh the evil they do to society, and the irreparable injury they bring upon the characters of individuals. In the following Work I have given those good properties their due weight: they have changed indignation into mirth, and turned, what would otherwise have been abhorrence, into derision.

THE NEWSPAPER

This not a Time favourable to poetical Composition; and why—Newspapers Enemies to Literature, and their general Influence—Their Numbers—The Sunday Monitor—Their general Character—Their Effect upon Individuals—upon Society—in the Country—The Village Freeholder—What Kind of Composition a Newspaper is; and the Amusement it affords—Of what Parts it is chiefly composed—Articles of Intelligence: Advertisements: The Stage: Quacks: Puffing—The Correspondents to a Newspaper; political and poetical—Advice to the latter—Conclusion.

A time like this, a busy, bustling time,
Suits ill with writers, very ill with rhyme:
Unheard we sing, when party-rage runs strong,
And mightier madness checks the flowing song:
Or, should we force the peaceful Muse to wield
Her feeble arms amid the furious field,
Where party-pens a wordy war maintain,
Poor is her anger, and her friendship vain;
And oft the foes who feel her sting, combine,
Till serious vengeance pays an idle line;
For party-poets are like wasps, who dart
Death to themselves, and to their foes but smart.
Hard then our fate: if general themes we choose,
Neglect awaits the song, and chills the Muse;
Or, should we sing the subject of the day,
To-morrow's wonder puffs our praise away.
More bless'd the bards of that poetic time,
When all found readers who could find a rhyme;
Green grew the bays on every teeming head,
And Cibber was enthroned, and Settle read.
Sing, drooping Muse, the cause of thy decline;
Why reign no more the once-triumphant Nine?
Alas! new charms the wavering many gain,
And rival sheets the reader's eye detain;
A daily swarm, that banish every Muse,
Come flying forth, and mortals call them NEWS:
For these unread the noblest volumes lie;
For these in sheets unsoil'd the Muses die;
Unbought, unbless'd, the virgin copies wait
In vain for fame, and sink, unseen, to fate.
Since, then, the town forsakes us for our foes,
The smoothest numbers for the harshest prose;
Let us, with generous scorn, the taste deride,
And sing our rivals with a rival's pride.
Ye gentle poets, who so oft complain
That foul neglect is all your labours gain;
That pity only checks your growing spite

To erring man, and prompts you still to write;
That your choice works on humble stalls are laid,
Or vainly grace the windows of the trade;
Be ye my friends, if friendship e'er can warm
Those rival bosoms whom the Muses charm:
Think of the common cause wherein we go,
Like gallant Greeks against the Trojan foe;
Nor let one peevish chief his leader blame,
Till, crown'd with conquest, we regain our fame;
And let us join our forces to subdue
This bold assuming but successful crew.

I sing of NEWS, and all those vapid sheets
The rattling hawker vends through gaping streets;
Whate'er their name, whate'er the time they fly,
Damp from the press, to charm the reader's eye:
For, soon as morning dawns with roseate hue,
The Herald of the morn arises too;
Post after Post succeeds, and, all day long,
Gazettes and Ledgers swarm, a noisy throng.
When evening comes, she comes with all her train
Of Ledgers, Chronicles, and Posts again—
Like bats, appearing, when the sun goes down,
From holes obscure and corners of the town.
Of all these triflers, all like these, I write;
Oh! like my subject could my song delight,
The crowd at Lloyd's one poet's name should raise,
And all the Alley echo to his praise.
In shoals the hours their constant numbers bring,
Like insects waking to th' advancing spring;
Which take their rise from grubs obscene that lie
In shallow pools, or thence ascend the sky:
Such are these base ephemeras, so born
To die before the next revolving morn.
Yet thus they differ: insect-tribes are lost
In the first visit of a winter's frost;
While these remain, a base but constant breed,
Whose swarming sons their short-lived sires succeed:
No changing season makes their number less,
Nor Sunday shines a sabbath on the press!
Then, lo! the sainted Monitor is born,
Whose pious face some sacred texts adorn:
As artful sinners cloak the secret sin,
To veil with seeming grace the guile within;
So Moral Essays on his front appear,
But all is carnal business in the rear;
The fresh-coin'd lie, the secret whisper'd last,
And all the gleanings of the six days past.

With these retired, through half the Sabbath-day,
The London-lounger yawns his hours away:
Not so, my little flock! your preacher fly,
Nor waste the time no worldly wealth can buy;
But let the decent maid and sober clown
Pray for these idlers of the sinful town:
This day, at least, on nobler themes bestow,
Nor give to Woodfall, or the world below.

But, Sunday pass'd, what numbers flourish then,
What wond'rous labours of the press and pen!
Diurnal most, some thrice each week affords,
Some only once—O avarice of words!
When thousand starving minds such manna seek,
To drop the precious food but once a week.
Endless it were to sing the powers of all,
Their names, their numbers; how they rise and fall:
Like baneful herbs the gazer's eye they seize,
Rush to the head, and poison where they please:
Like idle flies, a busy, buzzing train,
They drop their maggots in the trifler's brain;
That genial soil receives the fruitful store,
And there they grow, and breed a thousand more.

Now be their arts display'd, how first they choose
A cause and party, as the bard his muse;
Inspired by these, with clamorous zeal they cry,
And through the town their dreams and omens fly:
So the Sibylline leaves were blown about,
Disjointed scraps of fate involved in doubt;
So idle dreams, the journals of the night,
Are right and wrong by turns, and mingle wrong with right.
Some champions for the rights that prop the crown,
Some sturdy patriots, sworn to pull them down;
Some neutral powers, with secret forces fraught,
Wishing for war, but willing to be bought:
While some to every side and party go,
Shift every friend, and join with every foe;
Like sturdy rogues in privateers, they strike
This side and that, the foes of both alike;
A traitor-crew, who thrive in troubled times,
Fear'd for their force, and courted for their crimes.
Chief to the prosperous side the numbers sail,
Fickle and false, they veer with every gale;
As birds that migrate from a freezing shore,
In search of warmer climes, come skimming o'er,
Some bold adventurers first prepare to try
The doubtful sunshine of the distant sky;

But soon the growing Summer's certain sun
Wins more and more, till all at last are won:
So, on the early prospect of disgrace,
Fly in vast troops this apprehensive race;
Instinctive tribes! their failing food they dread,
And buy, with timely change, their future bread.

Such are our guides; how many a peaceful head,
Born to be still, have they to wrangling led!
How many an honest zealot stol'n from trade,
And factious tools of pious pastors made!
With clews like these they tread the maze of state,
These oracles explore, to learn our fate;
Pleased with the guides who can so well deceive,
Who cannot lie so fast as they believe.

Oft lend I, loth, to some sage friend an ear,
(For we who will not speak are doom'd to hear);
While he, bewilder'd, tells his anxious thought,
Infectious fear from tainted scribblers caught,
Or idiot hope; for each his mind assails,
As Lloyd's court-light or Stockdale's gloom prevails.
Yet stand I patient while but one declaims,
Or gives dull comments on the speech he maims:
But oh! ye Muses, keep your votary's feet
From tavern-haunts where politicians meet;
Where rector, doctor, and attorney pause,
First on each parish, then each public cause:
Indicted roads and rates that still increase;
The murmuring poor, who will not fast in peace;
Election-zeal and friendship, since declined;
A tax commuted, or a tithe in kind;
The Dutch and Germans kindling into strife;
Dull port and poachers vile, the serious ills of life.
Here comes the neighbouring justice, pleased to guide
His little club, and in the chair preside.
In private business his commands prevail,
On public themes his reasoning turns the scale;
Assenting silence soothes his happy ear,
And, in or out, his party triumphs here.

Nor here th' infectious rage for party stops,
But flits along from palaces to shops;
Our weekly journals o'er the land abound,
And spread their plague and influenzas round;
The village, too, the peaceful, pleasant plain,
Breeds the Whig-farmer and the Tory-swain;
Brookes' and St. Alban's boasts not, but, instead,

Stares the Red Ram, and swings the Rodney's Head:—
Hither, with all a patriot's care, comes he
Who owns the little hut that makes him free;
Whose yearly forty shillings buy the smile
Of mightier men, and never waste the while;
Who feels his freehold's worth, and looks elate,
A little prop and pillar of the state.
Here he delights the weekly news to con,
And mingle comments as he blunders on;
To swallow all their varying authors teach,
To spell a title, and confound a speech:
Till with a muddled mind he quits the news,
And claims his nation's licence to abuse;
Then joins the cry, "That all the courtly race
Are venal candidates for power and place";
Yet feels some joy, amid the general vice,
That his own vote will bring its wonted price.
These are the ills the teeming press supplies,
The pois'nous springs from learning's fountain rise;
Not there the wise alone their entrance find,
Imparting useful light to mortals blind;
But, blind themselves, these erring guides hold out
Alluring lights, to lead us far about;
Screen'd by such means, here Scandal whets her quill,
Here Slander shoots unseen, whene'er she will;
Here Fraud and Falsehood labour to deceive,
And Folly aids them both, impatient to believe.

Such, sons of Britain! are the guides ye trust;
So wise their counsel, their reports so just:—
Yet, though we cannot call their morals pure,
Their judgment nice, or their decisions sure;
Merit they have, to mightier works unknown,
A style, a manner, and a fate their own.
We, who for longer fame with labour strive,
Are pain'd to keep our sickly works alive;
Studious we toil, with patient care refine,
Nor let our love protect one languid line.
Severe ourselves, at last our works appear,
When, ah! we find our readers more severe;
For after all our care and pains, how few
Acquire applause, or keep it if they do!—
Not so these sheets, ordain'd to happier fate,
Praised through their day, and but that day their date;
Their careless authors only strive to join
As many words as make an even line;
As many lines as fill a row complete;
As many rows as furnish up a sheet:

From side to side, with ready types they run,
The measure's ended, and the work is done;
Oh, born with ease, how envied and how blest!
Your fate to-day and your to-morrow's rest.
To you all readers turn, and they can look
Pleased on a paper, who abhor a book;
Those, who ne'er deign'd their Bible to peruse,
Would think it hard to be denied their news;
Sinners and saints, the wisest with the weak,
Here mingle tastes, and one amusement seek;
This, like the public inn, provides a treat,
Where each promiscuous guest sits down to eat;
And such this mental food, as we may call
Something to all men, and to some men all.

Next, in what rare production shall we trace
Such various subjects in so small a space?
As the first ship upon the waters bore
Incongruous kinds who never met before;
Or as some curious virtuoso joins,
In one small room, moths, minerals, and coins,
Birds, beasts, and fishes; nor refuses place
To serpents, toads, and all the reptile race:
So here, compress'd within a single sheet,
Great things and small, the mean and mighty meet:
'Tis this which makes all Europe's business known,
Yet here a private man may place his own;
And, where he reads of Lords and Commons, he
May tell their honours that he sells rappee.
Add next th' amusement which the motley page
Affords to either sex and every age:
Lo! where it comes before the cheerful fire—
Damps from the press in smoky curls aspire
(As from the earth the sun exhales the dew),
Ere we can read the wonders that ensue:
Then, eager, every eye surveys the part,
That brings its favourite subject to the heart;
Grave politicians look for facts alone,
And gravely add conjectures of their own:
The sprightly nymph, who never broke her rest
For tottering crowns, or mighty lands oppress'd,
Finds broils and battles, but neglects them all
For songs and suits, a birth-day, or a ball;
The keen warm man o'erlooks each idle tale
For "Money's wanted," and "Estates on Sale";
While some with equal minds to all attend,
Pleased with each part, and grieved to find an end.

So charm the News; but we, who, far from town,
Wait till the postman brings the packet down,
Once in the week a vacant day behold,
And stay for tidings, till they're three days old:
That day arrives; no welcome post appears,
But the dull morn a sullen aspect wears;
We meet, but ah! without our wonted smile,
To talk of headaches, and complain of bile;
Sullen, we ponder o'er a dull repast,
Nor feast the body while the mind must fast.
A master-passion is the love of news,
Not music so commands, nor so the Muse:
Give poets claret, they grow idle soon;
Feed the musician, and he's out of tune;
But the sick mind, of this disease possess'd,
Flies from all cure, and sickens when at rest.

Now sing, my Muse, what various parts compose
These rival sheets of politics and prose.
First, from each brother's hoard a part they draw,
A mutual theft that never fear'd a law;
Whate'er they gain, to each man's portion fall,
And read it once, you read it through them all:
For this their runners ramble day and night,
To drag each lurking deed to open light;
For daily bread the dirty trade they ply,
Coin their fresh tales, and live upon the lie.
Like bees for honey, forth for news they spring—
Industrious creatures! ever on the wing;
Home to their several cells they bear the store,
Cull'd of all kinds, then roam abroad for more.

No anxious virgin flies to "fair Tweed-side";
No injured husband mourns his faithless bride;
No duel dooms the fiery youth to bleed,
But through the town transpires each vent'rous deed.

Should some fair frail-one drive her prancing pair,
Where rival peers contend to please the fair;
When, with new force, she aids her conquering eyes,
And beauty decks with all that beauty buys—
Quickly we learn whose heart her influence feels,
Whose acres melt before her glowing wheels.
To these a thousand idle themes succeed,
Deeds of all kinds, and comments to each deed.
Here stocks, the state-barometers, we view,
That rise or fall, by causes known to few;
Promotion's ladder who goes up or down;

Who wed, or who seduced, amuse the town;
What new-born heir has made his father blest;
What heir exults, his father now at rest;
That ample list the Tyburn-herald gives,
And each known knave, who still for Tyburn lives.

So grows the work, and now the printer tries
His powers no more, but leans on his allies.

When, lo! the advertising tribe succeed,
Pay to be read, yet find but few will read;
And chief th' illustrious race, whose drops and pills
Have patent powers to vanquish human ills:
These, with their cures, a constant aid remain,
To bless the pale composer's fertile brain;
Fertile it is, but still the noblest soil
Requires some pause, some intervals from toil;
And they at least a certain ease obtain
From Katterfelto's skill, and Graham's glowing strain.

I too must aid, and pay to see my name
Hung in these dirty avenues to fame;
Nor pay in vain, if aught the Muse has seen
And sung, could make those avenues more clean;
Could stop one slander ere it found its way,
And gave to public scorn its helpless prey.
By the same aid, the Stage invites her friends,
And kindly tells the banquet she intends;
Thither from real life the many run,
With Siddons weep, or laugh with Abingdon;
Pleased, in fictitious joy or grief, to see
The mimic passion with their own agree;
To steal a few enchanted hours away
From care, and drop the curtain on the day.
But who can steal from self that wretched wight,
Whose darling work is tried, some fatal night?
Most wretched man! when, bane to every bliss,
He hears the serpent-critic's rising hiss;
Then groans succeed; not traitors on the wheel
Can feel like him, or have such pangs to feel.
Nor end they here: next day he reads his fall
In every paper; critics are they all;
He sees his branded name, with wild affright,
And hears again the cat-calls of the night.

Such help the STAGE affords; a larger space
Is fill'd by PUFFS and all the puffing race.
Physic had once alone the lofty style,

The well-known boast, that ceased to raise a smile;
Now all the province of that tribe invade,
And we abound in quacks of every trade.

The simple barber, once an honest name—
Cervantes founded, Fielding raised his fame—
Barber no more, a gay perfumer comes,
On whose soft cheek his own cosmetic blooms;
Here he appears, each simple mind to move,
And advertises beauty, grace, and love.
—"Come, faded belles, who would your youth renew,
And learn the wonders of Olympian dew;
Restore the roses that begin to faint,
Nor think celestial washes vulgar paint;
Your former features, airs, and arts assume,
Circassian virtues, with Circassian bloom.
—Come, batter'd beaux, whose locks are turn'd to grey,
And crop Discretion's lying badge away;
Read where they vend these smart engaging things,
These flaxen frontlets with elastic springs;
No female eye the fair deception sees,
Not Nature's self so natural as these."
Such are their arts, but not confined to them,
The Muse impartial must her sons condemn:
For they, degenerate! join the venal throng,
And puff a lazy Pegasus along:
More guilty these, by Nature less design'd
For little arts that suit the vulgar-kind;
That barbers' boys, who would to trade advance,
Wish us to call them, smart Friseurs from France;
That he who builds a chop-house, on his door
Paints "The true old original Blue Boar!"
These are the arts by which a thousand live,
Where Truth may smile, and Justice may forgive;
But when, amid this rabble-rout, we find
A puffing poet to his honour blind;
Who slily drops quotations all about,
Packet or Post, and points their merit out;
Who advertises what reviewers say,
With sham editions every second day;
Who dares not trust his praises out of sight,
But hurries into fame with all his might;
Although the verse some transient praise obtains,
Contempt is all the anxious poet gains.
Now, puffs exhausted, advertisements past,
Their correspondents stand exposed at last;
These are a numerous tribe, to fame unknown,
Who for the public good forego their own;

Who, volunteers, in paper-war engage,
With double portion of their party's rage:
Such are the Bruti, Decii, who appear
Wooing the printer for admission here;
Whose generous souls can condescend to pray
For leave to throw their precious time away.
Oh! cruel Woodfall! when a patriot draws
His grey-goose quill in his dear country's cause,
To vex and maul a ministerial race,
Can thy stern soul refuse the champion place?
Alas! thou know'st not with what anxious heart
He longs his best-loved labours to impart;
How he has sent them to thy brethren round,
And still the same unkind reception found:
At length indignant will he damn the state,
Turn to his trade, and leave us to our fate.

These Roman souls, like Rome's great sons, are known
To live in cells on labours of their own.
Thus Milo, could we see the noble chief,
Feeds, for his country's good, on legs of beef;
Camillus copies deeds for sordid pay,
Yet fights the public battles twice a day;
E'en now the godlike Brutus views his score
Scroll'd on the bar-board, swinging with the door;
Where, tippling punch, grave Cato's self you'll see,
And Amor Patriæ vending smuggled tea.

Last in these ranks and least, their art's disgrace,
Neglected stand the Muse's meanest race:
Scribblers who court contempt, whose verse the eye
Disdainful views, and glances swiftly by:
This Poet's Corner is the place they choose,
A fatal nursery for an infant Muse;
Unlike that corner where true poets lie,
These cannot live, and they shall never die;
Hapless the lad whose mind such dreams invade,
And win to verse the talents due to trade.

Curb, then, O youth! these raptures as they rise;
Keep down the evil spirit and be wise;
Follow your calling, think the Muses foes,
Nor lean upon the pestle and compose.

I know your day-dreams, and I know the snare
Hid in your flow'ry path, and cry "Beware."
Thoughtless of ill, and to the future blind,
A sudden couplet rushes on your mind;

Here you may nameless print your idle rhymes,
And read your first-born work a thousand times;
Th' infection spreads, your couplet grows apace—
Stanzas to Delia's dog or Celia's face;
You take a name: Philander's odes are seen,
Printed, and praised, in every magazine;
Diarian sages greet their brother sage,
And your dark pages please th' enlighten'd age.—
Alas! what years you thus consume in vain,
Ruled by this wretched bias of the brain!

Go! to your desks and counters all return;
Your sonnets scatter, your acrostics burn;
Trade, and be rich; or, should your careful sires
Bequeath you wealth, indulge the nobler fires;
Should love of fame your youthful heart betray,
Pursue fair fame, but in a glorious way,
Nor in the idle scenes of Fancy's painting stray.

Of all the good that mortal men pursue,
The Muse has least to give, and gives to few;
Like some coquettish fair, she leads us on,
With smiles and hopes, till youth and peace are gone;
Then, wed for life, the restless wrangling pair
Forget how constant one, and one how fair:
Meanwhile, Ambition, like a blooming bride,
Brings power and wealth to grace her lover's side;
And, though she smiles not with such flattering charms,
The brave will sooner win her to their arms.
Then wed to her, if Virtue tie the bands,
Go spread your country's fame in hostile lands;
Her court, her senate, or her arms adorn,
And let her foes lament that you were born:
Or weigh her laws, their ancient rights defend,
Though hosts oppose, be theirs and Reason's friend;
Arm'd with strong powers, in their defence engage,
And rise the Thurlow of the future age!

THE PARISH REGISTER

IN THREE PARTS

INTRODUCTION

The Village Register considered, as containing principally the Annals of the Poor—State of the Peasantry as meliorated by Frugality and Industry—The Cottage of an industrious Peasant; its Ornaments—Prints and Books—The Garden; its Satisfactions—The State of the Poor, when improvident and vicious—The Row or Street, and its Inhabitants—The Dwelling of one of these—A Public House—Garden and its Appendages—Gamesters; rustic Sharpers, &c.—Conclusion of the Introductory Part.

PART I

BAPTISMS

The Child of the Miller's Daughter, and Relation of her Misfortune—A frugal Couple: their Kind of Frugality—Plea of the Mother of a natural Child: her Churching—Large Family of Gerard Ablett: his Apprehensions: Comparison between his State and that of the wealthy Farmer his Master: his Consolation—An old Man's Anxiety for an Heir: the Jealousy of another on having many—Characters of the Grocer Dawkins and his Friend: their different Kinds of Disappointment—Three Infants named—An Orphan Girl and Village School-mistress—Gardener's Child: Pedantry and Conceit of the Father: his Botanical Discourse: Method of fixing the Embryo-fruit of Cucumbers—Absurd Effects of Rustic Vanity: observed in the Names of their Children—Relation of the Vestry Debate on a Foundling: Sir Richard Monday—Children of various Inhabitants—The poor Farmer—Children of a Profligate: his Character and Fate—Conclusion.

Tum porro puer ut sævis projectus ab undis
Navita) nudus humi jacet, infans, indigus omni
Vitali auxilio—
Vagituque locum lugubri complet, ut æquum est,
Cui tantum in vitâ restet transire malorum.

Lucret. de Nat. Rerum, lib. v. [vv. 223—5, 227—8.]

The year revolves, and I again explore
The simple annals of my parish poor:
What infant-members in my flock appear;
What pairs I bless'd in the departed year;
And who, of old or young, or nymphs or swains,
Are lost to life, its pleasures and its pains.
No Muse I ask, before my view to bring
The humble actions of the swains I sing—
How pass'd the youthful, how the old their days;
Who sank in sloth, and who aspired to praise;
Their tempers, manners, morals, customs, arts;
What parts they had, and how they 'mploy'd their parts;
By what elated, soothed, seduced, depress'd,
Full well I know—these records give the rest.
Is there a place, save one the poet sees,
A land of love, of liberty and ease;
Where labour wearies not, nor cares suppress
Th' eternal flow of rustic happiness;
Where no proud mansion frowns in awful state,

Or keeps the sunshine from the cottage-gate,
Where young and old, intent on pleasure, throng,
And half man's life is holiday and song?
Vain search for scenes like these! no view appears,
By sighs unruffled or unstain'd by tears;
Since vice the world subdued and waters drown'd,
Auburn and Eden can no more be found.
Hence good and evil mix'd, but man has skill
And power to part them, when he feels the will!
Toil, care, and patience bless th' abstemious few,
Fear, shame, and want the thoughtless herd pursue.
Behold the cot! where thrives th' industrious swain,
Source of his pride, his pleasure, and his gain;
Screen'd from the winter's wind, the sun's last ray
Smiles on the window and prolongs the day;
Projecting thatch the woodbine's branches stop,
And turn their blossoms to the casement's top:
All need requires is in that cot contain'd,
And much that taste, untaught and unrestrain'd,
Surveys delighted; there she loves to trace,
In one gay picture, all the royal race;
Around the walls are heroes, lovers, kings;
The print that shows them and the verse that sings.
Here the last Lewis on his throne is seen,
And there he stands imprison'd, and his queen;
To these the mother takes her child, and shows
What grateful duty to his God he owes;
Who gives to him a happy home, where he
Lives and enjoys his freedom with the free;
When kings and queens, dethroned, insulted, tried,
Are all these blessings of the poor denied.
There is King Charles, and all his Golden Rules,
Who proved Misfortune's was the best of schools:
And there his son, who, tried by years of pain,
Proved that misfortunes may be sent in vain.
The magic-mill that grinds the gran'nams young,
Close at the side of kind Godiva hung;
She, of her favourite place the pride and joy,
Of charms at once most lavish and most coy,
By wanton act the purest fame could raise,
And give the boldest deed the chastest praise.
There stands the stoutest Ox in England fed;
There fights the boldest Jew, Whitechapel-bred;
And here Saint Monday's worthy votaries live
In all the joys that ale and skittles give.
Now, lo! in Egypt's coast that hostile fleet,
By nations dreaded and by Nelson beat;
And here shall soon another triumph come,

A deed of glory in a day of gloom—
Distressing glory! grievous boon of fate!
The proudest conquest, at the dearest rate.
On shelf of deal, beside the cuckoo-clock,
Of cottage-reading rests the chosen stock;
Learning we lack, not books, but have a kind
For all our wants, a meat for every mind:
The tale for wonder and the joke for whim,
The half-sung sermon and the half-groan'd hymn.
No need of classing; each within its place,
The feeling finger in the dark can trace;
"First from the corner, farthest from the wall":
Such all the rules, and they suffice for all.
There pious works for Sunday's use are found,
Companions for that Bible newly bound:
That Bible, bought by sixpence weekly saved,
Has choicest prints by famous hands engraved;
Has choicest notes by many a famous head,
Such as to doubt have rustic readers led;
Have made them stop to reason, why? and how?
And, where they once agreed, to cavil now.
Oh! rather give me commentators plain,
Who with no deep researches vex the brain;
Who from the dark and doubtful love to run,
And hold their glimmering tapers to the sun;
Who simple truth with nine-fold reasons back,
And guard the point no enemies attack.
Bunyan's famed Pilgrim rests that shelf upon;
A genius rare but rude was honest John:
Not one who, early by the Muse beguiled,
Drank from her well the waters undefiled;
Not one who slowly gain'd the hill sublime,
Then often sipp'd and little at a time;
But one who dabbled in the sacred springs,
And drank them muddy, mix'd with baser things.
Here, to interpret dreams we read the rules—
Science our own, and never taught in schools;
In moles and specks we Fortune's gifts discern,
And Fate's fix'd will from Nature's wanderings learn.
Of Hermit Quarle we read, in island rare,
Far from mankind and seeming far from care;
Safe from all want, and sound in every limb;
Yes! there was he, and there was care with him.
Unbound and heap'd, these valued works beside,
Lay humbler works the pedler's pack supplied;
Yet these, long since, have all acquired a name:
The Wandering Jew has found his way to fame;
And fame, denied to many a labour'd song,

Crowns Thumb the great, and Hickerthrift the strong.
There too is he, by wizard-power upheld,
Jack, by whose arm the giant-brood were quell'd:
His shoes of swiftness on his feet he placed;
His coat of darkness on his loins he braced;
His sword of sharpness in his hand he took,
And off the heads of doughty giants stroke:
Their glaring eyes beheld no mortal near;
No sound of feet alarm'd the drowsy ear;
No English blood their pagan sense could smell,
But heads dropp'd headlong, wondering why they fell.
These are the peasant's joy, when, placed at ease,
Half his delighted offspring mount his knees.
To every cot the lord's indulgent mind
Has a small space for garden-ground assign'd;
Here—till return of morn dismiss'd the farm—
The careful peasant plies the sinewy arm,
Warm'd as he works, and casts his look around
On every foot of that improving ground:
It is his own he sees; his master's eye
Peers not about, some secret fault to spy;
Nor voice severe is there, nor censure known;—
Hope, profit, pleasure,—they are all his own.
Here grow the humble chives, and, hard by them,
The leek with crown globose and reedy stem;
High climb his pulse in many an even row,
Deep strike the ponderous roots in soil below;
And herbs of potent smell and pungent taste
Give a warm relish to the night's repast;
Apples and cherries grafted by his hand,
And cluster'd nuts for neighbouring market stand.
Nor thus concludes his labour: near the cot,
The reed-fence rises round some fav'rite spot;
Where rich carnations, pinks with purple eyes,
Proud hyacinths, the least some florist's prize,
Tulips tall-stemm'd and pounced auriculas rise.
Here on a Sunday-eve, when service ends,
Meet and rejoice a family of friends;
All speak aloud, are happy and are free,
And glad they seem, and gaily they agree.
What, though fastidious ears may shun the speech,
Where all are talkers and where none can teach;
Where still the welcome and the words are old,
And the same stories are for ever told—
Yet theirs is joy that, bursting from the heart,
Prompts the glad tongue these nothings to impart;
That forms these tones of gladness we despise,
That lifts their steps, that sparkles in their eyes;

That talks or laughs or runs or shouts or plays,
And speaks in all their looks and all their ways.
Fair scenes of peace! ye might detain us long;
But vice and misery now demand the song,
And turn our view from dwellings simply neat,
To this infected row we term our street.
Here, in cabal, a disputatious crew
Each evening meet: the sot, the cheat, the shrew;
Riots are nightly heard—the curse, the cries
Of beaten wife, perverse in her replies;
While shrieking children hold each threat'ning hand,
And sometimes life, and sometimes food, demand:
Boys, in their first-stol'n rags, to swear begin,
And girls, who heed not dress, are skill'd in gin:
Snarers and smugglers here their gains divide;
Ensnaring females here their victims hide;
And here is one, the sibyl of the row,
Who knows all secrets, or affects to know.
Seeking their fate, to her the simple run,
To her the guilty, theirs awhile to shun;
Mistress of worthless arts, depraved in will,
Her care unbless'd and unrepaid her skill,
Slave to the tribe, to whose command she stoops,
And poorer than the poorest maid she dupes.
Between the road-way and the walls, offence
Invades all eyes and strikes on every sense:
There lie, obscene, at every open door,
Heaps from the hearth and sweepings from the floor;
And day by day the mingled masses grow,
As sinks are disembogued and kennels flow.
There hungry dogs from hungry children steal;
There pigs and chickens quarrel for a meal;
There dropsied infants wail without redress,
And all is want and wo and wretchedness:
Yet, should these boys, with bodies bronzed and bare,
High-swoln and hard, outlive that lack of care,
Forced on some farm, the unexerted strength,
Though loth to action, is compell'd at length,
When warm'd by health, as serpents in the spring
Aside their slough of indolence they fling.
Yet, ere they go, a greater evil comes—
See! crowded beds in those contiguous rooms;
Beds but ill parted by a paltry screen
Of paper'd lath or curtain dropp'd between;
Daughters and sons to yon compartments creep,
And parents here beside their children sleep.
Ye who have power, these thoughtless people part,
Nor let the ear be first to taint the heart!

Come! search within, nor sight nor smell regard;
The true physician walks the foulest ward.
See! on the floor what frouzy patches rest!
What nauseous fragments on yon fractured chest!
What downy dust beneath yon window-seat!
And round these posts that serve this bed for feet;
This bed, where all those tatter'd garments lie,
Worn by each sex, and now perforce thrown by!
See! as we gaze, an infant lifts its head,
Left by neglect and burrow'd in that bed;
The mother-gossip has the love suppress'd
An infant's cry once waken'd in her breast;
And daily prattles, as her round she takes,
(With strong resentment) of the want she makes.
Whence all these woes?—From want of virtuous will,
Of honest shame, of time-improving skill;
From want of care t'employ the vacant hour,
And want of ev'ry kind but want of power.
Here are no wheels for either wool or flax,
But packs of cards—made up of sundry packs;
Here is no clock, nor will they turn the glass.
And see how swift th'important moments pass;
Here are no books, but ballads on the wall
Are some abusive, and indecent all;
Pistols are here, unpair'd; with nets and hooks,
Of every kind, for rivers, ponds, and brooks;
An ample flask, that nightly rovers fill
With recent poison from the Dutchman's still;
A box of tools, with wires of various size,
Frocks, wigs, and hats, for night or day disguise,
And bludgeons stout to gain or guard a prize.
To every house belongs a space of ground,
Of equal size, once fenced with paling round;
That paling now by slothful waste destroy'd,
Dead gorse and stumps of elder fill the void,
Save in the centre-spot, whose walls of clay
Hide sots and striplings at their drink or play.
Within, a board, beneath a tiled retreat,
Allures the bubble and maintains the cheat;
Where heavy ale in spots like varnish shows;
Where chalky tallies yet remain in rows;
Black pipes and broken jugs the seats defile,
The walls and windows, rhymes and reck'nings vile;
Prints of the meanest kind disgrace the door,
And cards, in curses torn, lie fragments on the floor.
Here his poor bird th'inhuman cocker brings,
Arms his hard heel and clips his golden wings;
With spicy food th'impatient spirit feeds,

And shouts and curses as the battle bleeds.
Struck through the brain, deprived of both his eyes,
The vanquish'd bird must combat till he dies;
Must faintly peck at his victorious foe,
And reel and stagger at each feeble blow.
When fall'n, the savage grasps his dabbled plumes,
His blood-stain'd arms, for other deaths assumes;
And damns the craven-fowl, that lost his stake,
And only bled and perish'd for his sake.
Such are our peasants, those to whom we yield
Praise with relief, the fathers of the field;
And these who take, from our reluctant hands,
What Burn advises or the Bench commands.
Our farmers round, well pleased with constant gain,
Like other farmers, flourish and complain.—
These are our groups; our portraits next appear,
And close our exhibition for the year.

With evil omen we that year begin:
A Child of Shame—stern Justice adds, of Sin—
Is first recorded; I would hide the deed,
But vain the wish; I sigh and I proceed:
And could I well th' instructive truth convey,
'Twould warn the giddy and awake the gay.
Of all the nymphs who gave our village grace,
The Miller's daughter had the fairest face.
Proud was the Miller; money was his pride;
He rode to market, as our farmers ride;
And 'twas his boast, inspired by spirits, there,
His favourite Lucy should be rich as fair;
But she must meek and still obedient prove,
And not presume, without his leave, to love.
A youthful Sailor heard him;—"Ha!" quoth he,
"This Miller's maiden is a prize for me;
Her charms I love, his riches I desire,
And all his threats but fan the kindling fire;
My ebbing purse no more the foe shall fill,
But Love's kind act and Lucy at the mill."
Thus thought the youth, and soon the chase began,
Stretch'd all his sail, nor thought of pause or plan:
His trusty staff in his bold hand he took,
Like him and like his frigate, heart of oak;
Fresh were his features, his attire was new;
Clean was his linen, and his jacket blue:
Of finest jean, his trowsers, tight and trim,
Brush'd the large buckle at the silver rim.
He soon arrived, he traced the village-green;

There saw the maid, and was with pleasure seen;
Then talk'd of love, till Lucy's yielding heart
Confess'd 'twas painful, though 'twas right, to part.
"For ah! my father has a haughty soul;
Whom best he loves, he loves but to control;
Me to some churl in bargain he'll consign,
And make some tyrant of the parish mine:
Cold is his heart, and he with looks severe
Has often forced but never shed the tear;
Save, when my mother died, some drops express'd
A kind of sorrow for a wife at rest.—
To me a master's stern regard is shown,
I'm like his steed, prized highly as his own;
Stroked but corrected, threaten'd when supplied,
His slave and boast, his victim and his pride."
"Cheer up, my lass! I'll to thy father go—
The Miller cannot be the Sailor's foe;
Both live by Heaven's free gale, that plays aloud
In the stretch'd canvas and the piping shroud;
The rush of winds, the flapping sails above,
And rattling planks within, are sounds we love;
Calms are our dread; when tempests plough the deep,
We take a reef, and to the rocking sleep."
"Ha!" quoth the Miller, moved at speech so rash,
"Art thou like me? then, where thy notes and cash?
Away to Wapping, and a wife command,
With all thy wealth, a guinea, in thine hand;
There with thy messmates quaff the muddy cheer,
And leave my Lucy for thy betters here."
"Revenge! revenge!" the angry lover cried,
Then sought the nymph, and "Be thou now my bride."
Bride had she been, but they no priest could move
To bind in law the couple bound by love.
What sought these lovers then by day, by night,
But stolen moments of disturb'd delight—
Soft trembling tumults, terrors dearly prized,
Transports that pain'd, and joys that agonized:
Till the fond damsel, pleased with lad so trim,
Awed by her parent, and enticed by him,
Her lovely form from savage power to save,
Gave—not her hand, but ALL she could, she gave.
Then came the day of shame, the grievous night,
The varying look, the wandering appetite;
The joy assumed, while sorrow dimm'd the eyes;
The forced sad smiles that follow'd sudden sighs;
And every art, long used, but used in vain,
To hide thy progress, Nature, and thy pain.
Too eager caution shows some danger's near,

The bully's bluster proves the coward's fear;
His sober step the drunkard vainly tries,
And nymphs expose the failings they disguise.
First, whispering gossips were in parties seen;
Then louder Scandal walk'd the village-green;
Next babbling Folly told the growing ill,
And busy Malice dropp'd it at the mill.
"Go! to thy curse and mine," the Father said,
"Strife and confusion stalk around thy bed;
Want and a wailing brat thy portion be,
Plague to thy fondness, as thy fault to me.—
Where skulks the villain?"—"On the ocean wide
My William seeks a portion for his bride."—
"Vain be his search! but, till the traitor come,
The higgler's cottage be thy future home;
There with his ancient shrew and care abide,
And hide thy head—thy shame thou canst not hide."
Day after day was pass'd in pains and grief;
Week follow'd week—and still was no relief.
Her boy was born—no lads nor lasses came
To grace the rite or give the child a name;
Nor grave conceited nurse, of office proud,
Bore the young Christian roaring through the crowd:
In a small chamber was my office done,
Where blinks through paper'd panes the setting sun;
Where noisy sparrows, perch'd on penthouse near,
Chirp tuneless joy, and mock the frequent tear;
Bats on their webby wings in darkness move,
And feebly shriek their melancholy love.
No Sailor came; the months in terror fled!
Then news arrived: he fought, and he was DEAD!
At the lone cottage Lucy lives, and still
Walks for her weekly pittance to the mill;
A mean seraglio there her father keeps,
Whose mirth insults her, as she stands and weeps,
And sees the plenty, while compell'd to stay,
Her father's pride become his harlot's prey.
Throughout the lanes she glides, at evening's close,
And softly lulls her infant to repose;
Then sits and gazes, but with viewless look,
As gilds the moon the rippling of the brook;
And sings her vespers, but in voice so low,
She hears their murmurs as the waters flow:
And she too murmurs, and begins to find
The solemn wanderings of a wounded mind.
Visions of terror, views of wo succeed,
The mind's impatience, to the body's need;
By turns to that, by turns to this, a prey,

She knows what reason yields, and dreads what madness may.

Next, with their boy, a decent couple came,
And call'd him Robert, 'twas his father's name;
Three girls preceded, all by time endear'd,
And future births were neither hoped nor fear'd.
Bless'd in each other, but to no excess,
Health, quiet, comfort, form'd their happiness;
Love, all made up of torture and delight,
Was but mere madness in this couple's sight:
Susan could think, though not without a sigh,
If she were gone, who should her place supply;
And Robert, half in earnest, half in jest,
Talk of her spouse when he should be at rest:
Yet strange would either think it to be told,
Their love was cooling or their hearts were cold.
Few were their acres,—but, with these content,
They were, each pay-day, ready with their rent;
And few their wishes—what their farm denied,
The neighbouring town, at trifling cost, supplied.
If at the draper's window Susan cast
A longing look, as with her goods she pass'd,
And, with the produce of the wheel and churn,
Bought her a Sunday-robe on her return;
True to her maxim, she would take no rest,
Till care repaid that portion to the chest:
Or if, when loitering at the Whitsun-fair,
Her Robert spent some idle shillings there;
Up at the barn, before the break of day,
He made his labour for th'indulgence pay:
Thus both—that waste itself might work in vain—
Wrought double tides, and all was well again.
Yet, though so prudent, there were times of joy,
(The day they wed, the christening of the boy,)
When to the wealthier farmers there was shown
Welcome unfeign'd, and plenty like their own;
For Susan served the great, and had some pride
Among our topmost people to preside.
Yet in that plenty, in that welcome free,
There was the guiding nice frugality,
That, in the festal as the frugal day,
Has, in a different mode, a sovereign sway;
As tides the same attractive influence know,
In the least ebb and in their proudest flow:
The wise frugality, that does not give
A life to saving, but that saves to live;
Sparing, not pinching, mindful though not mean,
O'er all presiding, yet in nothing seen.

Recorded next, a babe of love I trace,
Of many loves the mother's fresh disgrace.—
"Again, thou harlot! could not all thy pain,
All my reproof, thy wanton thoughts restrain?"
"Alas! your reverence, wanton thoughts, I grant,
Were once my motive, now the thoughts of want;
Women, like me, as ducks in a decoy,
Swim down a stream, and seem to swim in joy;
Your sex pursue us, and our own disdain;
Return is dreadful, and escape is vain.
Would men forsake us, and would women strive
To help the fall'n, their virtue might revive."
For rite of churching soon she made her way,
In dread of scandal, should she miss the day.—
Two matrons came! with them she humbly knelt,
Their action copied and their comforts felt,
From that great pain and peril to be free,
Though still in peril of that pain to be;
Alas! what numbers, like this amorous dame,
Are quick to censure, but are dead to shame!

Twin-infants then appear: a girl, a boy,
Th' o'erflowing cup of Gerard Ablett's joy.
One had I named in every year that pass'd
Since Gerard wed, and twins behold at last!
Well pleased, the bridegroom smiled to hear—"A vine
Fruitful and spreading round the walls be thine,
And branch-like be thine offspring!"—Gerard then
Look'd joyful love, and softly said, "Amen."
Now of that vine he'd have no more increase,
Those playful branches now disturb his peace:
Them he beholds around his table spread,
But finds, the more the branch, the less the bread;
And while they run his humble walls about,
They keep the sunshine of good-humour out.
Cease, man, to grieve! thy master's lot survey,
Whom wife and children, thou and thine, obey;
A farmer proud beyond a farmer's pride,
Of all around the envy or the guide;
Who trots to market on a steed so fine,
That when I meet him, I'm ashamed of mine;
Whose board is high up-heap'd with generous fare,
Which five stout sons and three tall daughters share:
Cease, man, to grieve, and listen to his care.
A few years fled, and all thy boys shall be
Lords of a cot, and labourers like thee:
Thy girls, unportion'd, neighb'ring youths shall lead

Brides from my church, and thenceforth thou art freed;
But then thy master shall of cares complain,
Care after care, a long connected train;
His sons for farms shall ask a large supply,
For farmers' sons each gentle miss shall sigh;
Thy mistress, reasoning well of life's decay,
Shall ask a chaise, and hardly brook delay;
The smart young cornet who, with so much grace,
Rode in the ranks and betted at the race,
While the vex'd parent rails at deeds so rash,
Shall d—n his luck, and stretch his hand for cash.
Sad troubles, Gerard! now pertain to thee,
When thy rich master seems from trouble free;
But 'tis one fate at different times assign'd,
And thou shalt lose the cares that he must find.

"Ah!" quoth our village Grocer, rich and old,
"Would I might one such cause for care behold!"
To whom his Friend, "Mine greater bliss would be,
Would Heav'n take those my spouse assigns to me."

Aged were both, that Dawkins, Ditchem this,
Who much of marriage thought, and much amiss;
Both would delay, the one, till, riches gain'd,
The son he wish'd might be to honour train'd;
His Friend—lest fierce intruding heirs should come,
To waste his hoard and vex his quiet home.
Dawkins, a dealer once on burthen'd back
Bore his whole substance in a pedler's pack;
To dames discreet, the duties yet unpaid,
His stores of lace and hyson he convey'd.
When thus enrich'd, he chose at home to stop,
And fleece his neighbours in a new-built shop;
Then woo'd a spinster blithe, and hoped, when wed,
For love's fair favours and a fruitful bed.
Not so his Friend;—on widow fair and staid
He fix'd his eye; but he was much afraid,
Yet woo'd; while she his hair of silver hue
Demurely noticed, and her eye withdrew.
Doubtful he paused—"Ah! were I sure," he cried,
"No craving children would my gains divide:
Fair as she is, I would my widow take,
And live more largely for my partner's sake."
With such their views, some thoughtful years they pass'd,
And hoping, dreading, they were bound at last.
And what their fate? Observe them as they go,
Comparing fear with fear and wo with wo.
"Humphrey!" said Dawkins, "envy in my breast

Sickens to see thee in thy children bless'd;
They are thy joys, while I go grieving home
To a sad spouse, and our eternal gloom.
We look despondency; no infant near,
To bless the eye or win the parent's ear;
Our sudden heats and quarrels to allay,
And soothe the petty sufferings of the day.
Alike our want, yet both the want reprove;
Where are, I cry, these pledges of our love?
When she, like Jacob's wife, makes fierce reply,
Yet fond—'Oh! give me children, or I die';
And I return—still childless doom'd to live,
Like the vex'd patriarch—'Are they mine to give?'
Ah! much I envy thee thy boys, who ride
On poplar branch, and canter at thy side;
And girls, whose cheeks thy chin's fierce fondness know,
And with fresh beauty at the contact glow."
"Oh! simple friend," said Ditchem, "would'st thou gain
A father's pleasure by a husband's pain?
Alas! what pleasure—when some vig'rous boy
Should swell thy pride, some rosy girl thy joy—
Is it to doubt who grafted this sweet flower,
Or whence arose that spirit and that power?
"Four years I've wed; not one has pass'd in vain:
Behold the fifth! behold, a babe again!
My wife's gay friends th' unwelcome imp admire,
And fill the room with gratulation dire.
While I in silence sate, revolving all
That influence ancient men, or that befall,
A gay pert guest—Heav'n knows his business—came;
'A glorious boy,' he cried, 'and what the name?'
Angry I growl'd, 'My spirit cease to tease,
Name it yourselves,—Cain, Judas, if you please;
His father's give him—should you that explore,
The devil's or yours,' I said, and sought the door.
My tender partner not a word or sigh
Gives to my wrath, nor to my speech reply;
But takes her comforts, triumphs in my pain,
And looks undaunted for a birth again."
Heirs thus denied afflict the pining heart,
And, thus afforded, jealous pangs impart;
Let, therefore, none avoid, and none demand
These arrows number'd for the giant's hand.

Then with their infants three, the parents came,
And each assign'd—'twas all they had—a name:
Names of no mark or price; of them not one
Shall court our view on the sepulchral stone,

Or stop the clerk, th' engraven scrolls to spell,
Or keep the sexton from the sermon bell.

An orphan-girl succeeds; ere she was born
Her father died, her mother on that morn;
The pious mistress of the school sustains
Her parents' part, nor their affection feigns,
But pitying feels; with due respect and joy,
I trace the matron at her loved employ.
What time the striplings, wearied e'en with play,
Part at the closing of the summer's day,
And each by different path returns the well-known way—
Then I behold her at her cottage-door,
Frugal of light, her Bible laid before,
When on her double duty she proceeds,
Of time as frugal, knitting as she reads.
Her idle neighbours, who approach to tell
Some trifling tale, her serious looks compel,
To hear reluctant—while the lads who pass,
In pure respect walk silent on the grass.
Then sinks the day; but not to rest she goes,
Till solemn prayers the daily duties close.
But I digress, and lo! an infant train
Appear, and call me to my task again.
"Why Lonicera wilt thou name thy child?"
I ask'd the Gardener's wife, in accents mild.
"We have a right," replied the sturdy dame—
And Lonicera was the infant's name.
If next a son shall yield our Gardener joy,
Then Hyacinthus shall be that fair boy;
And if a girl, they will at length agree,
That Belladonna that fair maid shall be.
High-sounding words our worthy Gardener gets,
And at his club to wondering swains repeats;
He then of Rhus and Rhododendron speaks,
And Allium calls his onions and his leeks;
Nor weeds are now, for whence arose the weed,
Scarce plants, fair herbs, and curious flowers proceed;
Where Cuckoo-pints and Dandelions sprung,
(Gross names had they our plainer sires among,)
There Arums, there Leontodons we view,
And Artemisia grows, where Wormwood grew.
But though no weed exists his garden round,
From Rumex strong our Gardener frees his ground;
Takes soft Senicio from the yielding land,
And grasps the arm'd Urtica in his hand.
Not Darwin's self had more delight to sing
Of floral courtship, in th' awaken'd Spring,

Than Peter Pratt, who, simpering, loves to tell
How rise the Stamens, as the Pistils swell;
How bend and curl the moist-top to the spouse,
And give and take the vegetable vows;
How those esteem'd of old but tips and chives,
Are tender husbands and obedient wives;
Who live and love within the sacred bower—
That bridal bed the vulgar term a flower.
Hear Peter proudly, to some humble friend,
A wondrous secret in his science lend:—
"Would you advance the nuptial hour, and bring
The fruit of Autumn with the flowers of Spring:
View that light frame where Cucumis lies spread,
And trace the husbands in their golden bed,
Three powder'd Anthers;—then no more delay,
But to the Stigma's tip their dust convey;
Then by thyself, from prying glance secure,
Twirl the full tip and make your purpose sure;
A long-abiding race the deed shall pay,
Nor one unbless'd abortion pine away."
T' admire their friend's discourse our swains agree,
And call it science and philosophy.
'Tis good, 'tis pleasant, through th' advancing year,
To see unnumber'd growing forms appear.
What leafy-life from Earth's broad bosom rise!
What insect-myriads seek the summer skies!
What scaly tribes in every streamlet move!
What plumy people sing in every grove!
All with the year awaked to life, delight, and love.
Then names are good; for how, without their aid,
Is knowledge, gain'd by man, to man convey'd?
But from that source shall all our pleasures flow?
Shall all our knowledge be those names to know?
Then he, with memory bless'd, shall bear away
The palm from Grew, and Middleton, and Ray.
No! let us rather seek, in grove and field,
What food for wonder, what for use they yield;
Some just remark from Nature's people bring,
And some new source of homage for her King.

Pride lives with all; strange names our rustics give
To helpless infants, that their own may live;
Pleased to be known, they'll some attention claim,
And find some by-way to the house of fame.
The straightest furrow lifts the ploughman's art;
The hat he gain'd has warmth for head and heart;
The bowl that beats the greater number down
Of tottering nine-pins, gives to fame the clown;

Or, foil'd in these, he opes his ample jaws,
And lets a frog leap down, to gain applause;
Or grins for hours, or tipples for a week;
Or challenges a well-pinch'd pig to squeak.
Some idle deed, some child's preposterous name,
Shall make him known, and give his folly fame.
To name an infant meet our village-sires,
Assembled all, as such event requires;
Frequent and full, the rural sages sate,
And speakers many urged the long debate.
Some harden'd knaves, who roved the country round,
Had left a babe within the parish-bound.—
First, of the fact they question'd—"Was it true?"
The child was brought—"What then remain'd to do?
Was't dead or living?" This was fairly proved:
'Twas pinch'd, it roar'd, and every doubt removed.
Then by what name th' unwelcome guest to call
Was long a question, and it posed them all;
For he who lent it to a babe unknown,
Censorious men might take it for his own:
They look'd about, they gravely spoke to all,
And not one Richard answer'd to the call.
Next they inquired the day, when, passing by,
Th' unlucky peasant heard the stranger's cry:
This known, how food and raiment they might give,
Was next debated—for the rogue would live;
At last, with all their words and work content,
Back to their homes the prudent vestry went,
And Richard Monday to the workhouse sent.
There was he pinch'd and pitied, thump'd and fed,
And duly took his beatings and his bread;
Patient in all control, in all abuse,
He found contempt and kicking have their use—
Sad, silent, supple, bending to the blow,
A slave of slaves, the lowest of the low;
His pliant soul gave way to all things base;
He knew no shame, he dreaded no disgrace.
It seem'd, so well his passions he suppressed,
No feeling stirr'd his ever-torpid breast;
Him might the meanest pauper bruise and cheat,
He was a footstool for the beggar's feet;
His were the legs that ran at all commands;
They used on all occasions Richard's hands.
His very soul was not his own; he stole
As others order'd, and without a dole;
In all disputes, on either part he lied,
And freely pledged his oath on either side;
In all rebellions Richard join'd the rest,

In all detections Richard first confess'd.
Yet, though disgraced, he watch'd his time so well,
He rose in favour, when in fame he fell;
Base was his usage, vile his whole employ,
And all despised and fed the pliant boy.
At length, "'tis time he should abroad be sent,"
Was whisper'd near him—and abroad he went.
One morn they call'd him, Richard answered not;
They deem'd him hanging, and in time forgot;
Yet miss'd him long, as each, throughout the clan,
Found he "had better spared a better man."
Now Richard's talents for the world were fit,
He'd no small cunning, and had some small wit;
Had that calm look which seem'd to all assent,
And that complacent speech which nothing meant;
He'd but one care, and that he strove to hide,
How best for Richard Monday to provide.
Steel, through opposing plates, the magnet draws,
And steely atoms culls from dust and straws;
And thus our hero, to his interest true,
Gold through all bars and from each trifle drew;
But, still more surely round the world to go,
This fortune's child had neither friend nor foe.
Long lost to us, at last our man we trace—
Sir Richard Monday died at Monday-place.
His lady's worth, his daughter's, we peruse,
And find his grandsons all as rich as Jews;
He gave reforming charities a sum,
And bought the blessings of the blind and dumb;
Bequeathed to missions money from the stocks,
And Bibles issued from his private box;
But, to his native place severely just,
He left a pittance bound in rigid trust—
Two paltry pounds, on every quarter's-day,
(At church produced) for forty loaves should pay:
A stinted gift, that to the parish shows
He kept in mind their bounty and their blows!
To farmers three, the year has given a son:
Finch on the Moor, and French, and Middleton.
Twice in this year a female Giles I see:
A Spalding once, and once a Barnaby—
A humble man is he, and, when they meet,
Our farmers find him on a distant seat;
There for their wit he serves a constant theme—
They praise his dairy, they extol his team,
They ask the price of each unrivall'd steed.
And whence his sheep, that admirable breed?
His thriving arts they beg he would explain,

And where he puts the money he must gain.
They have their daughters, but they fear their friend
Would think his sons too much would condescend;
They have their sons who would their fortunes try,
But fear his daughters will their suit deny.
So runs the joke, while James, with sigh profound,
And face of care, looks moveless on the ground;
His cares, his sighs, provoke the insult more,
And point the jest—for Barnaby is poor.

Last in my list, five untaught lads appear;
Their father dead, compassion sent them here—
For still that rustic infidel denied
To have their names with solemn rite applied.
His, a lone house, by Deadman's Dyke-way stood;
And his, a nightly haunt, in Lonely-wood.
Each village inn has heard the ruffian boast,
That he believed in neither God nor ghost;
That, when the sod upon the sinner press'd,
He, like the saint, had everlasting rest;
That never priest believed his doctrines true,
But would, for profit, own himself a Jew,
Or worship wood and stone, as honest heathen do;
That fools alone on future worlds rely,
And all who die for faith, deserve to die.
These maxims, part th' attorney's clerk profess'd;
His own transcendent genius found the rest.
Our pious matrons heard, and, much amazed,
Gazed on the man, and trembled as they gazed;
And now his face explored, and now his feet,
Man's dreaded foe, in this bad man, to meet.
But him our drunkards as their champion raised,
Their bishop call'd, and as their hero praised;
Though most, when sober, and the rest, when sick,
Had little question whence his bishopric.
But he, triumphant spirit! all things dared,
He poach'd the wood, and on the warren snared;
'Twas his, at cards, each novice to trepan,
And call the wants of rogues the rights of man;
Wild as the winds, he let his offspring rove,
And deem'd the marriage-bond the bane of love.
What age and sickness, for a man so bold,
Had done, we know not—none beheld him old.
By night, as business urged, he sought the wood—
The ditch was deep—the rain had caused a flood—
The foot-bridge fail'd—he plunged beneath the deep,
And slept, if truth were his, th' eternal sleep.

These have we named; on life's rough sea they sail,
With many a prosperous, many an adverse gale!
Where passion soon, like powerful winds, will rage,
And prudence, wearied, with their strength engage.
Then each, in aid, shall some companion ask,
For help or comfort in the tedious task;
And what that help—what joys from union flow,
What good or ill, we next prepare to show;
And row, meantime, our weary bark ashore,
As Spenser his—but not with Spenser's oar.

PART II

MARRIAGES

Previous Consideration necessary: yet not too long Delay—Imprudent Marriage of old Kirk and his
Servant—Comparison between an ancient and youthful Partner to a young Man—Prudence of Donald
the Gardener—Parish Wedding: the compelled Bridegroom; Day of Marriage, how spent—Relation of
the Accomplishments of Phoebe Dawson, a rustic Beauty; her Lover: his Courtship; their Marriage—
Misery of Precipitation—The wealthy Couple: Reluctance in the Husband; why?—Unusually fair
Signatures in the Register: the common Kind—Seduction of Lucy Collins by Footman Daniel: her rustic
Lover; her Return to him—An ancient Couple: Comparisons on the Occasion—More pleasant View of
Village Matrimony: Farmers celebrating the Day of Marriage; their Wives—Reuben and Rachel, a happy
Pair: an Example of prudent Delay—Reflections on their State who were not so prudent, and its
Improvement towards the Termination of Life; an old Man so circumstanced—Attempt to seduce a
Village Beauty: Persuasion and Reply; the Event.

*Nubere si quà voles, quamvis properabitis ambo,
Differ; habent parvæ commoda magna moræ.*

Ovid. Fast. lib. iii. [vv. 393-4.]

"Disposed to wed, e'en while you hasten, stay;
There's great advantage in a small delay:"—
Thus Ovid sang, and much the wise approve
This prudent maxim of the priest of Love.
If poor, delay for future want prepares,
And eases humble life of half its cares;
If rich, delay shall brace the thoughtful mind,
T' endure the ills that e'en the happiest find:
Delay shall knowledge yield on either part,
And show the value of the vanquished heart;
The humours, passions, merits, failings prove,
And gently raise the veil that's worn by Love;
Love, that impatient guide—too proud to think

Of vulgar wants, of clothing, meat and drink—
Urges our amorous swains their joys to seize,
And then, at rags and hunger frighten'd, flees.—
Yet not too long in cold debate remain:
Till age, refrain not—but if old, refrain.

By no such rule would Gaffer Kirk be tried;
First in the year he led a blooming bride,
And stood a withered elder at her side.
Oh! Nathan! Nathan! at thy years, trepann'd
To take a wanton harlot by the hand!
Thou, who wert used so tartly to express
Thy sense of matrimonial happiness,
Till every youth, whose bans at church were read,
Strove not to meet, or meeting, hung his head;
And every lass forbore at thee to look,
A sly old fish, too cunning for the hook;—
And now at sixty, that pert dame to see
Of all thy savings mistress, and of thee;
Now will the lads, rememb'ring insults past,
Cry, "What, the wise-one in the trap at last!"
Fie! Nathan! fie! to let an artful jade
The close recesses of thine heart invade;
What grievous pangs, what suffering, she'll impart,
And fill with anguish that rebellious heart;
For thou wilt strive incessantly, in vain,
By threatening speech, thy freedom to regain:
But she for conquest married, nor will prove
A dupe to thee, thine anger, or thy love.
Clamorous her tongue will be;—of either sex,
She'll gather friends around thee, and perplex
Thy doubtful soul; thy money she will waste
In the vain ramblings of a vulgar taste;
And will be happy to exert her power,
In every eye, in thine, at every hour.
Then wilt thou bluster—"No! I will not rest,
And see consumed each shilling of my chest":
Thou wilt be valiant—"When thy cousins call,
I will abuse and shut my door on all";
Thou wilt be cruel—"What the law allows,
That be thy portion, my ungrateful spouse!
Nor other shillings shalt thou then receive,
And when I die—What! may I this believe?
Are these true tender tears? and does my Kitty grieve?
Ah! crafty vixen, thine old man has fears;
But weep no more! I'm melted by thy tears;
Spare but my money; thou shalt rule ME still,
And see thy cousins—there! I burn the will."—

Thus, with example sad, our year began,
A wanton vixen and a weary man;
But had this tale in other guise been told,
Young let the lover be, the lady old,
And that disparity of years shall prove
No bane of peace, although some bar to love:
'Tis not the worst, our nuptial ties among,
That joins the ancient bride and bridegroom young;—
Young wives, like changing winds, their power display,
By shifting points and varying day by day;
Now zephyrs mild, now whirlwinds in their force,
They sometimes speed, but often thwart our course;
And much experienced should that pilot be,
Who sails with them on life's tempestuous sea.
But like a trade-wind is the ancient dame,
Mild to your wish, and every day the same;
Steady as time, no sudden squalls you fear,
But set full sail and with assurance steer;
Till every danger in your way be pass'd,
And then she gently, mildly breathes her last;
Rich you arrive, in port awhile remain,
And for a second venture sail again.

For this, blithe Donald southward made his way,
And left the lasses on the banks of Tay;
Him to a neighbouring garden fortune sent,
Whom we beheld, aspiringly content:
Patient and mild, he sought the dame to please,
Who ruled the kitchen and who bore the keys.
Fair Lucy first, the laundry's grace and pride,
With smiles and gracious looks, her fortune tried;
But all in vain she praised his "pawky eyne,"
Where never fondness was for Lucy seen:
Him the mild Susan, boast of dairies, loved,
And found him civil, cautious, and unmoved:
From many a fragrant simple, Catharine's skill
Drew oil and essence from the boiling still;
But not her warmth, nor all her winning ways,
From his cool phlegm could Donald's spirit raise:
Of beauty heedless, with the merry mute,
To Mistress Dobson he preferr'd his suit;
There proved his service, there address'd his vows,
And saw her mistress—friend—protectress—spouse;
A butler now, he thanks his powerful bride,
And, like her keys, keeps constant at her side.

Next at our altar stood a luckless pair,
Brought by strong passions and a warrant there;

By long rent cloak, hung loosely, strove the bride,
From ev'ry eye what all perceived to hide;
While the boy-bridegroom, shuffling in his pace,
Now hid awhile and then exposed his face;
As shame alternately with anger strove
The brain confused with muddy ale to move.
In haste and stammering he perform'd his part,
And look'd the rage that rankled in his heart;
(So will each lover inly curse his fate,
Too soon made happy and made wise too late;)
I saw his features take a savage gloom,
And deeply threaten for the days to come.
Low spake the lass, and lisp'd and minced the while,
Look'd on the lad, and faintly tried to smile;
With soften'd speech and humbled tone she strove
To stir the embers of departed love:
While he, a tyrant, frowning walk'd before,
Felt the poor purse and sought the public door,
She, sadly following, in submission went,
And saw the final shilling foully spent;
Then to her father's hut the pair withdrew,
And bade to love and comfort long adieu!
Ah! fly temptation, youth, refrain! refrain!
I preach for ever; but I preach in vain!

Two summers since, I saw, at Lammas Fair,
The sweetest flower that ever blossom'd there,
When Phoebe Dawson gaily cross'd the Green,
In haste to see and happy to be seen:
Her air, her manners, all who saw admired,
Courteous though coy, and gentle though retired;
The joy of youth and health her eyes display'd,
And ease of heart her every look convey'd;
A native skill her simple robes express'd,
As with untutor'd elegance she dress'd;
The lads around admired so fair a sight,
And Phoebe felt, and felt she gave, delight.
Admirers soon of every age she gain'd,
Her beauty won them and her worth retain'd;
Envy itself could no contempt display,
They wish'd her well, whom yet they wish'd away.
Correct in thought, she judged a servant's place
Preserved a rustic beauty from disgrace;
But yet on Sunday-eve, in freedom's hour,
With secret joy she felt that beauty's power,
When some proud bliss upon the heart would steal,
That, poor or rich, a beauty still must feel.—
At length, the youth, ordain'd to move her breast,

Before the swains with bolder spirit press'd;
With looks less timid made his passion known,
And pleased by manners most unlike her own;
Loud though in love, and confident though young;
Fierce in his air, and voluble of tongue;
By trade a tailor, though, in scorn of trade,
He served the 'Squire, and brush'd the coat he made:
Yet now, would Phoebe her consent afford,
Her slave alone, again he'd mount the board;
With her should years of growing love be spent,
And growing wealth—she sigh'd and look'd consent.
Now, through the lane, up hill, and 'cross the green,
(Seen by but few, and blushing to be seen—
Dejected, thoughtful, anxious, and afraid,)
Led by the lover, walk'd the silent maid.
Slow through the meadows roved they many a mile,
Toy'd by each bank and trifled at each stile;
Where, as he painted every blissful view,
And highly colour'd what he strongly drew,
The pensive damsel, prone to tender fears,
Dimm'd the false prospect with prophetic tears.—
Thus pass'd th' allotted hours, till, lingering late,
The lover loiter'd at the master's gate;
There he pronounced adieu! and yet would stay,
Till chidden—soothed—entreated—forced away,
He would of coldness, though indulged, complain,
And oft retire and oft return again;
When, if his teasing vex'd her gentle mind,
The grief assumed, compell'd her to be kind!
For he would proof of plighted kindness crave,
That she resented first and then forgave,
And to his grief and penance yielded more
Than his presumption had required before.—
Ah! fly temptation, youth; refrain! refrain,
Each yielding maid and each presuming swain!

Lo! now with red rent cloak and bonnet black,
And torn green gown loose hanging at her back,
One who an infant in her arms sustains,
And seems in patience striving with her pains;
Pinch'd are her looks, as one who pines for bread,
Whose cares are growing and whose hopes are fled;
Pale her parch'd lips, her heavy eyes sunk low,
And tears unnoticed from their channels flow;
Serene her manner, till some sudden pain
Frets the meek soul, and then she's calm again.—
Her broken pitcher to the pool she takes,
And every step with cautious terror makes;

For not alone that infant in her arms,
But nearer cause, her anxious soul alarms.
With water burthen'd, then she picks her way,
Slowly and cautious, in the clinging clay;
Till, in mid-green, she trusts a place unsound,
And deeply plunges in th' adhesive ground;
Thence, but with pain, her slender foot she takes,
While hope the mind, as strength the frame, forsakes:
For, when so full the cup of sorrow grows,
Add but a drop, it instantly o'erflows.
And now her path, but not her peace, she gains,
Safe from her task, but shivering with her pains;
Her home she reaches, open leaves the door,
And, placing first her infant on the floor,
She bares her bosom to the wind, and sits,
And sobbing struggles with the rising fits.
In vain, they come; she feels th'inflating grief,
That shuts the swelling bosom from relief;
That speaks in feeble cries a soul distressed,
Or the sad laugh that cannot be repress'd.
The neighbour-matron leaves her wheel and flies
With all the aid her poverty supplies;
Unfee'd, the calls of Nature she obeys,
Not led by profit, nor allured by praise;
And, waiting long, till these contentions cease,
She speaks of comfort, and departs in peace.
Friend of distress! the mourner feels thy aid,
She cannot pay thee, but thou wilt be paid.

But who this child of weakness, want, and care?
'Tis Phoebe Dawson, pride of Lammas Fair;
Who took her lover for his sparkling eyes,
Expressions warm, and love-inspiring lies.
Compassion first assail'd her gentle heart,
For all his suffering, all his bosom's smart:
And then his prayers! they would a savage move,
And win the coldest of the sex to love.
But ah! too soon his looks success declared,
Too late her loss the marriage-rite repaired;
The faithless flatterer then his vows forgot,
A captious tyrant or a noisy sot:
If present, railing, till he saw her pain'd;
If absent, spending what their labours gain'd;
Till that fair form in want and sickness pined,
And hope and comfort fled that gentle mind.
Then fly temptation, youth; resist, refrain!
Nor let me preach for ever and in vain!

Next came a well-dress'd pair, who left their coach,
And made, in long procession, slow approach;
For this gay bride had many a female friend,
And youths were there, this favoured youth t' attend.
Silent, nor wanting due respect, the crowd
Stood humbly round, and gratulation bow'd;
But not that silent crowd, in wonder fix'd,
Not numerous friends, who praise and envy mix'd,
Nor nymphs attending near to swell the pride
Of one more fair, the ever-smiling bride;
Nor that gay bride, adorn'd with every grace,
Nor love nor joy triumphant in her face,
Could from the youth's sad signs of sorrow chase.
Why didst thou grieve? wealth, pleasure, freedom thine;
Vex'd it thy soul, that freedom to resign?
Spake Scandal truth? "Thou didst not then intend
So soon to bring thy wooing to an end"?
Or, was it, as our prating rustics say,
To end as soon, but in a different way?
'Tis told, thy Phillis is a skilful dame,
Who play'd uninjured with the dangerous flame:
That, while, like Lovelace, thou thy coat display'd,
And hid the snare for her affection laid,
Thee, with her net, she found the means to catch,
And, at the amorous see-saw, won the match.
Yet others tell, the Captain fix'd thy doubt,
He'd call thee brother, or he'd call thee out.—
But rest the motive—all retreat too late,
Joy like thy bride's should on thy brow have sate;
The deed had then appear'd thine own intent,
A glorious day, by gracious fortune sent,
In each revolving year to be in triumph spent.
Then in few weeks that cloudy brow had been
Without a wonder or a whisper seen;
And none had been so weak as to inquire,
"Why pouts my Lady?" or "why frowns the Squire?"

How fair these names, how much unlike they look
To all the blurr'd subscriptions in my book:
The bridegroom's letters stand in row above.
Tapering yet stout, like pine-trees in his grove;
While free and fine the bride's appear below,
As light and slender as her jasmines grow.
Mark now in what confusion, stoop or stand,
The crooked scrawls of many a clownish hand;
Now out, now in, they droop, they fall, they rise,
Like raw recruits drawn forth for exercise;
Ere yet reform'd and modell'd by the drill,

The free-born legs stand striding as they will.
Much have I tried to guide the fist along,
But still the blunderers placed their blottings wrong:
Behold these marks uncouth! how strange that men,
Who guide the plough, should fail to guide the pen.
For half a mile the furrows even lie;
For half an inch the letters stand awry;—
Our peasants, strong and sturdy in the field,
Cannot these arms of idle students wield;
Like them, in feudal days, their valiant lords
Resign'd the pen and grasp'd their conqu'ring swords;
They to robed clerks and poor dependent men
Left the light duties of the peaceful pen;
Nor to their ladies wrote, but sought to prove,
By deeds of death, their hearts were fill'd with love.
But yet, small arts have charms for female eyes;
Our rustic nymphs the beau and scholar prize;
Unletter'd swains and ploughmen coarse they slight,
For those who dress, and amorous scrolls indite.

For Lucy Collins happier days had been,
Had Footman Daniel scorn'd his native green;
Or when he came an idle coxcomb down,
Had he his love reserved for lass in town;
To Stephen Hill she then had pledged her truth,—
A sturdy, sober, kind, unpolish'd youth;
But from the day, that fatal day she spied
The pride of Daniel, Daniel was her pride.
In all concerns was Stephen just and true;
But coarse his doublet was and patch'd in view,
And felt his stockings were, and blacker than his shoe;
While Daniel's linen all was fine and fair—
His master wore it, and he deign'd to wear;
(To wear his livery, some respect might prove;
To wear his linen, must be sign of love:)
Blue was his coat, unsoil'd by spot or stain;
His hose were silk, his shoes of Spanish-grain;
A silver knot his breadth of shoulder bore;
A diamond buckle blazed his breast before—
Diamond he swore it was! and show'd it as he swore;
Rings on his fingers shone; his milk-white hand
Could pick-tooth case and box for snuff command:
And thus, with clouded cane, a fop complete,
He stalk'd, the jest and glory of the street.
Join'd with these powers, he could so sweetly sing,
Talk with such toss, and saunter with such swing;
Laugh with such glee, and trifle with such art,
That Lucy's promise fail'd to shield her heart.

Stephen, meantime, to ease his amorous cares,
Fix'd his full mind upon his farm's affairs;
Two pigs, a cow, and wethers half a score,
Increased his stock, and still he look'd for more.
He, for his acres few, so duly paid,
That yet more acres to his lot were laid;
Till our chaste nymphs no longer felt disdain,
And prudent matrons praised the frugal swain;
Who, thriving well, through many a fruitful year,
Now clothed himself anew, and acted overseer.
Just then poor Lucy, from her friend in town,
Fled in pure fear, and came a beggar down;
Trembling, at Stephen's door she knock'd for bread—
Was chidden first, next pitied, and then fed;
Then sat at Stephen's board, then shared in Stephen's bed
All hope of marriage lost in her disgrace,
He mourns a flame revived, and she a love of lace.

Now to be wed a well-match'd couple came;
Twice had old Lodge been tied, and twice the dame;
Tottering they came and toying, (odious scene!)
And fond and simple, as they'd always been.
Children from wedlock we by laws restrain;
Why not prevent them, when they're such again?
Why not forbid the doting souls, to prove
Th' indecent fondling of preposterous love?
In spite of prudence, uncontroll'd by shame,
The amorous senior woos the toothless dame,
Relating idly, at the closing eve,
The youthful follies he disdains to leave;
Till youthful follies wake a transient fire,
When arm in arm they totter and retire.
So a fond pair of solemn birds, all day,
Blink in their seat and doze the hours away;
Then, by the moon awaken'd, forth they move,
And fright the songsters with their cheerless love.
So two sear trees, dry, stunted, and unsound,
Each other catch, when dropping to the ground;
Entwine their wither'd arms 'gainst wind and weather,
And shake their leafless heads, and drop together.
So two cold limbs, touch'd by Galvani's wire,
Move with new life, and feel awaken'd fire;
Quivering awhile, their flaccid forms remain,
Then turn to cold torpidity again.

"But ever frowns your Hymen? man and maid,
Are all repenting, suffering, or betray'd?"
Forbid it, Love! we have our couples here

Who hail the day in each revolving year:
These are with us, as in the world around;
They are not frequent, but they may be found.
Our farmers, too; what, though they fail to prove,
In Hymen's bonds, the tenderest slaves of love,
(Nor, like those pairs whom sentiment unites,
Feel they the fervour of the mind's delights:)
Yet, coarsely kind and comfortably gay,
They heap the board and hail the happy day:
And, though the bride, now freed from school, admits
Of pride implanted there some transient fits;
Yet soon she casts her girlish flights aside,
And in substantial blessings rests her pride.
No more she moves in measured steps, no more
Runs, with bewilder'd ear, her music o'er;
No more recites her French the hinds among,
But chides her maidens in her mother-tongue;
Her tambour-frame she leaves and diet spare,
Plain work and plenty with her house to share;
Till, all her varnish lost, in few short years,
In all her worth, the farmer's wife appears.
Yet not the ancient kind; nor she who gave
Her soul to gain—a mistress and a slave:
Who not to sleep allow'd the needful time;
To whom repose was loss, and sport a crime;
Who, in her meanest room (and all were mean),
A noisy drudge, from morn till night was seen;—
But she, the daughter, boasts a decent room,
Adorn'd with carpet, form'd in Wilton's loom;
Fair prints along the paper'd wall are spread
There, Werter sees the sportive children fed,
And Charlotte, here, bewails her lover dead.
'Tis here, assembled, while in space apart
Their husbands, drinking, warm the opening heart,
Our neighbouring dames, on festal days, unite
With tongues more fluent and with hearts as light;
Theirs is that art, which English wives alone
Profess—a boast and privilege their own;
An art it is, where each at once attends
To all, and claims attention from her friends,
When they engage the tongue, the eye, the ear,
Reply when list'ning, and when speaking hear:
The ready converse knows no dull delays,
"But double are the pains, and double be the praise."

Yet not to those alone who bear command
Heaven gives a heart to hail the marriage band;
Among their servants, we the pairs can show,

Who much to love and more to prudence owe.
Reuben and Rachel, though as fond as doves,
Were yet discreet and cautious in their loves;
Nor would attend to Cupid's wild commands,
Till cool reflection bade them join their hands.
When both were poor, they thought it argued ill
Of hasty love to make them poorer still;
Year after year, with savings long laid by,
They bought the future dwelling's full supply;
Her frugal fancy cull'd the smaller ware,
The weightier purchase ask'd her Reuben's care;
Together then their last year's gain they threw,
And lo! an auction'd bed, with curtains neat and new.
Thus both, as prudence counsell'd, wisely stay'd,
And cheerful then the calls of Love obey'd:
What if, when Rachel gave her hand, 'twas one
Embrown'd by Winter's ice and Summer's sun?
What if, in Reuben's hair, the female eye
Usurping grey among the black could spy?
What if, in both, life's bloomy flush was lost,
And their full autumn felt the mellowing frost?
Yet time, who blow'd the rose of youth away,
Had left the vigorous stem without decay;
Like those tall elms, in Farmer Frankford's ground,
They'll grow no more—but all their growth is sound;
By time confirm'd and rooted in the land,
The storms they've stood, still promise they shall stand.

These are the happier pairs: their life has rest,
Their hopes are strong, their humble portion bless'd;
While those, more rash, to hasty marriage led,
Lament th' impatience which now stints their bread.
When such their union, years their cares increase;
Their love grows colder, and their pleasures cease;
In health just fed, in sickness just relieved;
By hardships harass'd and by children grieved;
In petty quarrels and in peevish strife
The once fond couple waste the spring of life;
But, when to age mature those children grown,
Find hopes and homes and hardships of their own,
The harass'd couple feel their lingering woes
Receding slowly, till they find repose.
Complaints and murmurs then are laid aside,
(By reason these subdued, and those by pride;)
And, taught by care, the patient man and wife
Agree to share the bitter-sweet of life;
(Life that has sorrow much and sorrow's cure,
Where they who most enjoy shall much endure;)

Their rest, their labours, duties, sufferings, prayers,
Compose the soul, and fit it for its cares;
Their graves before them, and their griefs behind,
Have each a med'cine for the rustic mind;
Nor has he care to whom his wealth shall go,
Or who shall labour with his spade and hoe;
But, as he lends the strength that yet remains,
And some dead neighbour on his bier sustains,
(One with whom oft he whirl'd the bounding flail,
Toss'd the broad coit, or took th' inspiring ale,)
"For me," (he meditates,) "shall soon be done
This friendly duty, when my race be run;
'Twas first in trouble as in error pass'd,
Dark clouds and stormy cares whole years o'ercast,
But calm my setting day, and sunshine smiles at last:
My vices punish'd and my follies spent,
Not loth to die, but yet to live content,
I rest";—then, casting on the grave his eye,
His friend compels a tear, and his own griefs a sigh.

Last on my list appears a match of love,
And one of virtue—happy may it prove!—
Sir Edward Archer is an amorous knight,
And maidens chaste and lovely shun his sight;
His bailiff's daughter suited much his taste,
For Fanny Price was lovely and was chaste;
To her the Knight with gentle looks drew near,
And timid voice assumed, to banish fear.—
"Hope of my life, dear sovereign of my breast,
Which, since I knew thee, knows not joy nor rest;
Know, thou art all that my delighted eyes,
My fondest thoughts, my proudest wishes prize;
And is that bosom—(what on earth so fair!)
To cradle some coarse peasant's sprawling heir?
To be that pillow which some surly swain
May treat with scorn and agonize with pain?
Art thou, sweet maid, a ploughman's wants to share,
To dread his insult, to support his care;
To hear his follies, his contempt to prove,
And (oh! the torment!) to endure his love;
Till want and deep regret those charms destroy,
That time would spare, if time were pass'd in joy?
With him, in varied pains, from morn till night,
Your hours shall pass, yourself a ruffian's right;
Your softest bed shall be the knotted wool;
Your purest drink the waters of the pool;
Your sweetest food will but your life sustain,
And your best pleasure be a rest from pain;

While, through each year, as health and strength abate,
You'll weep your woes and wonder at your fate;
And cry, 'Behold, as life's last cares come on,
My burthens growing when my strength is gone!'
"Now turn with me, and all the young desire,
That taste can form, that fancy can require;
All that excites enjoyment, or procures
Wealth, health, respect, delight, and love, are yours:
Sparkling, in cups of gold, your wines shall flow,
Grace that fair hand, in that dear bosom glow;
Fruits of each clime, and flowers, through all the year,
Shall on your walls and in your walks appear;
Where all, beholding, shall your praise repeat,
No fruit so tempting and no flower so sweet.
The softest carpets in your rooms shall lie,
Pictures of happiest loves shall meet your eye,
And tallest mirrors, reaching to the floor,
Shall show you all the object I adore;
Who, by the hands of wealth and fashion dress'd,
By slaves attended and by friends caress'd,
Shall move, a wonder, through the public ways,
And hear the whispers of adoring praise.
Your female friends, though gayest of the gay,
Shall see you happy, and shall, sighing, say,
While smother'd envy rises in the breast—
'Oh! that we lived so beauteous and so bless'd!'
"Come then, my mistress, and my wife; for she
Who trusts my honour is the wife for me;
Your slave, your husband, and your friend employ,
In search of pleasures we may both enjoy."
To this the damsel, meekly firm, replied:
"My mother loved, was married, toil'd, and died;
With joys, she'd griefs, had troubles in her course,
But not one grief was pointed by remorse;
My mind is fix'd, to Heaven I resign,
And be her love, her life, her comforts mine."
Tyrants have wept; and those with hearts of steel,
Unused the anguish of the heart to heal,
Have yet the transient power of virtue known,
And felt th' imparted joy promote their own.
Our Knight, relenting, now befriends a youth,
Who to the yielding maid had vow'd his truth;
And finds in that fair deed a sacred joy,
That will not perish, and that cannot cloy—
A living joy, that shall its spirit keep,
When every beauty fades, and all the passions sleep.

PART III

BURIALS

True Christian Resignation not frequently to be seen—The Register a melancholy Record—A dying Man, who at length sends for a Priest: for what Purpose? answered—Old Collett of the Inn, an Instance of Dr. Young's slow-sudden Death: his Character and Conduct—The Manners and Management of the Widow Goe: her successful Attention to Business; her Decease unexpected—The Infant-Boy of Gerard Ablett dies: Reflections on his Death, and the Survivor his Sister-Twin—The Funeral of the deceased Lady of the Manor described: her neglected Mansion; Undertaker and Train; the Character which her Monument will hereafter display—Burial of an ancient Maiden: some former Drawback on her Virgin-fame; Description of her House and Household; Her Manners, Apprehensions, Death—Isaac Ashford, a virtuous Peasant, dies: his manly Character; Reluctance to enter the Poor-House; and why—Misfortune and Derangement of Intellect in Robin Dingley: whence they proceeded: he is not restrained by Misery from a wandering Life; his various Returns to his Parish; his final Return—Wife of Farmer Frankford dies in Prime of Life; Affliction in Consequence of such Death; melancholy View of her House, &c. on her Family's Return from her Funeral: Address to Sorrow—Leah Cousins, a Midwife: her Character; and successful Practice; at length opposed by Doctor Glibb; Opposition in the Parish: Argument of the Doctor; of Leah: her Failure and Decease—Burial of Roger Cuff, a Sailor: his Enmity to his Family; how it originated: his Experiment and its Consequence—The Register terminates—A Bell heard: Inquiry, for whom? The Sexton—Character of old Dibble, and the five Rectors whom he served—Reflections—Conclusion.

Qui vultus Acherontis atri,
Qui Stygia tristem, non tristis, videt,—
. . . .
Par ille Regi, par Superis erit.

Seneca in Agamem. [Act III. vv. 606-8.]

There was, 'tis said, and I believe, a time,
When humble Christians died with views sublime;
When all were ready for their faith to bleed,
But few to write or wrangle for their creed;
When lively Faith upheld the sinking heart,
And friends, assured to meet, prepared to part;
When Love felt hope, when Sorrow grew serene,
And all was comfort in the death-bed scene.
Alas! when now the gloomy king they wait,
'Tis weakness yielding to resistless fate;
Like wretched men upon the ocean cast,
They labour hard and struggle to the last,
"Hope against hope," and wildly gaze around,
In search of help that never shall be found:
Nor, till the last strong billow stops the breath,
Will they believe them in the jaws of Death!

When these my records I reflecting read,
And find what ills these numerous births succeed;
What powerful griefs these nuptial ties attend,
With what regret these painful journeys end;
When from the cradle to the grave I look,
Mine I conceive a melancholy book.
Where now is perfect resignation seen?
Alas! it is not on the village-green:—
I've seldom known, though I have often read,
Of happy peasants on their dying-bed;
Whose looks proclaim'd that sunshine of the breast,
That more than hope, that Heaven itself express'd.
What I behold are feverish fits of strife,
'Twixt fears of dying and desire of life:
Those earthly hopes, that to the last endure;
Those fears, that hopes superior fail to cure;
At best a sad submission to the doom,
Which, turning from the danger, lets it come.

Sick lies the man, bewilder'd, lost, afraid,
His spirits vanquish'd and his strength decay'd;
No hope the friend, the nurse, the doctor lend—
"Call then a priest, and fit him for his end."
A priest is call'd; 'tis now, alas! too late,
Death enters with him at the cottage-gate;
Or, time allow'd, he goes, assured to find
The self-commending, all-confiding mind;
And sighs to hear, what we may justly call
Death's common-place, the train of thought in all.
"True, I'm a sinner," feebly he begins,
"But trust in Mercy to forgive my sins";
(Such cool confession no past crimes excite;
Such claim on Mercy seems the sinner's right!)
"I know, mankind are frail, that God is just,
And pardons those who in his mercy trust;
We're sorely tempted in a world like this;
All men have done, and I like all, amiss;
But now, if spared, it is my full intent
On all the past to ponder and repent:
Wrongs against me I pardon great and small,
And if I die, I die in peace with all."
His merits thus and not his sins confess'd,
He speaks his hopes, and leaves to Heaven the rest.
Alas! are these the prospects, dull and cold,
That dying Christians to their priests unfold?
Or mends the prospect when th' enthusiast cries,
"I die assured!" and in a rapture dies?

Ah, where that humble, self-abasing mind,
With that confiding spirit, shall we find—
The mind that, feeling what repentance brings,
Dejection's terrors and Contrition's stings,
Feels then the hope, that mounts all care above,
And the pure joy that flows from pardoning love?
Such have I seen in death, and much deplore,
So many dying, that I see no more.
Lo! now my records, where I grieve to trace,
How Death has triumph'd in so short a space;
Who are the dead, how died they, I relate,
And snatch some portion of their acts from fate.

With Andrew Collett we the year begin,
The blind, fat landlord of the Old Crown Inn—
Big as his butt, and, for the self-same use,
To take in stores of strong fermenting juice.
On his huge chair beside the fire he sate,
In revel chief, and umpire in debate;
Each night his string of vulgar tales he told,
When ale was cheap and bachelors were bold:
His heroes all were famous in their days,
Cheats were his boast and drunkards had his praise;
"One, in three draughts, three mugs of ale took down,
As mugs were then—the champion of the Crown;
For thrice three days another lived on ale,
And knew no change but that of mild and stale;
Two thirsty soakers watch'd a vessel's side,
When he the tap, with dexterous hand, applied;
Nor from their seats departed, till they found
That butt was out and heard the mournful sound."
He praised a poacher, precious child of fun!
Who shot the keeper with his own spring-gun;
Nor less the smuggler who the exciseman tied,
And left him hanging at the birch-wood side,
There to expire; but one who saw him hang
Cut the good cord—a traitor of the gang.
His own exploits with boastful glee he told,
What ponds he emptied and what pikes he sold;
And how, when bless'd with sight alert and gay,
The night's amusements kept him through the day.
He sang the praises of those times, when all
"For cards and dice, as for their drink, might call;
When justice wink'd on every jovial crew,
And ten-pins tumbled in the parson's view."
He told, when angry wives, provoked to rail,
Or drive a third-day drunkard from his ale,
What were his triumphs, and how great the skill

That won the vex'd virago to his will:
Who raving came—then talk'd in milder strain—
Then wept, then drank, and pledged her spouse again.
Such were his themes: how knaves o'er laws prevail,
Or, when made captives, how they fly from jail;
The young how brave, how subtle were the old;
And oaths attested all that Folly told.
On death like his what name shall we bestow,
So very sudden! yet so very slow?
'Twas slow:—Disease, augmenting year by year,
Show'd the grim king by gradual steps brought near.
'Twas not less sudden: in the night he died,
He drank, he swore, he jested, and he lied;
Thus aiding folly with departing breath.—
"Beware, Lorenzo, the slow-sudden death."

Next died the Widow Goe, an active dame,
Famed ten miles round, and worthy all her fame;
She lost her husband when their loves were young,
But kept her farm, her credit, and her tongue:
Full thirty years she ruled, with matchless skill,
With guiding judgment and resistless will;
Advice she scorn'd, rebellions she suppress'd,
And sons and servants bow'd at her behest.
Like that great man's, who to his Saviour came,
Were the strong words of this commanding dame:—
"Come," if she said, they came; if "go," were gone;
And if "do this,"—that instant it was done.
Her maidens told she was all eye and ear,
In darkness saw and could at distance hear;—
No parish-business in the place could stir,
Without direction or assent from her;
In turn she took each office as it fell,
Knew all their duties, and discharged them well;
The lazy vagrants in her presence shook,
And pregnant damsels fear'd her stern rebuke;
She look'd on want with judgment clear and cool,
And felt with reason and bestow'd by rule;
She match'd both sons and daughters to her mind,
And lent them eyes—for Love, she heard, was blind;
Yet ceaseless still she throve, alert, alive,
The working bee, in full or empty hive;
Busy and careful, like that working bee,
No time for love nor tender cares had she;
But when our farmers made their amorous vows,
She talk'd of market-steeds and patent-ploughs.
Not unemploy'd her evenings pass'd away,
Amusement closed, as business waked the day;

When to her toilet's brief concern she ran,
And conversation with her friends began,
Who all were welcome, what they saw, to share;
And joyous neighbours praised her Christmas fare,
That none around might, in their scorn, complain
Of Gossip Goe as greedy in her gain.
Thus long she reign'd, admired, if not approved;
Praised, if not honour'd; fear'd, if not beloved;—
When, as the busy days of Spring drew near,
That call'd for all the forecast of the year;
When lively hope the rising crops survey'd,
And April promised what September paid;
When stray'd her lambs where gorse and greenweed grow;
When rose her grass in richer vales below;
When pleased she look'd on all the smiling land,
And view'd the hinds who wrought at her command;
(Poultry in groups still follow'd where she went;)
Then dread o'ercame her—that her days were spent.
"Bless me! I die, and not a warning giv'n,—
With much to do on Earth, and ALL for Heav'n!—
No reparation for my soul's affairs,
No leave petition'd for the barn's repairs;
Accounts perplex'd, my interest yet unpaid,
My mind unsettled, and my will unmade;
A lawyer, haste, and, in your way, a priest;
And let me die in one good work at least."
She spake, and, trembling, dropp'd upon her knees,
Heaven in her eye, and in her hand her keys;
And still the more she found her life decay,
With greater force she grasp'd those signs of sway:
Then fell and died!—In haste her sons drew near,
And dropp'd, in haste, the tributary tear;
Then from th' adhering clasp the keys unbound,
And consolation for their sorrows found.

Death has his infant-train; his bony arm
Strikes from the baby-cheek the rosy charm;
The brightest eye his glazing film makes dim,
And his cold touch sets fast the lithest limb:
He seized the sick'ning boy to Gerard lent,
When three days' life, in feeble cries, were spent;
In pain brought forth, those painful hours to stay,
To breathe in pain and sigh its soul away!
"But why thus lent, if thus recall'd again,
To cause and feel, to live and die, in pain?"
Or rather say, Why grievous these appear,
If all it pays for Heaven's eternal year;
If these sad sobs and piteous sighs secure

Delights that live, when worlds no more endure?
The sister-spirit long may lodge below,
And pains from nature, pains from reason, know;
Through all the common ills of life may run,
By hope perverted and by love undone;
A wife's distress, a mother's pangs, may dread,
And widow-tears, in bitter anguish, shed;
May at old age arrive through numerous harms,
With children's children in those feeble arms:
Nor, till by years of want and grief oppress'd,
Shall the sad spirit flee and be at rest!
Yet happier therefore shall we deem the boy,
Secured from anxious care and dangerous joy?
Not so! for then would Love Divine in vain
Send all the burthens weary men sustain;
All that now curb the passions when they rage,
The checks of youth and the regrets of age;
All that now bid us hope, believe, endure,
Our sorrow's comfort and our vice's cure;
All that for Heaven's high joys the spirits train,
And charity, the crown of all, were vain.
Say, will you call the breathless infant bless'd,
Because no cares the silent grave molest?
So would you deem the nursling from the wing
Untimely thrust and never train'd to sing;
But far more bless'd the bird whose grateful voice
Sings its own joy and makes the woods rejoice,
Though, while untaught, ere yet he charm'd the ear,
Hard were his trials and his pains severe!

Next died the Lady who yon Hall possess'd;
And here they brought her noble bones to rest.
In Town she dwelt;—forsaken stood the Hall:
Worms ate the floors, the tap'stry fled the wall;
No fire the kitchen's cheerless grate display'd;
No cheerful light the long-closed sash convey'd;
The crawling worm, that turns a summer-fly,
Here spun his shroud and laid him up to die
The winter-death:—upon the bed of state,
The bat shrill-shrieking woo'd his flickering mate;
To empty rooms the curious came no more,
From empty cellars turn'd the angry poor,
And surly beggars cursed the ever-bolted door.
To one small room the steward found his way,
Where tenants follow'd to complain and pay;
Yet no complaint before the Lady came,
The feeling servant spared the feeble dame;
Who saw her farms with his observing eyes,

And answer'd all requests with his replies.
She came not down, her falling groves to view;
Why should she know, what one so faithful knew?
Why come, from many clamorous tongues to hear,
What one so just might whisper in her ear?
Her oaks or acres why with care explore;
Why learn the wants, the sufferings of the poor;
When one so knowing all their worth could trace,
And one so piteous govern'd in her place?
Lo! now, what dismal sons of Darkness come,
To bear this daughter of Indulgence home;
Tragedians all, and well arranged in black!
Who nature, feeling, force, expression lack;
Who cause no tear, but gloomily pass by,
And shake their sables in the wearied eye,
That turns disgusted from the pompous scene,
Proud without grandeur, with profusion, mean!
The tear for kindness past affection owes;
For worth deceased the sigh from reason flows;
E'en well-feign'd passions for our sorrows call,
And real tears for mimic miseries fall—
But this poor farce has neither truth nor art,
To please the fancy or to touch the heart;
Unlike the darkness of the sky, that pours
On the dry ground its fertilizing showers;
Unlike to that which strikes the soul with dread,
When thunders roar and forky fires are shed;
Dark but not awful, dismal but yet mean,
With anxious bustle moves the cumbrous scene;
Presents no objects tender or profound,
But spreads its cold unmeaning gloom around.
When woes are feign'd, how ill such forms appear;
And oh! how needless, when the wo's sincere.
Slow to the vault they come, with heavy tread,
Bending beneath the Lady and her lead;
A case of elm surrounds that ponderous chest,
Close on that case the crimson velvet's press'd;
Ungenerous this, that to the worm denies,
With niggard-caution, his appointed prize;
For now, ere yet he works his tedious way,
Through cloth and wood and metal to his prey,
That prey dissolving shall a mass remain,
That fancy loathes and worms themselves disdain.
But see! the master-mourner makes his way,
To end his office for the coffin'd clay;
Pleased that our rustic men and maids behold
His plate like silver, and his studs like gold,
As they approach to spell the age, the name,

And all the titles of th' illustrious dame.—
This as (my duty done) some scholar read,
A village-father look'd disdain and said:
"Away, my friends! why take such pains to know
What some brave marble soon in church shall show?
Where not alone her gracious name shall stand,
But how she lived—the blessing of the land;
How much we all deplored the noble dead,
What groans we utter'd and what tears we shed;
Tears, true as those, which in the sleepy eyes
Of weeping cherubs on the stone shall rise;
Tears, true as those, which, ere she found her grave,
The noble Lady to our sorrows gave."

Down by the church-way walk, and where the brook
Winds round the chancel like a shepherd's crook,
In that small house, with those green pales before,
Where jasmine trails on either side the door;
Where those dark shrubs that now grow wild at will,
Were clipp'd in form and tantalized with skill;
Where cockles blanch'd and pebbles neatly spread,
Form'd shining borders for the larkspurs' bed—
There lived a Lady, wise, austere, and nice,
Who show'd her virtue by her scorn of vice.
In the dear fashions of her youth she dress'd,
A pea-green Joseph was her favourite vest;
Erect she stood, she walk'd with stately mien,
Tight was her length of stays, and she was tall and lean.
There long she lived in maiden-state immured,
From looks of love and treacherous man secured;
Though evil fame (but that was long before)
Had blown her dubious blast at Catherine's door.
A Captain thither, rich from India, came,
And though a cousin call'd, it touch'd her fame:
Her annual stipend rose from his behest,
And all the long-prized treasures she possess'd:—
If aught like joy awhile appear'd to stay
In that stern face, and chase those frowns away,
'Twas when her treasures she disposed for view,
And heard the praises to their splendour due;
Silks beyond price, so rich, they'd stand alone,
And diamonds blazing on the buckled zone;
Rows of rare pearls by curious workmen set,
And bracelets fair in box of glossy jet;
Bright polish'd amber precious from its size,
Or forms the fairest fancy could devise.
Her drawers of cedar, shut with secret springs,
Conceal'd the watch of gold and rubied rings;

Letters, long proofs of love, and verses fine
Round the pink'd rims of crisped Valentine.
Her china-closet, cause of daily care,
For woman's wonder held her pencill'd ware;
That pictured wealth of China and Japan,
Like its cold mistress, shunn'd the eye of man.
Her neat small room, adorn'd with maiden-taste,
A clipp'd French puppy, first of favourites, graced;
A parrot next, but dead and stuff'd with art;
(For Poll, when living, lost the Lady's heart,
And then his life; for he was heard to speak
Such frightful words as tinged his Lady's cheek;)
Unhappy bird! who had no power to prove,
Save by such speech, his gratitude and love.
A grey old cat his whiskers lick'd beside;
A type of sadness in the house of pride.
The polish'd surface of an India chest,
A glassy globe, in frame of ivory, press'd;
Where swam two finny creatures: one of gold,
Of silver one, both beauteous to behold.
All these were form'd the guiding taste to suit;
The beasts well-manner'd and the fishes mute.
A widow'd Aunt was there, compelled by need
The nymph to flatter and her tribe to feed;
Who, veiling well her scorn, endured the clog,
Mute as the fish and fawning as the dog.
As years increased, these treasures, her delight,
Arose in value in their owner's sight:
A miser knows that, view it as he will,
A guinea kept is but a guinea still;
And so he puts it to its proper use,
That something more this guinea may produce:
But silks and rings, in the possessor's eyes,
The oft'ner seen, the more in value rise,
And thus are wisely hoarded to bestow
The kind of pleasure that with years will grow.
But what avail'd their worth—if worth had they—
In the sad summer of her slow decay?
Then we beheld her turn an anxious look
From trunks and chests, and fix it on her book—
A rich-bound Book of Prayer the Captain gave,
(Some Princess had it, or was said to have;)
And then once more, on all her stores, look round,
And draw a sigh so piteous and profound,
That told, "Alas! how hard from these to part,
And for new hopes and habits form the heart!
What shall I do," (she cried,) "my peace of mind
To gain in dying, and to die resign'd?"

"Hear," we return'd;—"these baubles cast aside,
Nor give thy God a rival in thy pride;
Thy closets shut, and ope thy kitchen's door;
There own thy failings, here invite the poor;
A friend of Mammon let thy bounty make;
For widows' prayers thy vanities forsake;
And let the hungry of thy pride partake:
Then shall thy inward eye with joy survey
The angel Mercy tempering Death's delay!"
Alas! 'twas hard; the treasures still had charms,
Hope still its flattery, sickness its alarms;
Still was the same unsettled, clouded view,
And the same plaintive cry, "What shall I do?"
Nor change appear'd: for when her race was run,
Doubtful we all exclaim'd, "What has been done?"
Apart she lived, and still she lies alone;
Yon earthy heap awaits the flattering stone,
On which invention shall be long employ'd,
To show the various worth of Catherine Lloyd.

Next to these ladies, but in nought allied,
A noble Peasant, Isaac Ashford, died.
Noble he was, contemning all things mean,
His truth unquestion'd and his soul serene;
Of no man's presence Isaac felt afraid;
At no man's question Isaac look'd dismay'd:
Shame knew him not, he dreaded no disgrace;
Truth, simple truth, was written in his face;
Yet while the serious thought his soul approved,
Cheerful he seem'd, and gentleness he loved.
To bliss domestic he his heart resign'd,
And, with the firmest, had the fondest mind.
Were others joyful, he look'd smiling on,
And gave allowance where he needed none;
Good he refused with future ill to buy,
Nor knew a joy that caused reflection's sigh;
A friend to virtue, his unclouded breast
No envy stung, no jealousy distress'd;
(Bane of the poor! it wounds their weaker mind,
To miss one favour which their neighbours find.)
Yet far was he from stoic pride removed;
He felt humanely, and he warmly loved.
I mark'd his action, when his infant died,
And his old neighbour for offence was tried;
The still tears, stealing down that furrow'd cheek,
Spoke pity, plainer than the tongue can speak.
If pride were his, 'twas not their vulgar pride,
Who, in their base contempt, the great deride;

Nor pride in learning,—though my clerk agreed,
If fate should call him, Ashford might succeed;
Nor pride in rustic skill, although we knew
None his superior, and his equals few:—
But, if that spirit in his soul had place,
It was the jealous pride that shuns disgrace:
A pride in honest fame, by virtue gain'd,
In sturdy boys to virtuous labours train'd;
Pride in the power that guards his country's coast,
And all that Englishmen enjoy and boast;
Pride in a life that slander's tongue defied,—
In fact, a noble passion, misnamed pride.
He had no party's rage, no sect'ry's whim;
Christian and countryman was all with him.
True to his church he came; no Sunday-shower
Kept him at home in that important hour;
Nor his firm feet could one persuading sect,
By the strong glare of their new light, direct;—
"On hope, in mine own sober light, I gaze,
But should be blind and lose it, in your blaze."
In times severe, when many a sturdy swain
Felt it his pride, his comfort, to complain,
Isaac their wants would soothe, his own would hide,
And feel in that his comfort and his pride.
At length he found, when seventy years were run,
His strength departed, and his labour done;
When he, save honest fame, retain'd no more,
But lost his wife and saw his children poor:
'Twas then, a spark of—say not, discontent—
Struck on his mind, and thus he gave it vent:
"Kind are your laws, ('tis not to be denied,)
That in yon house for ruin'd age provide,
And they are just;—when young, we give you all,
And for assistance in our weakness call.—
Why then this proud reluctance to be fed,
To join your poor, and eat the parish-bread?
But yet I linger, loth with him to feed,
Who gains his plenty by the sons of need;
He who, by contract, all your paupers took,
And gauges stomachs with an anxious look.
On some old master I could well depend;
See him with joy and thank him as a friend;
But ill on him, who doles the day's supply,
And counts our chances, who at night may die:
Yet help me, Heav'n! and let me not complain
Of what I suffer, but my fate sustain."
Such were his thoughts, and so resign'd he grew;
Daily he placed the workhouse in his view!

But came not there, for sudden was his fate:
He dropp'd, expiring, at his cottage-gate.
I feel his absence in the hours of prayer,
And view his seat and sigh for Isaac there:
I see no more those white locks thinly spread
Round the bald polish of that honoured head;
No more that awful glance on playful wight,
Compell'd to kneel and tremble at the sight,
To fold his fingers, all in dread the while,
Till Mister Ashford soften'd to a smile;
No more that meek and suppliant look in prayer,
Nor the pure faith (to give it force), are there;—
But he is bless'd, and I lament no more
A wise good man, contented to be poor.

Then died a Rambler: not the one who sails
And trucks, for female favours, beads and nails;
Not one, who posts from place to place—of men
And manners treating with a flying pen;
Not he, who climbs, for prospects, Snowdon's height,
And chides the clouds that intercept the sight;
No curious shell, rare plant, or brilliant spar,
Enticed our traveller from his home so far;
But all the reason, by himself assign'd
For so much rambling, was, a restless mind;
As on, from place to place, without intent,
Without reflection, Robin Dingley went.
Not thus by nature;—never man was found
Less prone to wander from his parish-bound:
Claudian's old Man, to whom all scenes were new,
Save those where he and where his apples grew,
Resembled Robin, who around would look,
And his horizon for the earth's mistook.
To this poor swain a keen Attorney came:—
"I give thee joy, good fellow! on thy name;
The rich old Dingley's dead;—no child has he,
Nor wife, nor will; his ALL is left for thee:
To be his fortune's heir thy claim is good;
Thou hast the name, and we will prove the blood."
The claim was made; 'twas tried—it would not stand;
They proved the blood, but were refused the land.
Assured of wealth, this man of simple heart,
To every friend had predisposed a part:
His wife had hopes indulged of various kind;
The three Miss Dingleys had their school assign'd,
Masters were sought for what they each required,
And books were bought and harpsichords were hired:
So high was hope;—the failure touch'd his brain,

And Robin never was himself again.
Yet he no wrath, no angry wish express'd,
But tried, in vain, to labour or to rest;
Then cast his bundle on his back, and went
He knew not whither, nor for what intent.
Years fled;—of Robin all remembrance past,
When home he wander'd in his rags at last.
A sailor's jacket on his limbs was thrown,
A sailor's story he had made his own;
Had suffer'd battles, prisons, tempests, storms,
Encountering death in all his ugliest forms.
His cheeks were haggard, hollow was his eye,
Where madness lurk'd, conceal'd in misery;
Want, and th' ungentle world, had taught a part,
And prompted cunning to that simple heart:
He now bethought him, he would roam no more,
But live at home and labour as before.
Here clothed and fed, no sooner he began
To round and redden, than away he ran;
His wife was dead, their children past his aid:
So, unmolested, from his home he stray'd.
Six years elapsed, when, worn with want and pain,
Came Robin, wrapt in all his rags, again.—
We chide, we pity;—placed among our poor,
He fed again, and was a man once more.
As when a gaunt and hungry fox is found,
Entrapp'd alive in some rich hunter's ground;
Fed for the field, although each day's a feast,
Fatten you may, but never tame the beast;
A house protects him, savoury viands sustain;
But loose his neck and off he goes again:
So stole our vagrant from his warm retreat,
To rove a prowler and be deem'd a cheat.
Hard was his fare; for, him at length we saw,
In cart convey'd and laid supine on straw.
His feeble voice now spoke a sinking heart;
His groans now told the motions of the cart;
And when it stopp'd, he tried in vain to stand;
Closed was his eye, and clench'd his clammy hand;
Life ebb'd apace, and our best aid no more
Could his weak sense or dying heart restore:
But now he fell, a victim to the snare,
That vile attorneys for the weak prepare—
They who, when profit or resentment call,
Heed not the groaning victim they enthrall.

Then died lamented, in the strength of life,
A valued Mother and a faithful Wife;

Call'd not away, when time had loosed each hold
On the fond heart, and each desire grew cold;
But when, to all that knit us to our kind,
She felt fast-bound, as charity can bind—
Not, when the ills of age, its pain, its care,
The drooping spirit for its fate prepare;
And each affection, failing, leaves the heart
Loosed from life's charm and willing to depart—
But all her ties the strong invader broke,
In all their strength, by one tremendous stroke!
Sudden and swift the eager pest came on,
And terror grew, till every hope was gone;
Still those around appear'd for hope to seek!
But view'd the sick, and were afraid to speak.—
Slowly they bore, with solemn step, the dead;
When grief grew loud and bitter tears were shed,
My part began; a crowd drew near the place,
Awe in each eye, alarm in every face:
So swift the ill, and of so fierce a kind,
That fear with pity mingled in each mind;
Friends with the husband came their griefs to blend;
For good-man Frankford was to all a friend.
The last-born boy they held above the bier;
He knew not grief, but cries express'd his fear;
Each different age and sex reveal'd its pain,
In now a louder, now a lower strain;
While the meek father, listening to their tones,
Swell'd the full cadence of the grief by groans.
The elder sister strove her pangs to hide,
And soothing words to younger minds applied
"Be still, be patient," oft she strove to say;
But fail'd as oft, and weeping turn'd away.
Curious and sad, upon the fresh-dug hill,
The village-lads stood melancholy still;
And idle children, wandering to-and-fro,
As Nature guided, took the tone of wo.
Arrived at home, how then they gazed around,
In every place—where she no more was found;
The seat at table she was wont to fill;
The fire-side chair, still set, but vacant still;
The garden-walks, a labour all her own,
The latticed bower, with trailing shrubs o'ergrown;
The Sunday-pew she fill'd with all her race—
Each place of hers, was now a sacred place,
That, while it call'd up sorrows in the eyes,
Pierced the full heart and forced them still to rise.
Oh sacred sorrow! by whom souls are tried,
Sent not to punish mortals, but to guide;

If thou art mine, (and who shall proudly dare
To tell his Maker, he has had his share?)
Still let me feel for what thy pangs are sent,
And be my guide and not my punishment!

Of Leah Cousins next the name appears,
With honours crown'd and bless'd with length of years,
Save that she lived to feel, in life's decay,
The pleasure die, the honours drop away.
A matron she, whom every village-wife
View'd as the help and guardian of her life;
Fathers and sons, indebted to her aid,
Respect to her and her profession paid;
Who in the house of plenty largely fed,
Yet took her station at the pauper's bed;
Nor from that duty could be bribed again,
While fear or danger urged her to remain.
In her experience all her friends relied;
Heaven was her help and nature was her guide.
Thus Leah lived, long trusted, much caress'd,
Till a Town-Dame a youthful Farmer bless'd;
A gay vain bride, who would example give
To that poor village where she deign'd to live;
Some few months past, she sent, in hour of need,
For Doctor Glibb, who came with wond'rous speed:
Two days he waited, all his art applied,
To save the mother when her infant died:—
"'Twas well I came," at last he deign'd to say;
"'Twas wondrous well"—and proudly rode away.
The news ran round:—"How vast the Doctor's pow'r!
He saved the Lady in the trying hour;
Saved her from death, when she was dead to hope,
And her fond husband had resign'd her up:
So all, like her, may evil fate defy,
If Doctor Glibb, with saving hand, be nigh."
Fame (now his friend), fear, novelty, and whim,
And fashion, sent the varying sex to him:
From this, contention in the village rose,
And these the Dame espoused, the Doctor those:
The wealthier part, to him and science went;
With luck and her the poor remain'd content.
The matron sigh'd; for she was vex'd at heart,
With so much profit, so much fame, to part:
"So long successful in my art," she cried,
"And this proud man, so young and so untried!"
"Nay," said the Doctor, "dare you trust your wives,
The joy, the pride, the solace of your lives,
To one who acts and knows no reason why,

But trusts, poor hag! to luck for an ally?—
Who, on experience, can her claims advance,
And own the powers of accident and chance?
A whining dame, who prays in danger's view,
(A proof she knows not what beside to do;)
What's her experience? In the time that's gone,
Blundering she wrought, and still she blunders on:—
What is Nature? One who acts in aid
Of gossips half asleep, and half afraid.
With such allies I scorn my fame to blend,
Skill is my luck and courage is my friend;
No slave to Nature, 'tis my chief delight
To win my way and act in her despite:—
"Trust then my art, that, in itself complete,
Needs no assistance and fears no defeat."
Warm'd by her well-spiced ale and aiding pipe,
The angry matron grew for contest ripe.
"Can you," she said, "ungrateful and unjust,
Before experience, ostentation trust!
What is your hazard, foolish daughters, tell?
If safe, you're certain; if secure, you're well:
That I have luck must friend and foe confess,
And what's good judgment but a lucky guess?
He boasts but what he can do:—will you run
From me, your friend! who, all he boasts, have done?
By proud and learned words his powers are known;
By healthy boys and handsome girls my own.
Wives! fathers! children! by my help you live;
Has this pale Doctor more than life to give?
No stunted cripple hops the village round;
Your hands are active and your heads are sound:
My lads are all your fields and flocks require;
My lasses all those sturdy lads admire.
Can this proud leech, with all his boasted skill,
Amend the soul or body, wit or will?
Does he for courts the sons of farmers frame,
Or make the daughter differ from the dame?
Or, whom he brings into this world of wo,
Prepares he them their part to undergo?
If not, this stranger from your doors repel,
And be content to be, and to be well."
She spake; but, ah! with words too strong and plain;
Her warmth offended, and her truth was vain:
The many left her, and the friendly few,
If never colder, yet they older grew;
Till, unemploy'd, she felt her spirits droop,
And took, insidious aid! th' inspiring cup;
Grew poor and peevish as her powers decay'd,

And propp'd the tottering frame with stronger aid;—
Then died!—I saw our careful swains convey,
From this our changeful world, the matron's clay,
Who to this world, at least, with equal care,
Brought them its changes, good and ill to share.
Now to his grave was Roger Cuff convey'd,
And strong resentment's lingering spirit laid.
Shipwreck'd in youth, he home return'd, and found
His brethren three—and thrice they wish'd him drown'd.
"Is this a landman's love? Be certain then,
We part for ever!"—and they cried, "Amen!"
His words were truth's.—Some forty summers fled;
His brethren died; his kin supposed him dead:
Three nephews these, one sprightly niece, and one,
Less near in blood—they call'd him surly John;
He work'd in woods apart from all his kind.
Fierce were his looks and moody was his mind.
For home the Sailor now began to sigh:—
"The dogs are dead, and I'll return and die;
When all I have, my gains, in years of care,
The younger Cuffs with kinder souls shall share.—
Yet hold! I'm rich;—with one consent they'll say,
'You're welcome, Uncle, as the flowers in May.'
No; I'll disguise me, be in tatters dress'd,
And best befriend the lads who treat me best."
Now all his kindred,—neither rich nor poor—
Kept the wolf want some distance from the door.
In piteous plight he knock'd at George's gate,
And begg'd for aid, as he described his state;—
But stern was George:—"Let them who had thee strong,
Help thee to drag thy weaken'd frame along;
To us a stranger, while your limbs would move,
From us depart and try a stranger's love:—
Ha! dost thou murmur?"—for, in Roger's throat,
Was "Rascal!" rising with disdainful note.
To pious James he then his prayer address'd;—
"Good lack," quoth James, "thy sorrows pierce my breast;
And, had I wealth, as have my brethren twain,
One board should feed us and one roof contain.
But plead I will thy cause and I will pray;
And so farewell! Heaven help thee on thy way!"
"Scoundrel!" said Roger, (but apart;)—and told
His case to Peter;—Peter too was cold;—
"The rates are high; we have a-many poor;
But I will think,"—he said, and shut the door.
Then the gay Niece the seeming pauper press'd:—
"Turn, Nancy, turn, and view this form distress'd;
Akin to thine is this declining frame,

And this poor beggar claims an Uncle's name."
"Avaunt! begone!" the courteous maiden said,
"Thou vile impostor! Uncle Roger's dead:
I hate thee, beast; thy look my spirit shocks!
Oh! that I saw thee starving in the stocks!"
"My gentle niece!" he said—and sought the wood.—
"I hunger, fellow; prithee, give me food!"
"Give! am I rich? This hatchet take, and try
Thy proper strength, nor give those limbs the lie;
Work, feed thyself, to thine own powers appeal,
Nor whine out woes, thine own right-hand can heal:
And while that hand is thine and thine a leg,
Scorn of the proud or of the base to beg."
"Come, surly John, thy wealthy kinsman view,"
Old Roger said:—"thy words are brave and true;
Come, live with me: we'll vex those scoundrel-boys,
And that prim shrew shall, envying, hear our joys.—
Tobacco's glorious fume all day we'll share,
With beef and brandy kill all kinds of care;
We'll beer and biscuit on our table heap,
And rail at rascals, till we fall asleep."
Such was their life; but when the woodman died,
His grieving kin for Roger's smiles applied—
In vain; he shut, with stern rebuke, the door,
And dying, built a refuge for the poor:
With this restriction, That no Cuff should share
One meal, or shelter for one moment there.

My record ends:—But hark! e'en now I hear
The bell of death, and know not whose to fear.
Our farmers all, and all our hinds were well;
In no man's cottage danger seem'd to dwell;—
Yet death of man proclaim these heavy chimes,
For thrice they sound, with pausing space, three times.
"Go; of my sexton seek, Whose days are sped?—
"What! he, himself!—and is old Dibble dead?"
His eightieth year he reach'd, still undecay'd,
And rectors five to one close vault convey'd:—
But he is gone; his care and skill I lose,
And gain a mournful subject for my Muse:
His masters lost, he'd oft in turn deplore,
And kindly add,—"Heaven grant, I lose no more!"
Yet, while he spake, a sly and pleasant glance
Appear'd at variance with his complaisance:
For, as he told their fate and varying worth,
He archly look'd,—"I yet may bear thee forth."
"When first"—(he so began)—"my trade I plied,
Good master Addle was the parish-guide;

His clerk and sexton, I beheld with fear
His stride majestic, and his frown severe;
A noble pillar of the church he stood,
Adorn'd with college-gown and parish-hood.
Then as he paced the hallow'd aisles about,
He fill'd the sevenfold surplice fairly out!
But in his pulpit, wearied down with prayer,
He sat and seem'd as in his study's chair;
For while the anthem swell'd, and when it ceased,
Th' expecting people view'd their slumbering priest:
Who, dozing, died.—Our Parson Peele was next;
'I will not spare you,' was his favourite text;
Nor did he spare, but raised them many a pound;
Ev'n me he mulct for my poor rood of ground;
Yet cared he nought, but with a gibing speech,
'What should I do,' quoth he, 'but what I preach?'
His piercing jokes (and he'd a plenteous store)
Were daily offer'd both to rich and poor;
His scorn, his love, in playful words he spoke;
His pity, praise, and promise, were a joke:
But though so young and bless'd with spirits high,
He died as grave as any judge could die:
The strong attack subdued his lively powers,—
His was the grave, and Doctor Grandspear ours.
Then were there golden times the village round;
In his abundance all appear'd t' abound;
Liberal and rich, a plenteous board he spread,
E'en cool Dissenters at his table fed,
Who wish'd, and hoped,—and thought a man so kind
A way to Heaven, though not their own, might find;
To them, to all, he was polite and free,
Kind to the poor, and, ah! most kind to me:
'Ralph,' would he say, 'Ralph Dibble, thou art old;
That doublet fit, 'twill keep thee from the cold.
How does my sexton?—What! the times are hard;
Drive that stout pig, and pen him in thy yard.'
But most, his rev'rence loved a mirthful jest:—
'Thy coat is thin; why, man, thou'rt barely dress'd;
It's worn to th' thread; but I have nappy beer;
Clap that within, and see how they will wear!'
"Gay days were these; but they were quickly past:
When first he came, we found he cou'dn't last:
A whoreson cough (and at the fall of leaf)
Upset him quite;—but what's the gain of grief?
"Then came the Author-Rector; his delight
Was all in books; to read them, or to write:
Women and men he strove alike to shun,
And hurried homeward when his tasks were done,

Courteous enough, but careless what he said,
For points of learning he reserved his head;
And, when addressing either poor or rich,
He knew no better than his cassock which.
He, like an osier, was of pliant kind,
Erect by nature, but to bend inclined;
Not like a creeper falling to the ground,
Or meanly catching on the neighbours round.—
Careless was he of surplice, hood, and band—
And kindly took them as they came to hand;
Nor, like the doctor, wore a world of hat,
As if he sought for dignity in that.
He talk'd, he gave, but not with cautious rules,
Nor turn'd from gipsies, vagabonds, or fools;
It was his nature, but they thought it whim,
And so our beaux and beauties turn'd from him.
Of questions much he wrote, profound and dark—
How spake the serpent, and where stopp'd the ark;
From what far land the Queen of Sheba came;
Who Salem's priest, and what his father's name;
He made the Song of Songs its mysteries yield,
And Revelations, to the world, reveal'd.
He sleeps i' the aisle—but not a stone records
His name or fame, his actions or his words:
And, truth, your reverence, when I look around,
And mark the tombs in our sepulchral ground,
(Though dare I not of one man's hope to doubt),
I'd join the party who repose without,
"Next came a youth from Cambridge, and, in truth,
He was a sober and a comely youth;
He blush'd in meekness as a modest man,
And gain'd attention ere his task began;
When preaching, seldom ventured on reproof,
But touch'd his neighbours tenderly enough.
Him, in his youth, a clamorous sect assail'd,
Advised and censured, flatter'd,—and prevail'd.—
Then did he much his sober hearers vex,
Confound the simple, and the sad perplex;
To a new style his reverence rashly took;
Loud grew his voice, to threat'ning swell'd his look;
Above, below, on either side, he gazed,
Amazing all, and most himself amazed:
No more he read his preachments pure and plain,
But launch'd outright, and rose and sank again:
At times he smiled in scorn, at times he wept,
And such sad coil with words of vengeance kept,
That our best sleepers started as they slept.
"'Conviction comes like lightning,' he would cry;

'In vain you seek it, and in vain you fly;
'Tis like the rushing of the mighty wind,
Unseen its progress, but its power you find;
It strikes the child ere yet its reason wakes;
His reason fled, the ancient sire it shakes.
The proud, learn'd man, and him who loves to know
How and from whence these gusts of grace will blow,
It shuns,—but sinners in their way impedes,
And sots and harlots visits in their deeds:
Of faith and penance it supplies the place;
Assures the vilest that they live by grace,
And, without running, makes them win the race.'
"Such was the doctrine our young prophet taught;
And here conviction, there confusion wrought;
When his thin cheek assumed a deadly hue,
And all the rose to one small spot withdrew:
They call'd it hectic; 'twas a fiery flush,
More fix'd and deeper than the maiden blush;
His paler lips the pearly teeth disclosed,
And lab'ring lungs the length'ning speech opposed.
No more his span-girth shanks and quiv'ring thighs
Upheld a body of the smaller size;
But down he sank upon his dying bed,
And gloomy crotchets fill'd his wandering head.—
"'Spite of my faith, all-saving faith,' he cried,
'I fear of worldly works the wicked pride;
Poor as I am, degraded, abject, blind,
The good I've wrought still rankles in my mind;
My alms-deeds all, and every deed I've done,
My moral-rags defile me, every one;
It should not be—what say'st thou? tell me, Ralph.'
Quoth I, 'Your reverence, I believe, you're safe;
Your faith's your prop, nor have you pass'd such time
In life's good-works as swell them to a crime.
If I of pardon for my sins were sure,
About my goodness I would rest secure.'
"Such was his end; and mine approaches fast;
I've seen my best of preachers—and my last."—
He bow'd, and archly smiled at what he said,
Civil but sly:—"And is old Dibble dead?"
Yes! he is gone: and WE are going all;
Like flowers we wither, and like leaves we fall;—
Here, with an infant, joyful sponsors come,
Then bear the new-made Christian to its home;
A few short years, and we behold him stand,
To ask a blessing, with his bride in hand:
A few, still seeming shorter, and we hear
His widow weeping at her husband's bier:—

Thus, as the months succeed, shall infants take
Their names; thus parents shall the child forsake;
Thus brides again and bridegrooms blithe shall kneel,
By love or law compell'd their vows to seal,
Ere I again, or one like me, explore
These simple annals of the VILLAGE POOR.

THE BIRTH OF FLATTERY

The Subject—Poverty and Cunning described—When united, a jarring Couple—Mutual Reproof—The Wife consoled by a Dream—Birth of a Daughter—Description and Prediction of Envy—How to be rendered ineffectual, explained in a Vision—Simulation foretells the future Success and Triumphs of Flattery—Her Power over various Characters and different Minds; over certain Classes of Men; over Envy himself—Her successful Art of softening the Evils of Life; of changing Characters; of meliorating Prospects, and affixing Value to Possessions, Pictures, &c.—Conclusion.

Omnia habeo, nec quicquam habeo
Quidquid dicunt, laudo; id rursum si negant, laudo id quoque.
Negat quis, nego; ait, aio. Postremò imperavi egomet mihi
Omnia assentari.

Terent. in Eunuch. [Act II. Sc. II.]

It has been held in ancient rules,
That flattery is the food of fools;
Yet now and then your men of wit
Will condescend to taste a bit.

Swift, Cadenus and Vanessa.

Muse of my Spenser, who so well could sing
The passions all, their bearings and their ties;
Who could in view those shadowy beings bring,
And with bold hand remove each dark disguise,
Wherein love, hatred, scorn, or anger lies:
Guide him to Fairy-land, who now intends
That way his flight; assist him as he flies,
To mark those passions, Virtue's foes and friends,
By whom when led she droops, when leading she ascends.

Yes! they appear, I see the fairy-train!
And who that modest nymph of meek address?
Not Vanity, though loved by all the vain;
Not Hope, though promising to all success;
Nor Mirth, nor Joy, though foe to all distress;

Thee, sprightly syren, from this train I choose,
Thy birth relate, thy soothing arts confess;
'Tis not in thy mild nature to refuse,
When poets ask thine aid, so oft their meed and muse.

In Fairy-land, on wide and cheerless plain,
Dwelt, in the house of Care, a sturdy swain;
A hireling he, who, when he till'd the soil,
Look'd to the pittance that repaid his toil;
And to a master left the mingled joy
And anxious care that follow'd his employ.
Sullen and patient he at once appear'd,
As one who murmur'd, yet as one who fear'd;
Th' attire was coarse that clothed his sinewy frame,
Rude his address, and Poverty his name.

In that same plain a nymph, of curious taste,
A cottage (plann'd with all her skill) had placed;
Strange the materials, and for what design'd
The various parts, no simple man might find;
What seem'd the door, each entering guest withstood,
What seem'd a window was but painted wood;
But by a secret spring the wall would move,
And day-light drop through glassy door above.
'Twas all her pride, new traps for praise to lay,
And all her wisdom was to hide her way;
In small attempts incessant were her pains,
And Cunning was her name among the swains.

Now, whether fate decreed this pair should wed,
And blindly drove them to the marriage-bed;
Or whether love in some soft hour inclined
The damsel's heart, and won her to be kind,
Is yet unsung: they were an ill-match'd pair,
But both disposed to wed—and wed they were.

Yet, though united in their fortune, still
Their ways were diverse; varying was their will;
Nor long the maid had bless'd the simple man,
Before dissensions rose, and she began:—

"Wretch that I am! since to thy fortune bound,
What plan, what project, with success is crown'd?
I, who a thousand secret arts possess,
Who every rank approach with right address;
Who've loosed a guinea from a miser's chest,
And worm'd his secret from a traitor's breast;

Thence gifts and gains collecting, great and small,
Have brought to thee, and thou consum'st them all:
For want like thine—a bog without a base—
Ingulfs all gains I gather for the place;
Feeding, unfill'd; destroying, undestroy'd;
It craves for ever, and is ever void:—
Wretch that I am! what misery have I found,
Since my sure craft was to thy calling bound!"

"Oh! vaunt of worthless art," the swain replied,
Scowling contempt, "how pitiful this pride!
What are these specious gifts, these paltry gains,
But base rewards for ignominious pains?
With all thy tricking, still for bread we strive;
Thine is, proud wretch! the care that cannot thrive;
By all thy boasted skill and baffled hooks
Thou gain'st no more than students by their books;
No more than I for my poor deeds am paid,
Whom none can blame, will help, or dare upbraid.
"Call this our need, a bog that all devours—
Then what thy petty arts but summer-flowers,
Gaudy and mean, and serving to betray
The place they make unprofitably gay?
Who know it not, some useless beauties see—
But ah! to prove it, was reserved for me."

Unhappy state! that, in decay of love,
Permits harsh truth his errors to disprove;
While he remains, to wrangle and to jar
Is friendly tournament, not fatal war;
Love in his play will borrow arms of hate,
Anger and rage, upbraiding and debate;
And by his power the desperate weapons thrown,
Become as safe and pleasant as his own;
But left by him, their natures they assume,
And fatal, in their poisoning force, become.

Time fled, and now the swain compell'd to see
New cause for fear—"Is this thy thrift?" quoth he.
To whom the wife with cheerful voice replied:—
"Thou moody man, lay all thy fears aside,
I've seen a vision;—they, from whom I came,
A daughter promise, promise wealth and fame;
Born with my features, with my arts, yet she
Shall patient, pliant, persevering be,
And in thy better ways resemble thee.
The fairies round shall at her birth attend;
The friend of all in all shall find a friend;

And, save that one sad star that hour must gleam
On our fair child, how glorious were my dream!"

This heard the husband, and, in surly smile,
Aim'd at contempt, but yet he hoped the while:
For as, when sinking, wretched men are found
To catch at rushes rather than be drown'd;
So on a dream our peasant placed his hope,
And found that rush as valid as a rope.

Swift fled the days, for now in hope they fled,
When a fair daughter bless'd the nuptial bed;
Her infant-face the mother's pains beguiled,
She look'd so pleasing, and so softly smiled;
Those smiles, those looks, with sweet sensations moved
The gazer's soul, and, as he look'd, he loved.

And now the fairies came, with gifts, to grace
So mild a nature and so fair a face.
They gave, with beauty, that bewitching art,
That holds in easy chains the human heart;
They gave her skill to win the stubborn mind,
To make the suffering to their sorrows blind,
To bring on pensive looks the pleasing smile,
And Care's stern brow of every frown beguile.
These magic favours graced the infant-maid,
Whose more enlivening smile the charming gifts repaid.

Now Fortune changed, who, were she constant long,
Would leave us few adventures for our song.
A wicked elfin roved this land around,
Whose joys proceeded from the griefs he found;
Envy his name:—his fascinating eye
From the light bosom drew the sudden sigh;
Unsocial he, but with malignant mind,
He dwelt with man, that he might curse mankind;
Like the first foe, he sought th' abode of Joy,
Grieved to behold, but eager to destroy;
Round blooming beauty, like the wasp, he flew,
Soil'd the fresh sweet, and changed the rosy hue;
The wise, the good, with anxious heart, he saw,
And here a failing found, and there a flaw;
Discord in families 'twas his to move,
Distrust in friendship, jealousy in love;
He told the poor, what joys the great possess'd,
The great—what calm content the cottage bless'd;
To part the learned and the rich he tried,
Till their slow friendship perish'd in their pride.

Such was the fiend, and so secure of prey,
That only Misery pass'd unstung away.

Soon as he heard the fairy-babe was born,
Scornful he smiled, but felt no more than scorn;
For why, when Fortune placed her state so low,
In useless spite his lofty malice show?
Why, in a mischief of the meaner kind,
Exhaust the vigour of a ranc'rous mind?
But, soon as Fame the fairy-gifts proclaim'd,
Quick-rising wrath his ready soul inflamed,
To swear, by vows that e'en the wicked tie,
The nymph should weep her varied destiny;
That every gift, that now appear'd to shine
In her fair face, and make her smiles divine,
Should all the poison of his magic prove,
And they should scorn her, whom she sought for love.

His spell prepared, in form an ancient dame,
A fiend in spirit, to the cot he came;
There gain'd admittance, and the infant press'd
(Muttering his wicked magic) to his breast;
And thus he said:—"Of all the powers, who wait
On Jove's decrees, and do the work of fate,
Was I alone, despised or worthless, found,
Weak to protect, or impotent to wound?
See then thy foe, regret the friendship lost,
And learn my skill, but learn it at your cost.
"Know then, O child! devote to fates severe,
The good shall hate thy name, the wise shall fear;
Wit shall deride, and no protecting friend
Thy shame shall cover, or thy name defend.
Thy gentle sex, who, more than ours, should spare
A humble foe, will greater scorn declare;
The base alone thy advocates shall be,
Or boast alliance with a wretch like thee."

He spake and vanish'd, other prey to find,
And waste in slow disease the conquer'd mind.

Awed by the elfin's threats, and fill'd with dread,
The parents wept, and sought their infant's bed:
Despair alone the father's soul possess'd,
But hope rose gently in the mother's breast;
For well she knew that neither grief nor joy
Pain'd without hope, or pleased without alloy;
And while these hopes and fears her heart divide,
A cheerful vision bade the fears subside.

She saw descending to the world below
An ancient form, with solemn pace and slow.

"Daughter, no more be sad," (the phantom cried,)
"Success is seldom to the wise denied;
In idle wishes fools supinely stay—
Be there a will, and wisdom finds a way:
Why art thou grieved? Be rather glad, that he,
Who hates the happy, aims his darts at thee,
But aims in vain; thy favour'd daughter lies,
Serenely blest, and shall to joy arise.
For, grant that curses on her name shall wait,
(So envy wills and such the voice of fate,)
Yet, if that name be prudently suppress'd,
She shall be courted, favour'd, and caress'd.
"For what are names? and where agree mankind
In those to persons or to acts assign'd?
Brave, learn'd, or wise, if some their favourites call,
Have they the titles or the praise from all?
Not so, but others will the brave disdain
As rash, and deem the sons of wisdom vain;
The self-same mind shall scorn or kindness move,
And the same deed attract contempt and love.
"So all the powers who move the human soul,
With all the passions who the will control,
Have various names—one giv'n by Truth Divine,
(As Simulation thus was fix'd for mine,)
The rest by man, who now, as wisdom's prize
My secret counsels, now as art despise;
One hour, as just, those counsels they embrace,
And spurn, the next, as pitiful and base.
"Thee, too, my child, those fools as Cunning fly,
Who on thy counsel and thy craft rely;
That worthy craft in others they condemn,
But 'tis their prudence, while conducting them.
"Be FLATTERY, then, thy happy infant's name,
Let Honour scorn her and let Wit defame;
Let all be true that Envy dooms, yet all,
Not on herself, but on her name, shall fall;
While she thy fortune and her own shall raise,
And decent Truth be call'd, and loved as modest Praise.
"O happy child! the glorious day shall shine,
When every ear shall to thy speech incline,
Thy words alluring and thy voice divine.
The sullen pedant and the sprightly wit,
To hear thy soothing eloquence, shall sit;
And both, abjuring Flattery, will agree

That truth inspires, and they must honour thee.
"Envy himself shall to thy accents bend,
Force a faint smile and sullenly attend,
When thou shalt call him Virtue's jealous friend,
Whose bosom glows with generous rage to find
How fools and knaves are flatter'd by mankind.
"The sage retired, who spends alone his days,
And flies th' obstreperous voice of public praise;
The vain, the vulgar cry shall gladly meet,
And bid thee welcome to his still retreat;
Much will he wonder, how thou cam'st to find
A man to glory dead, to peace consign'd.
'O Fame!' he'll cry, (for he will call thee Fame,)
'From thee I fly, from thee conceal my name.'
But thou shalt say, 'Though Genius takes his flight,
He leaves behind a glorious train of light,
And hides in vain;—yet prudent he that flies
The flatterer's art, and for himself is wise.'
"Yes, happy child! I mark th' approaching day,
When warring natures will confess thy sway;
When thou shalt Saturn's golden reign restore,
And vice and folly shall be known no more.
"Pride shall not then in human-kind have place,
Changed, by thy skill, to Dignity and Grace;
While Shame, who now betrays the inward sense
Of secret ill, shall be thy Diffidence;
Avarice shall thenceforth prudent Forecast be,
And bloody Vengeance, Magnanimity;
The lavish tongue shall honest truths impart,
The lavish hand shall show the generous heart,
And Indiscretion be contempt of art:
Folly and Vice shall then, no longer known,
Be, this as Virtue, that as Wisdom, shown.
"Then shall the Robber, as the Hero, rise
To seize the good that churlish law denies;
Throughout the world shall rove the generous band,
And deal the gifts of Heaven from hand to hand.
"In thy blest days no tyrant shall be seen,
Thy gracious king shall rule contented men;
In thy blest days shall not a rebel be,
But patriots all and well approved of thee.
"Such powers are thine, that man, by thee, shall wrest
The gainful secret from the cautious breast;
Nor then, with all his care, the good retain,
But yield to thee the secret and the gain.
In vain shall much experience guard the heart
Against the charm of thy prevailing art;
Admitted once, so soothing is thy strain,

It comes the sweeter, when it comes again;
And when confess'd as thine, what mind so strong
Forbears the pleasure it indulged so long?
"Soft'ner of every ill! of all our woes
The balmy solace! friend of fiercest foes!
Begin thy reign, and like the morning rise!
Bring joy, bring beauty, to our eager eyes;
Break on the drowsy world like opening day,
While grace and gladness join thy flow'ry way;
While every voice is praise, while every heart is gay.
"From thee all prospects shall new beauties take,
'Tis thine to seek them and 'tis thine to make;
On the cold fen I see thee turn thine eyes,
Its mists recede, its chilling vapour flies;
Th' enraptured lord th' improving ground surveys,
And for his Eden asks the traveller's praise,
Which yet, unview'd of thee, a bog had been,
Where spungy rushes hide the plashy green.
"I see thee breathing on the barren moor,
That seems to bloom although so bleak before;
There, if beneath the gorse the primrose spring,
Or the pied daisy smile below the ling,
They shall new charms, at thy command, disclose,
And none shall miss the myrtle or the rose.
The wiry moss, that whitens all the hill,
Shall live a beauty by thy matchless skill;
Gale from the bog shall yield Arabian balm,
And the grey willow wave a golden palm.
"I see thee smiling in the pictured room,
Now breathing beauty, now reviving bloom;
There, each immortal name 'tis thine to give
To graceless forms, and bid the lumber live.
Should'st thou coarse boors or gloomy martyrs see,
These shall thy Guidos those thy Teniers' be;
There shalt thou Raphael's saints and angels trace,
There make for Rubens and for Reynolds place,
And all the pride of art shalt find in her disgrace.
"Delight of either sex! thy reign commence;
With balmy sweetness soothe the weary sense,
And to the sickening soul thy cheering aid dispense.
Queen of the mind! thy golden age begin;
In mortal bosoms varnish shame and sin;
Let all be fair without, let all be calm within."

The Vision fled; the happy mother rose,
Kiss'd the fair infant, smiled at all her foes,
And FLATTERY made her name:—her reign began,
Her own dear sex she ruled, then vanquish'd man;

A smiling friend, to every class, she spoke,
Assumed their manners, and their habits took;
Her, for her humble mien, the modest loved;
Her cheerful looks the light and gay approved;
The just beheld her, firm; the valiant, brave;
Her mirth the free, her silence pleased the grave;
Zeal heard her voice, and, as he preach'd aloud,
Well-pleased he caught her whispers from the crowd—
(Those whispers, soothing-sweet to every ear,
Which some refuse to pay, but none to hear);
Shame fled her presence; at her gentle strain,
Care softly smiled, and guilt forgot its pain;
The wretched thought, the happy found her true;
The learn'd confess'd that she their merits knew;
The rich—could they a constant friend condemn?
The poor believed—for who should flatter them?

Thus on her name though all disgrace attend,
In every creature she beholds a friend.

REFLECTIONS

UPON THE SUBJECT—

Quid juvat errores, mersâ jam puppe, fateri?
Quid lacrymæ delicta juvant commissa secutæ?

Claudian. in Eutrop. lib. ii. lin. 7

What avails it, when shipwrecked, that error appears?
Are the crimes we commit wash'd away by our tears?

When all the fiercer passions cease
(The glory and disgrace of youth);
When the deluded soul, in peace,
Can listen to the voice of truth;
When we are taught in whom to trust,
And how to spare, to spend, to give,
(Our prudence kind, our pity just)—
'Tis then we rightly learn to live.

Its weakness when the body feels,
Nor danger in contempt defies;

To reason when desire appeals,
When on experience hope relies;
When every passing hour we prize,
Nor rashly on our follies spend;
But use it, as it quickly flies,
With sober aim to serious end;
When prudence bounds our utmost views,
And bids us wrath and wrong forgive;
When we can calmly gain or lose—
'Tis then we rightly learn to live.
Yet thus, when we our way discern,
And can upon our care depend,
To travel safely when we learn,
Behold! we're near our journey's end.
We've trod the maze of error round,
Long wand'ring in the winding glade;
And now the torch of truth is found,
It only shows us where we stray'd:
Light for ourselves, what is it worth,
When we no more our way can choose?
For others when we hold it forth,
They, in their pride, the boon refuse.

By long experience taught, we now
Can rightly judge of friends and foes,
Can all the worth of these allow,
And all their faults discern in those;
Relentless hatred, erring love,
We can for sacred truth forego;
We can the warmest friend reprove,
And bear to praise the fiercest foe:
To what effect? Our friends are gone,
Beyond reproof, regard, or care;
And of our foes remains there one,
The mild relenting thoughts to share?

Now 'tis our boast that we can quell
The wildest passions in their rage;
Can their destructive force repel,
And their impetuous wrath assuage:
Ah! Virtue, dost thou arm, when now
This bold rebellious race are fled;
When all these tyrants rest, and thou
Art warring with the mighty dead?
Revenge, ambition, scorn, and pride,
And strong desire and fierce disdain,
The giant-brood, by thee defied,
Lo! Time's resistless strokes have slain.

Yet Time, who could that race subdue,
(O'erpow'ring strength, appeasing rage,)
Leaves yet a persevering crew,
To try the failing powers of age.
Vex'd by the constant call of these,
Virtue awhile for conquest tries,
But weary grown and fond of ease,
She makes with them a compromise:
Av'rice himself she gives to rest,
But rules him with her strict commands;
Bids Pity touch his torpid breast,
And Justice hold his eager hands.

Yet is there nothing men can do,
When chilling Age comes creeping on?
Cannot we yet some good pursue?
Are talents buried? genius gone?
If passions slumber in the breast,
If follies from the heart be fled:
Of laurels let us go in quest,
And place them on the poet's head.

Yes, we'll redeem the wasted time,
And to neglected studies flee;
We'll build again the lofty rhyme,
Or live, Philosophy, with thee;
For reasoning clear, for flight sublime,
Eternal fame reward shall be;
And to what glorious heights we'll climb,
Th' admiring crowd shall envying see.

Begin the song! begin the theme!—
Alas! and is Invention dead?
Dream we no more the golden dream?
Is Mem'ry with her treasures fled?
Yes, 'tis too late—now Reason guides
The mind, sole judge in all debate;
And thus th' important point decides,
For laurels, 'tis, alas! too late.
What is possess'd we may retain,
But for new conquests strive in vain.
Beware then, Age, that what was won,
In life's past labours, studies, views,
Be lost not, now the labour's done,
When all thy part is—not to lose:
When thou canst toil or gain no more,
Destroy not what was gain'd before.

For, all that's gain'd of all that's good,
When time shall his weak frame destroy,
(Their use then rightly understood,)
Shall man, in happier state, enjoy.
Oh! argument for truth divine,
For study's cares, for virtue's strife:
To know th' enjoyment will be thine,
In that renew'd, that endless life!

SIR EUSTACE GREY

SCENE—A MAD-HOUSE

PERSONS—VISITOR, PHYSICIAN, AND PATIENT

Veris miscens falsa.—

Seneca in Herc. furente [Act IV. V. 1070].

VISITOR
I'll know no more;—the heart is torn
By views of wo we cannot heal;
Long shall I see these things forlorn,
And oft again their griefs shall feel,
As each upon the mind shall steal;
That wan projector's mystic style,
That lumpish idiot leering by,
That peevish idler's ceaseless wile,
And that poor maiden's half-form'd smile,
While struggling for the full-drawn sigh!—

I'll know no more.

PHYSICIAN
—Yes, turn again;
Then speed to happier scenes thy way,
When thou hast view'd, what yet remain,
The ruins of Sir Eustace Grey,
The sport of madness, misery's prey.
But he will no historian need;
His cares, his crimes, will he display,
And show (as one from frenzy freed)
The proud-lost mind, the rash-done deed.
That cell to him is Greyling Hall:—
Approach; he'll bid thee welcome there;

Will sometimes for his servant call,
And sometimes point the vacant chair:
He can, with free and easy air,
Appear attentive and polite;
Can veil his woes in manners fair,
And pity with respect excite.

PATIENT
Who comes?—Approach!—'tis kindly done:—
My learn'd physician, and a friend,
Their pleasures quit, to visit one
Who cannot to their ease attend,
Nor joys bestow, nor comforts lend,
As when I lived so bless'd, so well,
And dreamt not I must soon contend
With those malignant powers of hell.

PHYSICIAN
Less warmth, Sir Eustace, or we go.—

PATIENT
See! I am calm as infant-love,
A very child, but one of wo,
Whom you should pity, not reprove:—
But men at ease, who never strove
With passions wild, will calmly show
How soon we may their ills remove,
And masters of their madness grow.

Some twenty years I think are gone;—
(Time flies, I know not how, away;)—
The sun upon no happier shone,
Nor prouder man, than Eustace Grey.
Ask where you would, and all would say,
The man admired and praised of all,
By rich and poor, by grave and gay.
Was the young lord of Greyling Hall.
Yes! I had youth and rosy health;
Was nobly form'd, as man might be;
For sickness then, of all my wealth,
I never gave a single fee:
The ladies fair, the maidens free,
Were all accustom'd then to say,
Who would a handsome figure see
Should look upon Sir Eustace Grey.

He had a frank and pleasant look,
A cheerful eye and accent bland;

His very speech and manner spoke
The generous heart, the open hand;
About him all was gay or grand,
He had the praise of great and small;
He bought, improved, projected, plann'd,
And reign'd a prince at Greyling Hall.

My lady!—she was all we love;
All praise (to speak her worth) is faint;
Her manners show'd the yielding dove,
Her morals, the seraphic saint;
She never breathed nor look'd complaint;
No equal upon earth had she:—
Now, what is this fair thing I paint?
Alas! as all that live shall be.

There was, beside, a gallant youth,
And him my bosom's friend I had:—
Oh! I was rich in very truth,
It made me proud—it made me mad!—
Yes, I was lost—but there was cause!—
Where stood my tale?—I cannot find—
But I had all mankind's applause,
And all the smiles of womankind.

There were two cherub-things beside,
A gracious girl, a glorious boy;
Yet more to swell my full-blown pride,
To varnish higher my fading joy,
Pleasures were ours without alloy,
Nay, Paradise,—till my frail Eve
Our bliss was tempted to destroy,
Deceived and fated to deceive.

But I deserved; for all that time,
When I was loved, admired, caress'd,
There was within each secret crime,
Unfelt, uncancell'd, unconfess'd:
I never then my God address'd,
In grateful praise or humble prayer;
And, if His Word was not my jest,
(Dread thought!) it never was my care.

I doubted—fool I was to doubt!—
If that all-piercing eye could see;
If He who looks all worlds throughout,
Would so minute and careful be,
As to perceive and punish me:—

With man I would be great and high,
But with my God so lost, that He,
In his large view, should pass me by.

Thus bless'd with children, friend, and wife,
Bless'd far beyond the vulgar lot;
Of all that gladdens human life,
Where was the good, that I had not?
But my vile heart had sinful spot,
And Heaven beheld its deep'ning stain;
Eternal justice I forgot,
And mercy sought not to obtain.

Come near—I'll softly speak the rest!—
Alas! 'tis known to all the crowd,
Her guilty love was all confess'd,
And his, who so much truth avow'd,
My faithless friend's.—In pleasure proud
I sat, when these cursed tidings came;
Their guilt, their flight was told aloud,
And Envy smiled to hear my shame!

I call'd on Vengeance; at the word
She came:—Can I the deed forget?
I held the sword, th' accursed sword,
The blood of his false heart made wet;
And that fair victim paid her debt;
She pined, she died, she loath'd to live;—
I saw her dying—see her yet:
Fair fallen thing! my rage forgive!

Those cherubs still, my life to bless,
Were left; could I my fears remove,
Sad fears that checked each fond caress,
And poison'd all parental love?
Yet that with jealous feelings strove,
And would at last have won my will,
Had I not, wretch! been doom'd to prove
Th' extremes of mortal good and ill.

In youth! health! joy! in beauty's pride!
They droop'd: as flowers when blighted bow,
The dire infection came.—They died,
And I was cursed—as I am now.—
Nay, frown not, angry friend—allow
That I was deeply, sorely tried;
Hear then, and you must wonder how
I could such storms and strifes abide.

Storms!—not that clouds embattled make,
When they afflict this earthly globe;
But such as with their terrors shake
Man's breast, and to the bottom probe:
They make the hypocrite disrobe,
They try us all, if false or true;
For this, one devil had pow'r on Job;
And I was long the slave of two.

PHYSICIAN
Peace, peace, my friend; these subjects fly;
Collect thy thoughts—go calmly on.—

PATIENT
And shall I then the fact deny?
I was,—thou know'st—I was begone,
Like him who fill'd the eastern throne,
To whom the Watcher cried aloud;
That royal wretch of Babylon,
Who was so guilty and so proud.

Like him, with haughty, stubborn mind,
I, in my state, my comforts sought;
Delight and praise I hoped to find,
In what I builded, planted, bought!
Oh! arrogance! by misery taught—
Soon came a voice! I felt it come:
"Full be his cup, with evil fraught,
"Demons his guides, and death his doom!"

Then was I cast from out my state;
Two fiends of darkness led my way;
They waked me early, watch'd me late,
My dread by night, my plague by day!
Oh! I was made their sport, their play,
Through many a stormy troubled year;
And how they used their passive prey
Is sad to tell;—but you shall hear.

And first, before they sent me forth,
Through this unpitying world to run,
They robb'd Sir Eustace of his worth,
Lands, manors, lordships, every one;
So was that gracious man undone,
Was spurn'd as vile, was scorn'd as poor,
Whom every former friend would shun,
And menials drove from every door.

Then those ill-favour'd Ones, whom none
But my unhappy eyes could view,
Led me, with wild emotion, on,
And, with resistless terror, drew.
Through lands we fled, o'er seas we flew,
And halted on a boundless plain;
Where nothing fed, nor breathed, nor grew,
But silence ruled the still domain.

Upon that boundless plain, below,
The setting sun's last rays were shed,
And gave a mild and sober glow,
Where all were still, asleep, or dead;
Vast ruins in the midst were spread,
Pillars and pediments sublime,
Where the grey moss had form'd a bed,
And clothed the crumbling spoils of time.

There was I fix'd, I know not how,
Condemn'd for untold years to stay:
Yet years were not;—one dreadful now
Endured no change of night or day;
The same mild evening's sleeping ray
Shone softly-solemn and serene,
And all that time I gazed away,
The setting sun's sad rays were seen.

At length a moment's sleep stole on—
Again came my commission'd foes;
Again through sea and land we're gone,
No peace, no respite, no repose:
Above the dark broad sea we rose,
We ran through bleak and frozen land;
I had no strength their strength t' oppose,
An infant in a giant's hand.

They placed me where those streamers play,
Those nimble beams of brilliant light;
It would the stoutest heart dismay,
To see, to feel, that dreadful sight:
So swift, so pure, so cold, so bright,
They pierced my frame with icy wound,
And, all that half-year's polar night,
Those dancing streamers wrapp'd me round.

Slowly that darkness pass'd away,
When down upon the earth I fell;—

Some hurried sleep was mine by day;
But, soon as toll'd the evening bell,
They forced me on, where ever dwell
Far-distant men in cities fair,
Cities of whom no trav'lers tell,
Nor feet but mine were wanderers there.

Their watchmen stare, and stand aghast,
As on we hurry through the dark;
The watch-light blinks as we go past,
The watch-dog shrinks and fears to bark;
The watch-tower's bell sounds shrill; and, hark!
The free wind blows—we've left the town—
A wide sepulchral ground I mark,
And on a tombstone place me down.

What monuments of mighty dead!
What tombs of various kinds are found!
And stones erect their shadows shed
On humble graves, with wickers bound;
Some risen fresh, above the ground,
Some level with the native clay,
What sleeping millions wait the sound,
"Arise, ye dead, and come away!"

Alas! they stay not for that call;
Spare me this wo! ye demons, spare!—
They come! the shrouded shadows all—
'Tis more than mortal brain can bear;
Rustling they rise, they sternly glare
At man, upheld by vital breath;
Who, led by wicked fiends, should dare
To join the shadowy troops of death!

Yes, I have felt all man can feel,
Till he shall pay his nature's debt:
Ills that no hope has strength to heal,
No mind the comfort to forget:
Whatever cares the heart can fret,
The spirits wear, the temper gall,
Wo, want, dread, anguish, all beset
My sinful soul!—together all!

Those fiends upon a shaking fen
Fix'd me, in dark tempestuous night;
There never trod the foot of men;
There flock'd the fowl in wint'ry flight;
There danced the moor's deceitful light

Above the pool where sedges grow;
And, when the morning-sun shone bright,
It shone upon a field of snow.

They hung me on a bough so small.
The rook could build her nest no higher;
They fix'd me on the trembling ball
That crowns the steeple's quiv'ring spire;
They set me where the seas retire,
But drown with their returning tide;
And made me flee the mountain's fire,
When rolling from its burning side.

I've hung upon the ridgy steep
Of cliffs, and held the rambling brier;
I've plunged below the billowy deep,
Where air was sent me to respire;
I've been where hungry wolves retire;
And (to complete my woes) I've ran
Where Bedlam's crazy crew conspire
Against the life of reasoning man.

I've furl'd in storms the flapping sail,
By hanging from the topmast-head;
I've served the vilest slaves in jail,
And pick'd the dunghill's spoil for bread;
I've made the badger's hole my bed,
I've wander'd with a gipsy crew;
I've dreaded all the guilty dread,
And done what they would fear to do.

On sand, where ebbs and flows the flood,
Midway they placed and bade me die;
Propp'd on my staff, I stoutly stood,
When the swift waves came rolling by;
And high they rose, and still more high,
Till my lips drank the bitter brine;
I sobb'd convulsed, then cast mine eye,
And saw the tide's re-flowing sign.

And then, my dreams were such as nought
Could yield but my unhappy case;
I've been of thousand devils caught,
And thrust into that horrid place,
Where reign dismay, despair, disgrace;
Furies with iron fangs were there,
To torture that accursed race,
Doomed to dismay, disgrace, despair.

Harmless I was, yet hunted down
For treasons, to my soul unfit;
I've been pursued through many a town,
For crimes that petty knaves commit;
I've been adjudged t' have lost my wit,
Because I preach'd so loud and well;
And thrown into the dungeon's pit,
For trampling on the pit of hell.

Such were the evils, man of sin.
That I was fated to sustain;
And add to all, without—within,
A soul defiled with every stain
That man's reflecting mind can pain;
That pride, wrong, rage, despair, can make;
In fact, they'd nearly touch'd my brain,
And reason on her throne would shake.

But pity will the vilest seek,
If punish'd guilt will not repine;—
I heard a heavenly teacher speak,
And felt the SUN OF MERCY shine:
I hail'd the light! the birth divine!
And then was seal'd among the few;
Those angry fiends beheld the sign,
And from me in an instant flew.

Come, hear how thus the charmers cry
To wandering sheep, the strays of sin,
While some the wicket-gate pass by,
And some will knock and enter in:
Full joyful 'tis a soul to win,
For he that winneth souls is wise;
Now, hark! the holy strains begin,
And thus the sainted preacher cries:—

"Pilgrim, burthen'd with thy sin,
Come the way to Zion's gate,
There, till Mercy let thee in,
Knock and weep, and watch and wait.
Knock!—He knows the sinner's cry;
Weep!—He loves the mourner's tears;
Watch!—for saving grace is nigh;
Wait!—till heavenly light appears.

"Hark! it is the Bridegroom's voice;
Welcome, pilgrim, to thy rest;

Now within the gate rejoice,
Safe and seal'd, and bought and bless'd!
Safe—from all the lures of vice;
Seal'd—by signs the chosen know;
Bought—by love and life the price;
Bless'd—the mighty debt to owe.

"Holy Pilgrim! what for thee
In a world like this remain?
From thy guarded breast shall flee
Fear and shame, and doubt and pain.
Fear—the hope of Heaven shall fly;
Shame—from glory's view retire;
Doubt—in certain rapture die;
Pain—in endless bliss expire."

But though my day of grace was come,
Yet still my days of grief I find;
The former clouds' collected gloom
Still sadden the reflecting mind;
The soul, to evil things consign'd,
Will of their evil some retain;
The man will seem to earth inclined,
And will not look erect again.

Thus, though elect, I feel it hard
To lose what I possess'd before,
To be from all my wealth debarr'd:—
The brave Sir Eustace is no more.
But old I wax and passing poor,
Stern, rugged men my conduct view;
They chide my wish, they bar my door,
'Tis hard—I weep—you see I do.—

Must you, my friends, no longer stay?
Thus quickly all my pleasures end;
But I'll remember, when I pray,
My kind physician and his friend;
And those sad hours you deign to spend
With me, I shall requite them all;
Sir Eustace for his friends shall send,
And thank their love at Greyling Hall.

VISITOR
The poor Sir Eustace!—Yet his hope
Leads him to think of joys again;
And when his earthly visions droop,
His views of heavenly kind remain.—

But whence that meek and humbled strain,
That spirit wounded, lost, resign'd?
Would not so proud a soul disdain
The madness of the poorest mind?

PHYSICIAN

No! for the more he swell'd with pride,
The more he felt misfortune's blow;
Disgrace and grief he could not hide,
And poverty had laid him low:
Thus shame and sorrow working slow,
At length this humble spirit gave;
Madness on these began to grow,
And bound him to his fiends a slave.

Though the wild thoughts had touch'd his brain,
Then was he free.—So, forth he ran;
To soothe or threat, alike were vain:
He spake of fiends; look'd wild and wan;
Year after year, the hurried man
Obey'd those fiends from place to place;
Till his religious change began
To form a frenzied child of grace.

For, as the fury lost its strength,
The mind reposed; by slow degrees
Came lingering hope, and brought at length,
To the tormented spirit ease:
This slave of sin, whom fiends could seize,
Felt or believed their power had end;—
"'Tis faith," he cried, "my bosom frees,
And now my SAVIOUR is my friend."

But ah! though time can yield relief,
And soften woes it cannot cure,
Would we not suffer pain and grief,
To have our reason sound and sure?
Then let us keep our bosoms pure,
Our fancy's favourite flights suppress;
Prepare the body to endure,
And bend the mind to meet distress;
And then HIS guardian care implore,
Whom demons dread and men adore.

THE HALL OF JUSTICE

PART I

Confiteor facere hoc annos; sed et altera causa est,
Anxietas animi, continuusque dolor.

Ovid [Epp. ex Ponto Lib. I. Ep. iv. vv. 7-8].

MAGISTRATE, VAGRANT, CONSTABLE, &c.

VAGRANT
Take, take away thy barbarous hand,
And let me to thy master speak;
Remit awhile the harsh command,
And hear me, or my heart will break.

MAGISTRATE
Fond wretch! and what canst thou relate,
But deeds of sorrow, shame, and sin?
Thy crime is proved, thou know'st thy fate;
But come, thy tale!—begin, begin!—

VAGRANT
My crime!—This sick'ning child to feed,
I seized the food your witness saw;
I knew your laws forbade the deed,
But yielded to a stronger law.

Know'st thou, to Nature's great command
All human laws are frail and weak?
Nay! frown not—stay his eager hand,
And hear me, or my heart will break.

In this, th' adopted babe I hold
With anxious fondness to my breast,
My heart's sole comfort I behold,
More dear than life, when life was bless'd;
I saw her pining, fainting, cold,
I begg'd—but vain was my request.

I saw the tempting food, and seized—
My infant-sufferer found relief;
And, in the pilfer'd treasure pleased,
Smiled on my guilt, and hush'd my grief.

But I have griefs of other kind,

Troubles and sorrows more severe;
Give me to ease my tortured mind,
Lend to my woes a patient ear;
And let me—if I may not find
A friend to help—find one to hear.

Yet nameless let me plead—my name
Would only wake the cry of scorn;
A child of sin, conceived in shame,
Brought forth in wo, to misery born.

My mother dead, my father lost,
I wander'd with a vagrant crew;
A common care, a common cost,
Their sorrows and their sins I knew;
With them, by want on error forced,
Like them, I base and guilty grew.

Few are my years, not so my crimes;
The age, which these sad looks declare,
Is Sorrow's work, it is not Time's,
And I am old in shame and care.

Taught to believe the world a place
Where every stranger was a foe,
Train'd in the arts that mark our race,
To what new people could I go?
Could I a better life embrace,
Or live as virtue dictates? No!—

So through the land I wandering went,
And little found of grief or joy;
But lost my bosom's sweet content
When first I loved—the Gipsy-Boy.

A sturdy youth he was and tall,
His looks would all his soul declare;
His piercing eyes were deep and small,
And strongly curl'd his raven-hair.

Yes, Aaron had each manly charm,
All in the May of youthful pride;
He scarcely fear'd his father's arm,
And every other arm defied.—
Oft, when they grew in anger warm,
(Whom will not love and power divide?)
I rose, their wrathful souls to calm,
Not yet in sinful combat tried.

His father was our party's chief,
And dark and dreadful was his look;
His presence fill'd my heart with grief;
Although to me he kindly spoke.

With Aaron I delighted went,
His favour was my bliss and pride;
In growing hope our days we spent,
Love growing charms in either spied;
It saw them, all which Nature lent,
It lent them all which she denied.

Could I the father's kindness prize,
Or grateful looks on him bestow,
Whom I beheld in wrath arise,
When Aaron sunk beneath his blow?

He drove him down with wicked hand,—
It was a dreadful sight to see;
Then vex'd him, till he left the land,
And told his cruel love to me;—
The clan were all at his command,
Whatever his command might be.

The night was dark, the lanes were deep,
And one by one they took their way;
He bade me lay me down and sleep,
I only wept and wish'd for day.

Accursèd be the love he bore.
Accursèd was the force he used;
So let him of his God implore
For mercy, and be so refused!

You frown again;—to show my wrong,
Can I in gentle language speak?
My woes are deep, my words are strong;—
And hear me, or my heart will break.

MAGISTRATE
I hear thy words, I feel thy pain;
Forbear awhile to speak thy woes;
Receive our aid, and then again
The story of thy life disclose.

For, though seduced and led astray,
Thou'st travell'd far and wander'd long;

Thy God hath seen thee all the way,
And all the turns that led thee wrong.

PART II

Quondam ridentes oculi, nunc fonte perenni
Deplorant poenas nocte dieque suas.

Corn. Galli [Maximiniani (Pseudo-Galli)] Eleg. [I. vv. 137-8.]

MAGISTRATE
Come, now again thy woes impart,
Tell all thy sorrows, all thy sin;
We cannot heal the throbbing heart
Till we discern the wounds within.

Compunction weeps our guilt away,
The sinner's safety is his pain;
Such pangs for our offences pay,
And these severer griefs are gain.

VAGRANT
The son came back—he found us wed;
Then dreadful was the oath he swore;—
His way through Blackburn Forest led;—
His father we beheld no more.

Of all our daring clan not one
Would on the doubtful subject dwell;
For all esteem'd the injured son,
And fear'd the tale which he could tell.

But I had mightier cause for fear;
For slow and mournful round my bed
I saw a dreadful form appear—
It came when I and Aaron wed.

(Yes! we were wed, I know my crime,—
We slept beneath the elmen tree;
But I was grieving all the time,
And Aaron frown'd my tears to see.

For he not yet had felt the pain
That rankles in a wounded breast;
He waked to sin, then slept again,

Forsook his God, yet took his rest.—

But I was forced to feign delight,
And joy in mirth and music sought;
And mem'ry now recalls the night,
With such surprise and horror fraught,
That reason felt a moment's flight,
And left a mind to madness wrought.)

When waking, on my heaving breast
I felt a hand as cold as death;
A sudden fear my voice suppress'd,
A chilling terror stopp'd my breath.—

I seem'd—no words can utter how!
For there my father-husband stood—
And thus he said:—"Will God allow,
"The great avenger, just and good,
A wife to break her marriage vow,
A son to shed his father's blood?"

I trembled at the dismal sounds,
But vainly strove a word to say;
So, pointing to his bleeding wounds,
The threat'ning spectre stalk'd away.

I brought a lovely daughter forth,
His father's child, in Aaron's bed;
He took her from me in his wrath;—
"Where is my child?"—"Thy child is dead."

'Twas false—we wander'd far and wide,
Through town and country, field and fen,
Till Aaron, fighting, fell and died,
And I became a wife again.

I then was young:—my husband sold
My fancièd charms for wicked price;
He gave me oft, for sinful gold,
The slave, but not the friend, of vice—
Behold me, Heaven! my pains behold,
And let them for my sins suffice!

The wretch, who lent me thus for gain,
Despised me when my youth was fled;
Then came disease, and brought me pain—
Come, death, and bear me to the dead!
For, though I grieve, my grief is vain,

And fruitless all the tears I shed.

True, I was not to virtue train'd;
Yet well I knew my deeds were ill;
By each offence my heart was pain'd—
I wept, but I offended still;
My better thoughts my life disdain'd,
But yet the viler led my will.

My husband died, and now no more
My smile was sought, or ask'd my hand—
A widow'd vagrant, vile and poor,
Beneath a vagrant's vile command.

Ceaseless I roved the country round,
To win my bread by fraudful arts,
And long a poor subsistence found,
By spreading nets for simple hearts.

Though poor, and abject, and despised,
Their fortunes to the crowd I told;
I gave the young the love they prized,
And promised wealth to bless the old;
Schemes for the doubtful I devised,
And charms for the forsaken sold.

At length for arts like these confined
In prison with a lawless crew,
I soon perceived a kindred mind,
And there my long-lost daughter knew:

His father's child, whom Aaron gave
To wander with a distant clan,
The miseries of the world to brave,
And be the slave of vice and man.

She knew my name—we met in pain;
Our parting pangs can I express?
She sail'd a convict o'er the main,
And left an heir to her distress.

This is that heir to shame and pain,
For whom I only could descry
A world of trouble and disdain—
Yet, could I bear to see her die,
Or stretch her feeble hand in vain,
And, weeping, beg of me supply?

No! though the fate thy mother knew
Was shameful! shameful though thy race
Have wander'd all, a lawless crew,
Outcasts, despised in every place:

Yet, as the dark and muddy tide,
When far from its polluted source,
Becomes more pure, and, purified,
Flows in a clear and happy course—

In thee, dear infant! so may end
Our shame, in thee our sorrows cease!
And thy pure course will then extend,
In floods of joy, o'er vales of peace.
Oh! by the God who loves to spare,
Deny me not the boon I crave;
Let this loved child your mercy share,
And let me find a peaceful grave;
Make her yet spotless soul your care,
And let my sins their portion have;
Her for a better fate prepare,
And punish whom 'twere sin to save!

MAGISTRATE
Recall the word, renounce the thought,
Command thy heart and bend thy knee.
There is to all a pardon brought,
A ransom rich, assured and free;
'Tis full when found, 'tis found if sought,
Oh! seek it, till 'tis seal'd to thee.

VAGRANT
But how my pardon shall I know?

MAGISTRATE
By feeling dread that 'tis not sent;
By tears, for sin that freely flow;
By grief, that all thy tears are spent;
By thoughts on that great debt we owe,
With all the mercy God has lent;
By suffering what thou canst not show,
Yet showing how thine heart is rent:
Till thou canst feel thy bosom glow,
And say, "MY SAVIOUR, I REPENT!"

WOMAN!

MR. LEDYARD, AS QUOTED BY M. PARKE IN HIS TRAVELS INTO AFRIC:

"To a Woman I never addressed myself in the language of decency and friendship, without receiving a decent and friendly answer. If I was hungry or thirsty, wet or sick, they did not hesitate, like Men, to perform a generous action: in so free and kind a manner did they contribute to my relief, that if I was dry, I drank the sweetest draught; and if hungry, I ate the coarsest morsel with a double relish."

Place the white man on Afric's coast,
Whose swarthy sons in blood delight,
Who of their scorn to Europe boast,
And paint their very demons white:
There, while the sterner sex disdains
To soothe the woes they cannot feel,
Woman will strive to heal his pains,
And weep for those she cannot heal.
Hers is warm pity's sacred glow;
From all her stores she bears a part,
And bids the spring of hope re-flow,
That languish'd in the fainting heart.

"What, though so pale his haggard face,
So sunk and sad his looks,"—she cries—
"And far unlike our nobler race,
With crisped locks and rolling eyes:
Yet misery marks him of our kind;
We see him lost, alone, afraid;
And pangs of body, griefs in mind,
Pronounce him man, and ask our aid.

"Perhaps, in some far-distant shore,
There are who in these forms delight;
Whose milky features please them more,
Than ours of jet thus burnish'd bright.
Of such may be his weeping wife,
Such children for their sire may call;
And, if we spare his ebbing life,
Our kindness may preserve them all."

Thus her compassion woman shows,
Beneath the line her acts are these;
Nor the wide waste of Lapland-snows
Can her warm flow of pity freeze:—
"From some sad land the stranger comes,
Where joys, like ours, are never found;
Let's soothe him in our happy homes,
Where freedom sits, with plenty crown'd.

"'Tis good the fainting soul to cheer,
To see the famish'd stranger fed;
To milk for him the mother-deer,
To smooth for him the furry bed.
The powers above our Lapland bless
With good no other people know,
T' enlarge the joys that we possess,
By feeling those that we bestow!"

Thus, in extremes of cold and heat,
Where wandering man may trace his kind;
Wherever grief and want retreat,
In Woman they compassion find;
She makes the female breast her seat,
And dictates mercy to the mind.

Man may the sterner virtues know,
Determined justice, truth severe;
But female hearts with pity glow,
And Woman holds affliction dear.
For guiltless woes her sorrows flow,
And suffering vice compels her tear;
'Tis hers to soothe the ills below,
And bid life's fairer views appear.
To Woman's gentle kind we owe
What comforts and delights us here;
They its gay hopes on youth bestow,
And care they soothe, and age they cheer.

George Crabbe – A Short Biography

George Crabbe was born on December 24th, 1754 in Aldeburgh, Suffolk, and was the eldest of six children fathered by George Crabbe Sr.

Crabbe was sent to school at a very young age and soon developed an avid and precocious interest in books. His father would often read passages from Milton and various 18th-century poets to him.

The family also subscribed to a country magazine called Martin's Philosophical Magazine. The Poet's Corner section was always given to Crabbe.

His father supported his son's interest in literature although obviously at that time thought his career would be in other areas.

Crabbe was sent first to a boarding-school at Bungay near his home, and a few years later to a more important school at Stowmarket, where he learnt mathematics and Latin, and a familiarity with the Latin classics. His early reading included the works of William Shakespeare, Alexander Pope, Abraham Cowley, Sir Walter Raleigh and Edmund Spenser.

Medicine had now been settled on as his future career and, after three years at Stowmarket, in 1768, he was apprenticed to a local doctor at Wickhambrook, near Bury St Edmunds. The doctor also kept a small farm, and Crabbe eventually spent more time doing farm labour and errands than medical work.

In 1771 he changed masters and moved to Woodbridge, here he joined a small club of young men who met at an inn for evening discussions. It was here that he also met his future wife, Sarah Elmy. Crabbe called her "Mira", and now, writing poetry, he would often refer to her as such in his poems.

In 1772, a lady's magazine offered a prize for the best poem on 'hope'. Crabbe entered and won. The magazine then printed other short pieces of his during the year.

His first major work, a satirical poem of nearly 400 lines called Inebriety, was self-published in 1775. Crabbe later said of the poem, which received little attention at the time, "Pray let not this be seen... there is very little of it that I'm not heartily ashamed of."

By this time he had completed his medical training and had returned to Aldeburgh. Low finances meant his intention to go to London to study at a hospital was abandoned and a job was taken as a warehouseman.

The following year, 1777, Crabbe did travel to London to practice medicine, but returned home with financial woes after a year. He continued to practice as a surgeon after returning, but with limited surgical skills, he received only the poorest of patients, together with small and undependable fees. This hurt his chances of an early marriage, but Sarah stayed devoted to him.

He moved to London again in April 1780, to see if he could make it as a poet, or, if that failed, as a doctor. By the end of May he had been forced to pawn his surgical instruments. But he had composed a number of works but, sadly, all failed to be published. He now wrote several letters seeking patronage, but these were also refused.

Crabbe was able to publish a poem at this time entitled The Candidate, but it was badly received by critics.

He continued to rack up debts, and was pressed by his creditors. In early 1781 he wrote a letter to Edmund Burke asking for help, in which he included samples of his poetry. Burke was swayed by Crabbe's letter and by meeting with him, giving him money to relieve his immediate wants, and assuring him that he would do all in his power to further Crabbe's literary career.

A short time later Burke told his friend Sir Joshua Reynolds that Crabbe had "the mind and feelings of a gentleman." Burke admitted Crabbe to his family circle at Beaconsfield. The time he spent with Burke and his family exposed him to further knowledge and ideas as well as new and valuable friends including Samuel Johnson. He completed his unfinished poems and revised others with the help of Burke's criticism. Burke helped him have his poem, The Library, published anonymously in June 1781, it was greeted with modest praise by critics, and some public appreciation.

Burke realised that Crabbe was more suited to be a clergyman than a surgeon. On his recommendation he was ordained to the curacy and then returned to Aldeburgh. His fellow townsmen resented his rise in social class. Burke now manoeuvred for Crabbe to be made chaplain to the Duke of Rutland at Belvoir Castle in Leicestershire.

The Duke and Duchess, were kind and generous to him as were their friends who enjoyed his literary works. But his relationship with the others in the household was tense. With the publication in May 1783 of his poem The Village, Crabbe achieved popularity with both the public and critics. Samuel Johnson said of it in a letter to Reynolds "I have sent you back Mr. Crabbe's poem, which I read with great delight. It is original, vigorous, and elegant."

It was decided that, as Chaplain to a noble family, Crabbe was in need of a college degree, and his name was entered on the boards of Trinity College, Cambridge, and through various influences Crabbe obtained a degree without residence. This was 1783, but almost immediately he received an LL.B. degree from the Archbishop of Canterbury. This allowed Crabbe to be given two small livings in Dorsetshire, Frome St Quintin and Evershot.

On the strength of these preferments and a promise of future assistance from the Duke, Crabbe and Sarah Elmy were married in December 1783, in the parish church of Beccles.

In 1784 the Duke of Rutland became Lord Lieutenant of Ireland. It was agreed that Crabbe would not go to Ireland, though the two men parted as close friends. The newly-weds stayed on at Belvoir for another eighteen months before Crabbe accepted a vacant curacy in Stathern in Leicestershire, moving there in 1785. The couple had four children of which only two sons survived; George (1785) and John (1787).

In October 1787, at age 35, the Duke of Rutland died in Dublin, after a short illness. The Duchess, anxious to have their former chaplain close by, was able to get Crabbe the two livings of Muston, Leicestershire, and Allington, Lincolnshire, in exchange for his old livings. Crabbe brought his family to Muston in February 1789.

Crabbe was also a coleopterist and recorder of beetles, and is credited for discovering the first specimen of Calosoma sycophanta L. to be recorded from Suffolk. He published an essay, in 1790, on the Natural History of the Vale of Belvoir. It includes over 70 species of local coleopterans.

In 1792, through the death of one of Sarah's relations and her older sister, the Crabbe family came into possession of an estate in Parham, which, at a stroke, removed all of their financial worries. Crabbe soon moved his family to the inheritance.

Crabbe's life at Parham was not happy. The former owner of the estate had been popular for his hospitality, while Crabbe's lifestyle was much more private. His solace here was the company of his friend Dudley Long North and his fellow Whigs who lived nearby.

After four years at Parham, the Crabbes moved to a home in Great Glemham, Suffolk, placed at his disposal by Dudley North.

In 1796 their third son, Edmund, died at the age of six. The death shredded Sarah's mental health and she never recovered. Crabbe, a devoted husband, tended her until her death many years later.

During his time at Glemham, Crabbe composed several novels, none of which were published. After Glemham, Crabbe moved to the village of Rendham in Suffolk, where he stayed until 1805. His poem The Parish Register was all but completed whilst here, and The Borough was also begun.

In September 1807, Crabbe published a new volume of poems which included The Library, The Newspaper, The Village and The Parish Register, to which were added Sir Eustace Grey and The Hall of Justice. It has been decades since his last publication but now, with this, he was seen as an important poet. Four editions were issued in 18 months. The reviews were unanimous in approval, headed by Francis Jeffrey in the critically important Edinburgh Review.

In 1809 Crabbe sent a copy of his poems to Walter Scott, who, in reply told Crabbe "how for more than twenty years he had desired the pleasure of a personal introduction to him, and how, as a lad of eighteen, he had met with selections from The Village and The Library in The Annual Register." This exchange of letters led to a friendship that lasted for the rest of their lives.

The success of The Parish Register encouraged Crabbe to proceed with a far longer poem, which he had been working on for several years. The Borough was begun at Rendham in Suffolk in 1801, continued at Muston after his return in 1805, and finally completed during a long visit to Aldeburgh in the autumn of 1809. It was published in 1810. In spite of its defects, The Borough was an outright success and went through six editions in the next six years. (Benjamin Britten's opera Peter Grimes is based on The Borough).

The following three years were especially lonely for him. His two sons, George and John, and were now clergymen themselves, each holding a local curacy enabling them to live under the parental roof, but Sarah's health was very poor, and Crabbe had no-one to help him with her care for most of the time.

Crabbe's next volume of poetry, Tales was published in the summer of 1812. It received a warm welcome from the poet's admirers, and was again warmly reviewed by Jeffrey in the Edinburgh Review. It is now considered Crabbe's masterpiece.

In the summer of 1813, Sarah felt well enough to visit London again. Crabbe, Sarah and their two sons spent nearly three months there. Crabbe was able to visit Dudley North and some of his other old friends, and to visit and help the poor and distressed, remembering his own want and misery in the great city thirty years earlier. The family returned to Muston in September, and at October's end Sarah died at the age of 63. Within days of her death Crabbe fell seriously ill. He rallied, however, and returned to the duties of his parish.

In 1814, he became Rector of Trowbridge in Wiltshire, a position given to him by the new Duke of Rutland. He now remained at Trowbridge for the rest of his life.

His two sons followed him, as soon as their existing engagements allowed them to leave Leicestershire. The younger son, John, became his father's curate, and the elder, became curate at Pucklechurch, also nearby. Crabbe's reputation as a poet continued to grow in these years. This made him a welcome guest in many houses. Nearby was the poet William Lisle Bowles, who introduced Crabbe to the noble family at Bowood House, home of the Marquess of Lansdowne, who was always ready to welcome those distinguished in literature and the arts. It was at Bowood House that Crabbe first met the poet Samuel Rogers, who became a close friend and had an influence on Crabbe's poetry. In 1817, on the advice of

Rogers, Crabbe stayed in London in the early summer to enjoy the literary society of the capital. Here he met Thomas Campbell, and through him and Rogers was introduced to his future publisher John Murray.

In June 1819, Crabbe published his collection Tales of the Hall.

Around 1820 Crabbe began suffering from frequent severe attacks of neuralgia, and this, together with his advancing years, made him less and less able to travel to London.

In the spring of 1822, Crabbe met Walter Scott for the first time in London, and promised to visit him in Scotland in the fall. He kept this promise during George IV's visit to Edinburgh.

Later in 1822, Crabbe was invited to spend Christmas at Belvoir Castle, but weather made the trip impossible. While at home, he continued to write a large amount of poetry (eventually leaving 21 manuscript volumes at his death).

Crabbe continued to visit at Hampstead throughout the 1820s, often meeting the writer Joanna Baillie and her sister Agnes.

In November 1832 he went to see his son George, at Pucklechurch. He was able to preach twice for his son, who congratulated him on the power of his voice, and other encouraging signs of strength. "I will venture a good sum, sir," he said, "that you will be assisting me ten years hence." "Ten weeks" was Crabbe's answer, and the prediction proved eerily accurate. Crabbe now returned to Trowbridge.

Early in January of the New Year he reported more drowsiness and increasing weakness. Later in the month he was laid low by a severe cold. Further complications arose, and it soon became apparent that he would not live much longer.

George Crabbe died on February 3rd, 1832, aged 77 at Trowbridge, Wiltshire with his two sons by his side.

George Crabbe – A Concise Bibliography

Sketch of Crabbe (1826)
Inebriety (1775)
The Candidate (1780)
The Library (1781)
The Village (1782)
The Newspaper (1785)
Poems (1807)
The Borough (1810)
Tales in Verse (1812)
Tales of the Hall (1819)
Posthumous Tales (1834)

Printed in Great Britain
by Amazon